International Entrepreneurship

International Entrepreneurship

Antonella Zucchella

Full Professor, Department of Economics and Management, University of Pavia, Italy

Birgit Hagen

Assistant Professor, Department of Economics and Management, University of Pavia, Italy

Manuel G. Serapio

Associate Professor of International Business and Entrepreneurship, Business School, University of Colorado, Denver, USA

Edward Elgar
PUBLISHING

Cheltenham, UK • Northampton, MA, USA

Cover image: Jeremy Bishop on Unsplash

Published by
Edward Elgar Publishing Limited
The Lypiatts
15 Lansdown Road
Cheltenham
Glos GL50 2JA
UK

Edward Elgar Publishing, Inc.
William Pratt House
9 Dewey Court
Northampton
Massachusetts 01060
USA

A catalogue record for this book
is available from the British Library

Library of Congress Control Number: 2018939976

ISBN 978 1 78536 544 7 (cased)
ISBN 978 1 78536 546 1 (paperback)
ISBN 978 1 78536 545 4 (eBook)

Typeset by Servis Filmsetting Ltd, Stockport, Cheshire
Printed by CPI Group (UK) Ltd, Croydon CR0 4YY

Contents in brief

Full contents

Foreword

This is the book I wish I had written. For years, publishers asked me to write a book on international entrepreneurship, but other projects always seemed to come first, even though I felt that the field needed a definitive book. Now, almost three decades since I published the first journal article on international entrepreneurship (IE) in a 1989 issue of the *Journal of Business Venturing*, I am pleased that IE has that definitive book.

Using dynamic cases to illustrate IE theory and practice, the book combines an evolutionary overview of the most important IE research content with a forward look to the modern and extremely fast-moving international environment. The authors raise important debates in IE that are sure to trigger thoughtful discussion. This book focuses specifically on IE, not solely on international business or entrepreneurship. Rather it is accurately set at the *interface* of these two disciplines.

The co-authors' complementary expertise enables them to combine theory and practice in a way that makes the book interesting and relevant to both graduate students and IE academic scholars. Antonella Zucchella, an international marketing professor and pioneer scholar in IE, has deep knowledge of IE research, having authored what many regard as the earliest scholarly book overviewing this area. Birgit Hagen, who has special expertise in small- and medium firm internationalization, is a junior IE scholar and thus brings her knowledge of the most recent research to the project. Antonella and Birgit bring a rich European perspective to the book. Manuel Serapio, whose early academic background was in international business, has extensive Asian and US consulting experience coupled with his practical knowledge of today's dynamic international environment. Manuel draws upon the rich teaching materials and cases he has developed for both his classroom and his summer IE workshop. More than 175 professors from 25 different countries have participated in Manuel's summer IE workshops in preparation for conducting IE research and teaching IE at their respective institutions.

The book offers maximum flexibility of use, allowing the instructor to adapt and enrich the content to suit any course. Masters-level students will find the cases on how entrepreneurial firms handle international issues particularly interesting. The cases, which lend themselves to easy updating and enrichment by other sources, offer rich application of theoretical content by dealing with real companies, many of which offer novel products and services. For those who wish to dive deeper into IE theory, the book's extensive references allow for more in-depth further reading. The book is essential for IE courses, and its focus on entrepreneurial firms engaging in international business offers a valuable reading supplement for courses in international business or entrepreneurship.

I applaud the co-authors for making a needed and welcome contribution to the teaching of international entrepreneurship.

Patricia McDougall-Covin
William L. Haeberle Professor of Entrepreneurship
Faculty Director, Institute for International Business
Kelley School of Business, Indiana University

1

Setting the field

1.1 International entrepreneurship: what, who, why

What is international entrepreneurship about? According to Oviatt and McDougall (2005, p. 540) it is about "the discovery, enactment, evaluation and exploitation of opportunities – across national borders – to create future goods and services". This widely accepted definition permits to highlight two key processes characterizing international entrepreneurship (IE from now on): the formation of opportunities and their exploitation. A second element is represented by proactivity and innovativeness, which accompany the formation and exploitation of opportunities and are both key attributes of entrepreneurs and their organizations: the creation of future goods and services is the aim of their action. Jones and Coviello (2005, p. 300) confirm that international entrepreneurship is an "evolutionary and potentially discontinuous process determined by innovation, and influenced by environmental change and human volition, action or decision". A third element, which distinguishes IE is the geographic perspective: the formation and exploitation of opportunities happen across national borders. IE also encompasses cross-country comparisons between entrepreneurial behaviour in individuals and their organizations (comparative international entrepreneurship).

IE is a relatively recent phenomenon: the first studies date back to the end of the 1980s. In 1989 Patricia McDougall published her work on international new ventures (INVs), defined as "start-ups that, from their inception, engage in international business, thus viewing their operating domain as international from the initial stages of the firm's operation" (McDougall, 1989, p. 390). Later, Oviatt and McDougall (2005, p. 537) defined the INV as "as a business organization that, from inception, seeks to derive significant competitive advantage from the use of resources and the sale of outputs in multiple countries". In 1993 Rennie published his research on Australian born global firms (BGs), that is, companies which started internationalizing in their first years of life: "Being born global means that exporting was the primary goal of the firm even upon its inception. These firms have been able to attain as much as 76% of their sales from exports after only two years of operation" (Rennie, 1993, p. 45). Rennie's focus was on early and fast exporters, but – as we can argue from the INV conceptualization – we can observe different typologies in international entrepreneurship (see next chapter). Knight and Cavusgil (2004) conceptualized further born global firms, highlighting their innovativeness and distinctive capabilities.

After the mentioned seminal contributions, studies on these types of firms flourished and still represent a main topic in IE studies. At the same time, the above definition of IE departs from the exclusive interest in international new ventures and born globals and embraces a variety of entrepreneurs and organizations in their quest for opportunities across the world. When opportunities are formed and exploited, a new growth path is disclosed: this happens both in new ventures and in established firms. In both cases, IE shows a fourth distinctive element: the attention to the temporal dimension of entrepreneurial phenomena. Time has a central role in IE and can be expressed through dimensions like precocity (firms going international very early in their life) and speed (fast international growth).

The above definitions of IE encompass the innovative, proactive and risk-taking behaviour of both individuals (entrepreneurs) and their organizations. The *who?* in IE studies thus involves paying attention to the individuals who found firms, who make them grow over time in international markets through processes of exploration and exploitation of opportunities.

And *why* has international entrepreneurship been emerging and fast growing in the last three decades? Its surge can be explained by a context of increasing globalization, which characterized the world economy since the beginning of the 1980s. The process has many facets: progresses in information and telecommunication technologies, reduction of trade barriers in different parts of the world, increasing efficiency in transportation means, and so on. McDougall-Covin, Jones and Serapio (2014, p. 2) in their introduction to the special issue of *Entrepreneurship Theory and Practice* devoted to international entrepreneurship discuss how "dramatic globalization drivers such as lower cost and faster communication technologies, lowering of trade and investment barriers, industry deregulations, and advances in cheaper and more efficient means of transportation converged and accelerated the world into the internationally dynamic and complex world of today". A new generation of entrepreneurs with a global mindset increasingly explore opportunities in international markets. Nowadays, an international orientation characterizes a growing number of entrepreneurs and the organizations they establish (Figure 1.1).

However, IE is not an entirely new phenomenon: in the history of humankind, periods of easier communications and trading facilities opened the way to international entrepreneurship. The last and major wave in IE is accompanied by unprecedented technological innovations, which have made the world a smaller place.

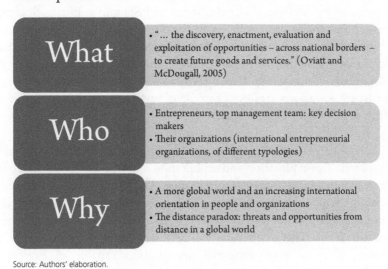

Source: Authors' elaboration.

Figure 1.1 International entrepreneurship: what, who and why

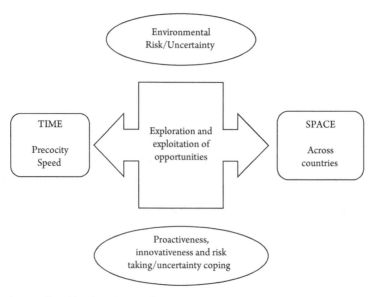

Source: Authors' elaboration.

Figure 1.2 IE in a nutshell: its five distinctive elements

Easier and faster communication and transportation across the globe have not diminished the need to understand deeply the various dimensions of distance (geographic, cultural and institutional, administrative and economic, following the distance dimensions suggested by Ghemawat in 2001). The world might have become smaller but not less complex, as the above comment by McDougall-Covin, Jones and Serapio confirms. International entrepreneurship has ample room for developing further, but also increasing challenges arising from this increasing complexity. The exploration and exploitation of international opportunities thus takes place in a context shrouded in uncertainty. The capacity to take risks (Covin and Slevin, 1991) or to cope with uncertainty (Zucchella and Magnani, 2016) represents the fifth key element for IE (Figure 1.2).

The above five elements, and particularly the core processes of (international) opportunities exploration and exploitation require – as mentioned above – an international entrepreneurial orientation. The latter represents the spectacles through which the entrepreneurs and their ventures see the world, discover and create opportunities that others have overlooked, thus shaping their environment. This orientation should characterize the entire organization. Establishing an entrepreneurial organization capable of exploring and exploiting successfully international opportunities (IEO, international entrepreneurial organization) is a major driver of growth and value creation

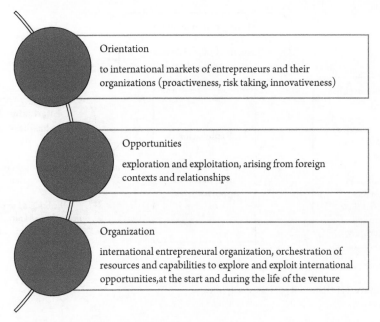

Orientation

to international markets of entrepreneurs and their organizations (proactiveness, risk taking, innovativeness)

Opportunities

exploration and exploitation, arising from foreign contexts and relationships

Organization

international entrepreneural organization, orchestration of resources and capabilities to explore and exploit international opportunities,at the start and during the life of the venture

Source: Adapted from Zucchella and Magnani (2016).

Figure 1.3 The triple O in international entrepreneurship

(Figure 1.3). In this book, we frequently refer to "organizations" and – more specifically – to IEO (international entrepreneurial organizations, following Zucchella and Magnani (2016), because IE encompasses the activities of companies and profit-oriented ventures as well as other typologies of organizations, like social ventures, NGOs, and so on. We agree with Knight (2016) that IE "emphasizes entrepreneurial internationalization of young or small firms or of ventures in established firms". At the same time, we support the idea that IE also encompasses social entrepreneurship across borders and any case of exploration of international opportunities exploration and exploitation, in order to create new value, economic and/or social.

The term organizations thus refers to a system of interconnected actors, resources, capabilities, processes and activities, pursuing common goals and aiming at creating value for their stakeholders.

1.2   Theory perspectives

As an emerging field, IE needs to be understood in terms of its theoretical positioning. Figure 1.4 positions IE at the crossroads of international business (IB) and entrepreneurship (E) studies. However, as Zucchella and Magnani

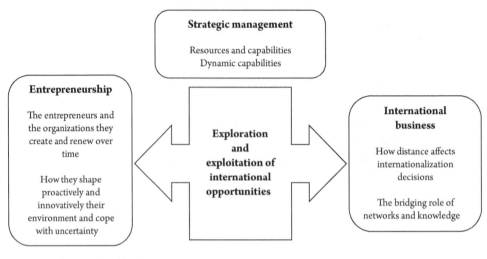

Source: Authors' elaboration.

Figure 1.4 IE and its parent disciplines

(2016) discuss, IE is also indebted to strategic management, especially in relation to concepts and models, which permit to understand and manage innovation and fast growth in international markets.

Regarding IB studies, IE established a particularly fertile debate with the internationalization process literature. When Johanson and Vahlne in 1977 outlined their seminal model in the IB process literature, they were observing mature large multinationals in Sweden, characterized by an incremental commitment to foreign markets: they started from countries, which they perceived "closer", then they gradually extended their scope. At the same time, in each country they increased their commitment (from export to foreign direct investments) as they gained experiential learning. This model (also Uppsala model) is still valid for many firms, but the growth in studies about INVs and BGs challenged some of its assumptions and outcomes. In the following years, Johanson and Vahlne (2003; 2009) progressively clarified and modified their original model, in order to explain why firms do not necessarily grow late and slow in foreign markets. The former experience of the entrepreneurs/decision makers and the role of networks were found as key factors capable of explaining early and fast global growth. A growing body of literature in IB focused on both social and inter-organizational ties as vehicles for rapid internationalization. This represents a major area of convergence between IB and IE, as well as the previously mentioned attention to the characteristics of key decision makers. Notwithstanding an increasing convergence between the IB internationalization process models and IE, a major difference persists between IB and IE: it is in the perspective they adopt in looking at foreign markets. IB theory is built upon the concept of the liability of foreignness (Hymer, 1976). Venturing abroad is a matter of risk/uncertainty due to "the unfamiliarity of the environment, from cultural, political, and economic differences, and from the need for coordination across geographic distance" (Zaheer, 1995, p. 343). Thus, firms entering new countries face higher costs when compared to local competitors. The mentioned different facets of distance and their combined effect make internationalization costly and gradual. International entrepreneurship tells us a different story: it views foreign markets as a realm of novel opportunities to be either discovered or created. It does not overlook uncertainty: instead, it requires readiness to cope with it in an innovative manner. It does not involve passively reacting to an unfavourable environment: instead, it means proactively shaping it. International entrepreneurial ventures do this thanks to their orientation, which represents their DNA, as discussed above.

Another major stream of literature, which has profoundly influenced IE is represented by entrepreneurship studies. They provide some of its distinctive traits, such as the attention to both the role of entrepreneurs and their organizations, with their attributes of risk taking, proactivity and innovativeness, and the importance of the processes of opportunities exploration and exploitation (Covin and Slevin, 1991; Shane and Venkataraman, 2000; Alvarez and Barney, 2007). Entrepreneurship studies also highlight the entrepreneurial decision-making processes and how entrepreneurs can shape their environment, leveraging on their (limited) actual resources and ties (Sarasvathy, 2001).

Finally, as mentioned above, IE borrows from strategic management studies some important concepts and theories. For example, the resource-based view (RBV) helps in explaining the role of resources – and particularly some resources and key capabilities (the entrepreneurial ones, the networks . . .) for the early and fast international growth of the firm (Peng, 2001; Westhead, Wright, and Ucbasaran, 2001; Weerawardena et al., 2007). A definition of IE according to Karra, Phillips and Tracey (2008, p. 441) resembles the strategic management and the RBV approach: "IE involves building competitive advantage by developing complex international resource configurations." A specific stream, which plays a relevant role in IE, is represented by dynamic capabilities, defined as "the firm's ability to integrate, build, and reconfigure internal and external competences to address rapidly changing environments" (Teece, Pisano and Shuen, 1997, p. 516). Dynamic capabilities support the capacity of international organizations to renew their abilities, products and processes over time and to face the challenges of fast moving and complex global endeavours (Weerawardena et al., 2007; Teece, 2014). In this last contribution, Teece supports a fertilization of IB theory with an entrepreneurial and dynamic capabilities approach, arguing (Teece, 2014, p. 8) that "dynamic capabilities coupled with good strategy are seen as necessary to sustain superior enterprise performance, especially in fast-moving global environments. Entrepreneurial management and transformational leadership are incorporated into a capabilities theory of the MNE."

Dynamic capabilities help in understanding how international firms can be entrepreneurial (i.e. innovative, proactive and risk taking/uncertainty coping) not only at their start-up stage but also during the course of their life, when they turn into established organizations (Zucchella and Magnani, 2016).

1.3 The environment of international entrepreneurship: across countries and cultures

1.3.1 The environment or the entrepreneur?

In this section the environment[1] and external drivers (or inhibitors) of international entrepreneurship are at the centre of attention. Here we take the view that IE emerges from and develops within an environment. However, such interaction, or the question of how much interaction and influence ensue from the wider firm environment is subject to lively discussion and not only in the international entrepreneurship literature.

On one side, the advocates of the "independent" view of entrepreneurship argue that it is the entrepreneurs and their particular traits, capabilities and resources they hold and develop. Entrepreneurial and firm-internal drivers here are seen to explain IE processes much more than do external environmental drivers. Such an argumentation is mainly based on the resource-based view (RBV) and similar theoretical frameworks (e.g. the knowledge-based view, dynamic capabilities) following the idea of the RBV that the firm's internal bundle of resources determines international growth and performance. On the other side, institutional scholars and industrial organization scholars argue that the external environment, that is, institutions or the industry, account for and determine any entrepreneurial action. Most recently, the intermediate position, the view that entrepreneurs draw strategically on their environment and the resources it offers, bridges the overly deterministic view of institutional theory with the overly independent view of entrepreneurship. It links the micro-, that is, entrepreneurs, and the macro-foundations, that is, environment, in an attempt to better explain IE processes and to account for the fact that there are convincing arguments for both positions.

Here, we adopt such an intermediate position to make the case for IE: international entrepreneurs and their firms interact with their multiple, different, dynamic and interrelated environments in order to explore and exploit international entrepreneurial opportunities.

The fact that IE deals with multiple and interdependent environments requires a stance which aims at identifying environmental factors which are common across country/cultural borders as well as a comparative stance (please see section 1.4). Hence, in this section, we focus on the identification and the description of past and future global trends which are considered external drivers and important framework conditions of IE.

As mentioned before, critically important topics in this context are technological innovation, industrial and social upgrading, national competitiveness but also global governance which trigger global trends and globalization. They gave rise to and reinforced concepts such as the "global village", "borderless world", and "worldwide society" in order to express the idea that the world is becoming smaller and an interdependent place.

1.3.2　A new and changed economic landscape for IE

Of all the trends affecting global business – and with it IE – definitely the economic growth of the 1990s was a main driver which affected substantially the amount of international activity. The growth came with the deregulation of markets, rapid growth of regional free-trade areas such as the EU, the NAFTA, ASEAN and APEC.[2]

At the same time the Soviet Union broke up and emerging countries such as Brazil, China, India, Turkey, Poland and so on realized impressive growth. The largest of these economies now account for more than a third of the world's largest economies and they are growing at around three times faster than the advanced ones (World Bank, 2011). Increased wealth and growth in many parts of the world bring enhanced purchasing power to an exponentially expanding middle class in these countries. Overall, a definite shift in economic power and influence away from industrialized countries – that is, the triad US, Europe and Japan – to countries in Asia, Latin America, Eastern Europe and Africa opens a new and challenging economic landscape for IE.

1.3.3 The role of technology

The availability of advanced methods of communication and transportation due to developments in information technology helped decrease significantly costs of international activity, opened new markets and made smaller markets grow large enough to offer viable business opportunities.

"Internetization" and entrepreneurship on Internet-enabled markets or international online markets make faster international growth possible for all firms, but for small firms in particular and provide platforms for internationalizing both new and existing businesses (e.g. Hagen and Zucchella, 2014; Katz, Safranski and Khan, 2003).

Put more broadly, digitization has not only meant increasing rates of Internet or online marketplaces. Adoption and "consumption" of digital technologies in everyday life and its ensuing constant connectivity also have a profound influence on the way other goods and services are consumed. For instance, products are increasingly examined, compared, purchased and paid for on the Internet and through mobile services. Consumption-related information is disseminated and discussed on blogs and forums. Consumers self-organize on social networking sites and take active roles in production processes. Not surprisingly then, digital virtual consumption is on the rise: millions of people around the world, that is, a global segment of consumers, are now spending billions per year on virtual items, characters and currencies in online games, social networking sites and the like (Lehdonvirta and Ernkvist, 2011). In this sense, digitization, and the many international business opportunities it creates, compares to a Cambrian moment (*The Economist*, 2014) for international entrepreneurship.

The quickly evolving scenario of the so-called industry 4.0 provides a set of technologies, which are supposed to be disruptive to a number of industries and firms (Strange and Zucchella, 2017). For international entrepreneurial organizations they represent a new realm of opportunities to be either discovered or created.

1.3.4 Exploiting opportunities of globalization

Technology, and in particular ICT, was also described as the driving force for the convergence of consumer preferences in Levitt's (1983) seminal contribution on the globalization of markets. Globalization of markets in the sense of convergence of consumer preferences has been advocated as one of the main factors enhancing the internationalization of new ventures because it increases the extent to which marketing strategy elements, for example, elements of the marketing mix, can be transferred effectively across countries and so provides an increased number of opportunities abroad.

Hannerz (1990, p. 237) stated that a world consumer culture is emerging as a result of the "increasing interconnectedness of varied local cultures as well as through the development of cultures without a clear anchorage in any one territory". Although the degree of convergence of consumer culture is still subject to lively debate, globalization definitely shapes the formation of global consumer segments. The Euromonitor profiles global consumers as of today as value-conscious, interactive, multicultural, health-driven, socially responsible and always connected. Such a profile is mirrored for example in the sharing economy and the many entrepreneurial businesses it comprises: Uber or BlaBlaCar, AirBnB or Couch surfing satisfy multiple facets of such a global consumer segment. Another trend related to health, wellbeing and social responsibility which cuts across countries and cultures is the tendency towards greener, healthier and more local food, to go for premium and organic ingredients or the tendency to control health (and live) through smart devices (Daphne, 2016).

1.3.5   Political-legal institutions conform

While the above-mentioned trends of globalization of consumer preferences relate essentially to the cultural environment, there are many other developments in political-legal institutions that reduce the differences between countries and so foster international activity and entrepreneurship. For instance, the demise of communism and its centrally planned economies, the rise of free-trade areas, and the even more extensive integration in regions like the European Union, together with the influence of the US, have led to more harmonization among the national institutions. Anti-trust law, for example, had, in comparison with the USA, always been more relaxed in most European countries. Under the influence of European regulations, anti-trust law and its enforcement have become harmonized (and stricter) across the area. Extant research also shows the influence of legal institutions, that is, laws and regulations, on shareholder protection, and the time and costs associated with opening a new business. Similarly, when examining new venture growth rates across markets, differences in regulatory environments have been found to influence growth. Further, differences in legal environments influence the timing of the dispute handling procedures in contract violations, therefore influencing the overall governance of international transactions. Firms (and investors) adapt their strategies to formal and informal institutions prevailing at the host location, especially when entering new markets. It follows that the more similar the country institutional environments, the easier it is to understand the requirements for international operations and for responses appropriate to local demands and the faster and broader internationalization may occur.

1.3.6 IE across industry environments

The environmental elements of industries and factor markets are less obviously tied to countries or culture. We discuss industry and factor market issues here as they comprise drivers that pertain to a group of businesses and so constitute part of the wider external environment.

Extant research shows that industry maturity and structure constitute relevant environmental factors that influence intensity, scope and speed of internationalization.

From the IE perspective, the distinction between global industries, in which the pressures for global integration prevail, versus multidomestic industries, in which pressures for local responsiveness prevail, is relevant. Firms in global industries serve universal customer needs, demands of multinational customers, and they face the presence of global competitors and pressures of cost reduction (Prahalad and Doz, 1987). The distinction between just the two is of course simplified but for IE it has an important implication: in the case of global customer needs, the firm approaches many markets simultaneously with the same product or service without the (costly and time consuming) need to respond to local adaptation pressures and so is able to accelerate international expansion and broaden international scope. Mathews and Zander (2007, p. 388) illustrate the influence of global industries further and make the case for a biotech firm, PSL, which rapidly enfolded into the global biotech economy as "the natural place in which to do business – dealing with sophisticated suppliers of protein science instrumentation, and sophisticated customers, around the world. It would have been perverse or outright impossible for PSL to limit its business to one country only."

In fact, there is a frequent association between the rise in INVs and their affiliation to high-tech or knowledge-intensive industries. It is agreed that these make part of naturally global market spheres, but there is also mounting evidence of born global firms in traditional industries (Gabrielsson et al., 2008; Rialp, Rialp and Knight, 2005; Andersson, Evers and Kuivalainen, 2014; Hagen and Zucchella, 2014).

Similar considerations apply to factor markets. Some factor markets are already very global and so trigger and determine global business approaches.

An example is the capital market, in which investors can move their funds from a country to another in a split second, following market opportunities. The labour market instead is highly "local". While, for instance, the American labour market facilitates rapid change from one company to the other, this is discouraged in Germany. It follows that for newly established US ventures it is much easier to attract experienced people than it is for new German companies. In the EU attempts have been made to create a common market with a free flow not only of goods but also capital and people. In IE literature, some factor market observations have been made by Mathews and Zander (2007) who note that rapid internationalization may occur in order to gain access to resources wherever they are available and because of a potential lack of adequate resources at home. Lenovo's founder Yang Yuanqing quote illustrates this well: "In a world with just one time zone – 'now' – business must source materials, innovation, talent, logistics, infrastructure and production wherever they are best available" (Accenture, 2008, p. 4). Also, the notion of knowledge environments (networks and clusters) as a source of international experience and reputation is emerging, which brings a fresh view to the analysis of the wider firm-environment (Jones, Coviello and Tang, 2011).

1.3.7 A new breed of entrepreneurs

We have started with and we conclude this section with the consideration of individuals involved in international entrepreneurship. One of the drivers (Figure 1.5) most commonly described in literature is a new "breed" of people with international experience and an international mindset, people who have benefitted from a more interconnected and smaller world in terms of education, work experience, travel and information. These new entrepreneurs are more able to bridge different environments, that is, institutional bridging (Karra, Phillips and Tracey, 2008), they have a worldview which is focused on international context and they have built, through their various international experiences, social and business networks they can tap.

In short, it is the interaction of environment and international entrepreneurs and their firms which bring international entrepreneurial processes to the fore. The interplay of globalization of markets, the enabling role and pervasive nature of technology and ICT in particular (Oviatt and McDougall, 2005), together with the emergence of global segments/customers in a growing number of industries, are major influencing factors for entrepreneurial action on an international or global scale. The interaction of environment and business activities of international new ventures also can create or help to develop local, national or international markets not only for their products and services but also for others by boosting demand and employment. In any

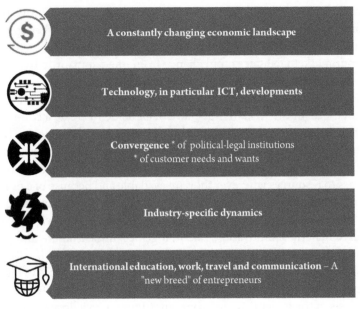

A constantly changing economic landscape

Technology, in particular ICT, developments

Convergence * of political-legal institutions
* of customer needs and wants

Industry-specific dynamics

International education, work, travel and communication – A
"new breed" of entrepreneurs

Source: Authors' elaboration.

Figure 1.5 Key environmental drivers of IE

case, IE adds an additional dose of uncertainty and "creative destruction" to the environment.

1.4 IE and comparative entrepreneurship

According to Oviatt and McDougall (2005) there are two streams in the study of international entrepreneurship. One of these streams focuses on the cross-national border behaviour of entrepreneurial actors and another focusing on the cross-national border comparison of entrepreneurs, their behaviours, and the circumstances in which they are embedded. Thus, research in the comparative branch of IE, or *comparative international entrepreneurship* (CIE), involves cross-national comparisons of *domestic entrepreneurship* (e.g. differences in entrepreneurial activity rates across countries) and of *entrepreneurial internationalization* (e.g. cross-country differences in the drivers of new venture internationalization) (Terjesen, Hessels and Li, 2016). Therefore, the focus of comparative entrepreneurship is how and why entrepreneurial activity differs across national contexts.

Comparative data from the Global Entrepreneurship Monitor (GEM),[3] the Global University Entrepreneurial Spirit Students' Study (GUESSS), the Community Innovation Survey and the like reveal important differences in entrepreneurial attitudes, intentions and activity across countries. The GEM for example depicts for 18 years such entrepreneurial information in more than 100 countries on an individual basis and complements this data with the survey of national experts (NS). GEM was one of the first initiatives to collect harmonized international data. As of today, continued policy interested in entrepreneurship has led to several large-scale initiatives to collect data. These include Eurostat, OECD and the World Bank.[4]

A conceptual rationale for the relationship between national environment and entrepreneurial activity (and consequently an explanation for the pronounced diversity) is that the political-legal, cultural and economic context determines the supportiveness of the environment so as to make it more legitimate, more attractive or easier to form a new business, to innovate or to internationalize. It may also be the case that the culture (or informal institutions) present in a society influences the motives, values and beliefs of individuals and so create more (or less) potential entrepreneurs.

Despite a convincing conceptual rationale and the pronounced diversity in entrepreneurial activity across countries (and societies), Terjesen, Hessels and Li (2016) in their recent review on CIE note that only limited theoretical insights and explanations are available.

According to these authors, research as of today, in line with descriptive data reported in the global or community surveys, identifies cross-national difference in entrepreneurship with regard to firm (e.g. financial and export performance) and country-level (e.g. economic growth) outcomes. Importantly, also the national antecedents, the drivers of IE (e.g. culture) differ, a fact which highlights the crucial role of a supportive or constraining context in which such entrepreneurial activity and the entrepreneurs are embedded.

We have already touched upon the external environment, namely economic, political-legal, and cultural conditions when identifying universal, global drivers of IE. Here we come back to these environments with an emphasis on the discussion of differences in national, country-specific setups. In comparative research institutional theory assumes an important role because institutions characterize the different environments and so affect economic and social development and with it IE. Their main function is uncertainty reduction because they establish a stable structure for all human and economic interaction, or, in different words, they define "the rules of the game" (North, 1990; Scott, 1995). Institutions which define the environment can be either formal – such as laws, economic rules and contracts – or informal – such as codes of conduct, attitudes, values, norms of behaviour, and conventions, or rather the culture of a determined society. The influence institutions exert differs in a temporal and control dimension: whereas a governing body can influence the evolution of a society's formal institutions in a rather direct and quick way, informal institutions are much less tangible and usually fall outside the direct influence of public policy. They can be moulded, but tend to resist change and take time to evolve towards new social norms.

1.4.1   Comparative entrepreneurship

The role and the nature of context

National economic, political-legal and sociocultural conditions, are seen to impact both the "supply" of potential entrepreneurs and the market room that presents (or limits) opportunities (i.e. the "demand" side) for new businesses and consequently the entry into and outcomes of entrepreneurship. The need for and the value of a comparative approach therefore is evidenced by government policy makers and business leaders worldwide as well as by scholars who challenge universally generalizable entrepreneurship theory for all contexts.

We will now examine in more detail research findings with respect to antecedents and outcomes of entrepreneurship across countries. In order to make the case for the large diversity we will provide illustrative examination of how countries or societies differ (e.g. in terms of specific institutions, processes, and attributes of entrepreneurs and entrepreneurial activity) and discuss evidence of the current explanations that are available from research.

We had touched upon change and *convergence* of society and markets as a result of global pressures emanating from technological, commercial and cultural trends. Here we stress that if we want to understand the effects of globalization[5] on domestic entrepreneurship and as a corollary on individuals and firms, we also need to study whether and how globalization tendencies and national institutions are complementary to each other. Hence, we have to take resilience, destabilizing or reinforcing effects in national systems into account.[6]

This reflects the view of institutional scholars (e.g. North, 1990) that the "rules of the game" in a society or the broader institutional context play an important role in explaining economic performance and entrepreneurship (Baumol, 1990). Baumol (1990) pioneered the role of institutions for entrepreneurial behaviour, that is, how "the social structure of payoffs" channelled entrepreneurship to different activities – some of which are productive, some unproductive, and some destructive or predatory. If institutions are such that it is beneficial for the individual to spend entrepreneurial effort on circumventing them, the individual will do so, rather than benefiting from institutions that reduce uncertainty[7] and enhance contract and product quality. The outcome in this case is expected to be one where corruption and predatory activities prevail over socially productive entrepreneurship. The underlying thought is that trust in the functioning of legal, political and economic systems arising from laws, norms, and standards is positively related to economic development. It follows that countries with a strong and supportive institutional environment will be more conducive to "productive" (e.g. high growth, innovative) entrepreneurship than those countries which are characterized by voids in their formal and informal environments.

(Potential) entrepreneurs as influenced by societies

We turn now to research findings which are concerned with the individuals, the potential entrepreneurs, and their embeddedness in context.

Unlike the idealized individualist, achievement-oriented "American" entrepreneur (e.g. McClelland, 1961), who is described so frequently in literature, there is growing evidence that entrepreneurial characteristics, traits, and values vary across contexts. Weber (1930) for example very early argued that society level differences in entrepreneurial activity can be explained by cultural and religious factors, namely Protestantism. He predicted that societies based on Protestantism, attached to an ethic of "working hard" and achievement would form people accordingly and in turn exhibit greater levels of entrepreneurship than societies with other religious traditions.

The "cultural mechanism" operates through cognition, beliefs and values and the individual's needs and motivations. Therefore, they affect how individuals recognize opportunities for entrepreneurial action and how they evaluate the feasibility and desirability of the pursuit of those opportunities by themselves. Beyond such individual effects, also collective mechanisms are at work: they influence individual behaviour through joint expectations and preferences and shared behavioural norms. For example, if entrepreneurs are seen favourably in a society and entrepreneurial examples, that is, an entrepreneurial role model, are strongly promoted, individuals in this society will have more positive beliefs and values and more confidence that such activities are feasible than individuals who live in societies where such an entrepreneurial atmosphere is not instilled. Business education is another example which can play an important role in this regard, by providing not only technical tools (i.e. accounting, marketing, finance, etc.), but by also helping to orient individuals towards self reliance, independent action, creativity, and flexible thinking.

Characteristics of individuals which have been found to differ across societies are, for example, their tolerance for ambiguity, autonomy or their locus of control[8] and risk-taking propensity. In a sample of students of business, economics, and engineering across nine countries, Thomas and Mueller (2000) asked whether traits associated with entrepreneurship differed systematically with cultural distance from the United States, a highly entrepreneurial nation. The traits examined were innovativeness, locus of control, risk-taking propensity, and energy levels. The authors found that as cultural distance with the US increased, the internal locus of control, risk taking, and energy levels decreased. A study with a total of 2,225 students in 13 developed and developing countries (Iakloveva, Kolvereid and Stephan, 2011) showed that the intentions to start a business were stronger in developing countries than in developed countries, a finding which is confirmed by GEM data and explained with "necessity" to form a business because of the lack of other employment opportunities. Rather than examining traits or intentions, Scheinberg and MacMillan (1988) asked whether motivations to start a business differed systematically across the 11 nations they surveyed. They did: whether one starts the venture because of wealth reasons, need for personal development, independence "to be my own boss" or because of a need to escape varied significantly across the countries.

Despite this evidence, there is also support for the expectation that entrepreneurs *do not* reflect the dominant values of their national society and share some universal traits. Entrepreneurs face similar challenges, regardless of context. For instance, in order to start international ventures, entrepreneurs require foresight and energy, passion and perseverance, initiative and drive, traits which speak to their "universal" traits. The entrepreneurial ability and will therefore have been described as anthropological constants. Research has also confirmed that central characteristics such as the combination of calculated risk-taking, innovativeness, and proactivity, that is, an entrepreneurial orientation (Covin and Slevin, 1991; Lumpkin and Dess, 1996), apply across cultural contexts. Similarly, across countries and cultures entrepreneurs have been shown to share a predictable set of values that are different from their non-entrepreneurial counterparts. For example, in comparison to others, entrepreneurs believed in taking the initiative and controlling their own destiny, were willing to take charge and direct others, and were positively oriented toward adaptation and change. This group of studies highlighted some consistent differences between entrepreneurs and non-entrepreneurs across cultures.

In summary, studies provide evidence for the role of national culture in that different cultures emphasize different motivational needs. The other key insight is that national culture is likely to influence national (or regional) rates of entrepreneurship by the creation of a larger supply of potential entrepreneurs: in order to be motivated to act, potential entrepreneurs must perceive themselves as capable and equipped to face the challenges of a global marketplace. Then, a formal regulatory framework intended to support entrepreneurship will have a much more potent impact on entrepreneurial activity levels. This suggests, that in addition to support from political-legal, and economic contexts, also informal institutions play an important role. It follows that a supportive environment for entrepreneurship is a combination of the "right" institutions, that is, the "right" drivers in a determined context.

Entrepreneurial activity and behaviour embedded in context

Not only the traits, the motivations or the values of individuals can be considered culturally bound, also entrepreneurial activity and behaviour is embedded in context. For instance, some countries are ripe with entrepreneurs who found firms in many different industries (e.g. the United States), while in other countries new firm formation is more of an exception (e.g. Germany, Italy). Not only the potential for and the level of entrepreneurship, also the type of entrepreneurship has been shown to be associated with the existence (or lack) of institutions.

While entrepreneurship in industrialized nations is mainly motivated by improvement and opportunity reasons, entrepreneurial activity in developing countries is more necessity-driven, implying that determinants of opportunity- and necessity-entrepreneurship are different. GEM data (Table 1.1) shows that such necessity entrepreneurship accounts for 27 per cent of new business creation across all countries studied, but that it is much more common in poorer countries. Rates of necessity entrepreneurship in China, Brazil, Argentina and Uganda were found to be at least five times higher than those reported in Belgium, France, the Netherlands, Sweden and Denmark (Reynolds, Bygrave and Autio, 2004).

Also, innovation is highly nation-specific (Nelson, 1993). For example, the combination of venture capital, which allows high risk taking, an active labour market of the scientists and professionals needed to form start-up companies, and strong financial incentives based on share options helps us to explain the competitive position of the US and UK firms in radical forms of innovation. Conversely, constraints on the provision of venture capital created by bank-centred capital markets as is the case in Germany, more

Table 1.1 An illustration of GEM (Global Entrepreneurship Monitor) data

Country	Entrepr. Inten- tions	Total early stage entrepr. Activity (TEA)	Perceived opportu- nities	Perceived capabili- ties	Innovation	Motiva- tional index[1]	Fear of failure
Brazil	28	20	53	36	12.4	1	36
Germany	6	5	37	41	24.7	2.7	41
China	21	10	30	49	28.8	1.5	49
Hong Kong	16	9	32	37	27.7	4.4	37
Italy	10	4	31	50	27	3.7	49
United States	12	13	55	33	37	6.4	33

Note: Percentages of aged 18–64 population who agree with the statement; indicate to have the required skills to start a business; who intend to start a business within 3 years; who are nascent entrepreneur or manager of a new business. 1) Percentage of those involved in TEA that are improvement-driven opportunity motivated, divided by the percentage of TEA that is necessity-motivated.

Source: www.gemconsortium.org /data.

rigidities in the labour market, and less adequate performance incentives within German firms, help to explain the position of German firms in more incremental types of innovation.

Therefore, the pronounced diversity of entrepreneurial activity and the ensuing differences in economic development and growth has led to much attention to the investigation of institutions to create favourable positive entrepreneurial framework conditions and a supportive environment.

The economic and the regulatory environment (formal institutions)

The set of possible determinants of entrepreneurship that has been examined in scholarly research in the economic-regulatory arena is very large. It includes, for example, demography, the level of economic development, the level of government intervention, availability of finance, the degree of administrative complexity/bureaucracy, the tax environment, the intellectual property rights regime and its enforcement, competition law, labour laws, bankruptcy law, corruption and so on (Table 1.2).

Here, the most frequently mentioned obstacles to entrepreneurs are excessive bureaucracy, taxes, labour and social security regulations, and access to finance. In particular, the role of and the access to capital and various facets

Table 1.2 A comparison of the "Ease of doing business" across some selected countries (2017)

	Ease of doing Business	Starting a Business	Register-ing Property	Getting Credit	Trading across Borders	Paying Taxes	Enfor-cing Contracts	Resolving Insolvency
New Zealand	1	1	1	1	55	11	13	34
Hong Kong SAR, China	4	3	61	20	42	3	21	28
US	8	51	36	2	35	36	20	5
Germany	17	114	79	32	38	48	17	3
Italy	50	63	24	101	1	126	108	25
Brazil	123	175	128	101	149	181	37	67

Note: Ranks from 1 to 190; a high ease of doing business ranking mean that the regulatory environment is more conducive to the starting and operation of a focal firm.

Source: Doing Business, www.doingbusiness.org; more indicators and subnational data are also available.

of financial institutions (e.g. provision of venture capital, access to international capital markets, lending policies) emerge as one of the most crucial conditions of entrepreneurship (e.g. Bruton and Ahlstrom, 2002; George and Prabhu, 2000, 2003). Additionally, the importance of well defined and enforced intellectual property rights for entrepreneurial activity is stressed. Overall, a dynamic economic environment, legal and regulatory quality, government intervention, as well as financial sector development and financial depth create a climate for innovation and entrepreneurship and are relevant to explaining the prevalence of entrepreneurial activity. Beyond creating trust, strong institutions also influence how much value from an opportunity is appropriable, a factor which plays an important role in evaluating the attractiveness of an opportunity. Figure 1.6 illustrates some indicators of economic and regulatory strength in various countries.

Bowen and De Clercq (2008) note that the entrepreneurship literature has focused largely on identifying the determinants of the level, rather than the type, of entrepreneurial activity. They hypothesize that the country's institutional environment will influence the allocation of entrepreneurial effort, and in particular will influence the extent to which entrepreneurial activity is directed toward high-growth activities. They use 40 countries to test their hypothesis and show that high-growth activities are positively related to a country's financial and educational activities targeted at entrepreneurship and are negatively related to a country's level of corruption,

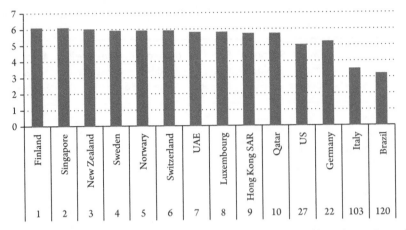

Note: Rank 1–7 (best); includes public institutions such as property rights, IPP; ethics and corruption; undue influence; public sector performance (e.g. burden of government regulation; efficiency of legal framework in settling disputes), security (e.g. business cost of terrorism, organized crime); and private institutions (corporate ethics, accountability).

Source: World Economic Forum – Global Competitiveness Index (data platform).

Figure 1.6 The top 10 countries – 1st pillar – Institutions of the World Economic Forum and US, Germany, Italy and Brazil

thereby identifying dimensions and channels to improve a nation's economic growth.

The informal – cultural – environment

In spite of growing knowledge in research, formal institutions alone do have limited explanatory value to explain differences across countries. For example, Van Stel, Carree and Thurik (2005) note that countries such as Belgium, France, Japan, Switzerland, Australia, Canada, and the US all have the same level of development, but that the first four have a low level of entrepreneurial activity, while the last three have a high level,[9] a difference that is shown to be persistent. While variations in entrepreneurial activities and their relative stability over time point to the influence of economic development, or rather to technological development and new markets coming forward, variations across countries and regions seem to be the result of institutional and cultural contexts. In other words, the relative stability in the differences observed for a group of countries or regions suggests that there are other explanatory factors than just economic factors at work. Work by Lafuente, Vaillant and Rialp (2007) provides empirical support for this premise that regions with different informal institutional frameworks will react differently to identical formal institutions and policies.

Therefore, in addition to economic and political-legal institutions, culture is widely thought to influence both the quality and the level of entrepreneurial activity across countries.

Most prominently, country cultural dimensions like individualism or collectivism, uncertainty avoidance or performance orientation[10] have been related to different aspects of entrepreneurial activity, processes and strategies. Recently, Autio, Pathak and Wennberg (2013) provided evidence for the influence of cultural practices (e.g. uncertainty avoidance, performance orientation, collectivism as defined by the GLOBE study) on start-up activity and growth aspiration of entrepreneurs in 42 countries. As one would expect, practices of uncertainty avoidance are negatively associated with business formation, whereas the cultural practices of performance orientation are associated positively with start-up activity. Collectivism is associated negatively with entry but positively with growth, revealing the differentiated impact of collectivism on different phases of the entrepreneurial process: in a phase of growth collectivism seems to facilitate resource mobilization. A socially supportive culture and social capital thus strongly support entrepreneurship rates.

Similarly, the presences of an entrepreneurial role or norms and commonly held positive perceptions regarding the status and reward of entrepreneurship models fosters start-up activity.

On the flip side, social stigma, that is, the informal social repercussions (beyond legal and financial consequences implied by bankruptcy) towards entrepreneurial failure in a society acts as a significant obstacle to entrepreneurial activity. The stigma associated with failure does not only condition the decision to become an entrepreneur, but also the character of the venture to be launched and the decision to terminate an entrepreneurial project (Landier, 2005). For example, Japanese entrepreneurs who tried and failed at a venture faced diminished career prospects, diminished social status and personal shame while in other social contexts, such as Silicon Valley, failure is treated much less seriously and failure is seen as a necessary step towards learning. Recognizing the importance of overcoming the stigma of business failure, the EU has introduced its "second chance policy" in 2007 and devoted the second of its 10 principles to this in the Small Business Act for Europe.

Other studies depart from the study of entrepreneurship rates or types and focus on cultural implications for entrepreneurial firm strategies. Using a seven-nation sample, Steensma, Marino and Weaver (2000) find that entrepreneurs from feminine, collectivist, and uncertainty avoiding societies appreciate cooperative strategies more than their counterparts. Moreover, entrepreneurs from feminine societies place greater emphasis on partner similarity in terms of objectives and values to ensure cooperative success, whereas those from individualistic societies emphasize contractual safeguards. Institutions also impact resource mobilizing (Desa, 2012). In situations of institutional voids, less entrepreneurial activity, more informal activity and more bricolage (making do – entrepreneurs do with what they have at hand) is observed. In contexts with no or little formal rules of the game informal practices are established to fill the voids confirming the view that in situations of weak, uncertain or emergent regulatory institutions, entrepreneurship moves towards informal activity to survive and develop.

In summary, the environment and institutions matter. They influence the supply and the demand side of entrepreneurial activity which shows pronounced variation across countries and societies. Moreover, the research illustrated above comes with important implications: it is the *combination of institutions* which matters. Formal institutions need to be complemented with the "right" informal institutions to guarantee an environment conducive to entrepreneurial activity and growth.

For policy, the findings demonstrate the need for greater attention to the combination and adaptation of entrepreneurship support and promotion more than a uniform layout across political and administrative boundaries.

1.4.2 Comparative international entrepreneurship – entrepreneurial internationalization across different countries

An additional field of comparative investigation relevant to IE is entrepreneurial internationalization across various countries, a field which is yet to be explored. As noted by Baker, Gedajlovic and Lubatkin (2005), compared to noncomparative entrepreneurial internationalization research (i.e. the stream on international new ventures/born global firms), the comparative IE stream has not developed at a similar pace and limited insights are available despite the large cross-national variations identified. Keupp and Gassmann in their review (2009) find that only 11 over 167 (6.6 per cent) of the international entrepreneurship articles published employed country-level factors. Just a few employ a multi-country design to study different resource stocks in various countries (e.g. Loane and Bell, 2006) but then do not elaborate on potential country-strategy associations. In other words, we know that entrepreneurial internationalization and resources important to internationalization are different across country contexts but we have little understanding of the how and why of such differences.

However, similar to the rationale above we may expect that the institutional setup influences not only start-up activity but also venture internationalization and entrepreneur's intention to internationalize. Economic, regulatory and cultural conditions of a country will determine whether a company is facilitated or hindered, pulled or pushed into markets abroad and how its internationalization strategy will develop.

The entrepreneur's intention to internationalize may be influenced by cognition and the self-confidence they exhibit regarding their knowledge, skills and competencies to internationalize. For example, international entrepreneurial education, and exchange programmes to build international first-hand experience and the like will foster an international entrepreneurial mindset, conducive to starting international new ventures.

Now, with respect to extant research on comparative firm internationalization, the conceptual and the empirical contributions are mainly confined to the drivers of internationalization. We may posit that countries with strong economic, regulatory and normative institutions offer resources and conditions that strengthen new venture competitive advantage that in turn leads them to internationalize in an entrepreneurial (born global) manner. On the contrary, we may also expect that new ventures with growth ambitions are pushed abroad because of weak contextual conditions which do not offer adequate resources for development (Mathews and Zander, 2007). In the same vein, small markets, economically non-attractive markets (e.g. competitive rivalry, demand patterns) may push new ventures abroad or affect the likelihood to start up internationally right from inception.

External environment aspects conducive to internationalization include intellectual property protection (Gassmann and Keupp, 2007), policy changes (Bell, McNaughton and Young, 2001), and openness to international trade (De Clercq, Hessels and Van Stel, 2008) similar to the drivers described for general entrepreneurial activity. Culture, with respect to industry, instead seems to play a small role in determining firm internationalization in the work, for example, by Boter and Holmquist (1996) and Perks and Hughes (2008). Cannone and Ughetto (2014) in their cross-country survey of drivers of born global firms show that the existence of a small domestic market positively and significantly affects the likelihood of a start-up internationalizing right from its inception. The level of internal competition neither helps nor hurts the propensity of born globals to diversify geographically quickly. Other elements (the degree of patent protection and the availability of private equity finance in the home country) do not seem to influence the internationalization choice or the degree of born-globalness of the sample firms. These results are in contrast with theoretical predictions that consider a weak appropriability regime and poor availability of private equity finance in the home country as strong determinants for firms that choose to internationalize from the outset.

In summary, comparative research in the field of entrepreneurial internationalization is still limited and prevents from drawing meaningful conclusions regarding cross-country patterns.

1.5 Beyond for-profit entrepreneurship: international social entrepreneurship

Social entrepreneurship (SE) is attracting growing attention both in business press and scholarly research. One of the reasons for the growing interest is that it signals the imperative to drive social change and its transformational benefit to society. Another reason is that social entrepreneurship is seen as a new phenomenon that is reshaping the way we think about social value creation and that challenges traditional assumptions of business and traditional models of entrepreneurship.

We will discuss social entrepreneurship and its international dimension in more detail in Chapter 2. The aim here is to give an introduction and an analysis of the extent to which elements applicable to the "traditional", commercial entrepreneurship are transferable to other types of entrepreneurship, namely social entrepreneurship. Gartner (2004) argued for considering the "critical mess" and challenged the field to consider different types of entrepreneurship to get a more complete idea of the process itself. Without entering into the discussion on the degree of distinctiveness of social entrepreneurship, we think that social entrepreneurship is an instance useful to outline elements which help to increase understanding of entrepreneurial processes and to illustrate how different contexts (country and firm-context) shape such processes. Since SE illustrates the interaction between different contours of contexts[11] and entrepreneurial action, it informs on an issue which is core to international entrepreneurship, the impact that the multiplicity of environments and differences may have on the entrepreneurial process.

Common across the many understandings and definitions of social entrepreneurship is the element of social value creation as the primary underlying driver, rather than personal and shareholder wealth. A second commonly accepted element is the fact that the activity is characterized by any of the

Schumpeterian "new combinations". Dacin, Dacin and Matear (2010) add consideration of different outcomes, both positive and negative, related to creating social value as a third definitional element.

Austin, Stevenson and Wei Skillern (2006) in their comparison of business and social entrepreneurship list four dimensions along which they evaluate the distinctiveness of SE against the traditional, commercial form of entrepreneurship, namely market failure, mission, resource mobilization, and performance management. They depart with the source and nature of opportunity and argue that social opportunities emerge from market failure and social needs which conventional entrepreneurship is not able to satisfy profitably. What then is a problem for the conventional entrepreneur is an opportunity for the social entrepreneurs. They note that the definition of the opportunity is not necessarily shared between the various stakeholders of a firm, which, as we will argue here below, are many and of many different types for the SE. Motivation for joint action then will greatly depend on the entrepreneur's ability to create a common shared view of opportunity.

Second, the same authors see differences in purpose and reward to differentiate traditional from social entrepreneurship. They argue that the fact that the primary mission of the SE is social value creation will have consequences for the firm's management and personnel motivation. Resource mobilization, a key phase of the entrepreneurial process and an important determinant of entrepreneurial success as described in conventional literature, will present a prevailing difference as social enterprises have more and very different stakeholders (from philanthropic investors to governmental bodies, to private investors, to individuals), making it more complex than in a conventional venture. Social enterprises may face more restraints in attracting crucial resources: for example, they may not be able to pay market rates for their people and so may not be able to attract talent. The need to rely on volunteers, for example, also requires the capacity to motivate and attract people who are tied to the specific social need, additionally constraining the room to move for SE. An additional question for SEs is how to balance and how to weave social and economic concerns into organization management, to the mutual satisfaction of the variety of internal and external stakeholders. Dacin, Dacin and Matear (2010) in this respect believe that a further distinguishing factor is the competency-based factors of social entrepreneurs to focus on and to engage external resources. Finally, the social mission creates greater challenges for measuring performance as relatively tangible and quantifiable measures of performance, that is, financial indicators, market share, customer satisfaction, are not readily applicable, a fact, which again adds complexity to stakeholder relationships.

As is clear from the above, the distinction between social and commercial entrepreneurship along these dimensions is not dichotomous, it is rather a continuum with the extremes of purely social to purely economic. Such an analysis, however, is useful to show how different contextual conditions impact on entrepreneurial processes.

To conclude, we briefly add some considerations with regard to the general external context, more than the "industry" context.[12] The factors that we have described in sections 1.3 and 1.4 as affecting the nature and the outcome of the entrepreneurial opportunity and activity, have considerable overlap for commercial and social entrepreneurship. Economic, political-legal and sociocultural environments can be equally important for both sectors. For instance, funding, philanthropic and non, originates from commercial enterprises and individual contributions depend on the populations' discretionary income and general economic conditions. Entrepreneurs, conventional and social, must know regulations and the specific types of laws relevant to their business. Overall, however, as discussed above, a country's political, economic and social conditions affect the need and the resources for certain types of activity, social activity such as education, environment, health, housing and so on. According to the many differences in such conditions, supply of entrepreneurs and their firm strategic responses will differ.

For example, social entrepreneurship may inform a resource-mobilizing strategy in adverse environments or in situations of institutional voids (given the fact that social opportunities may be more accentuated in poor or institutionally underdeveloped contexts). More reliance on external resources and a more cooperative stance on the side of SEs will inform conventional entrepreneurship which is more concerned with assembling unique firm internal resources. In the same vein, Dacin, Dacin and Matear (2010) suggest that SE are more likely to pay attention to the external sources and develop creative mechanisms to circumvent environmental barriers. More than circumvent, we add, SE have also been reported to actively change adverse conditions and act as institutional entrepreneurs. Institutional entrepreneurship, however, is beyond the scope of this book.

Finally, SE shows the importance of cultural understanding and cultural resources external to the firm. The ability to collect, understand and leverage cultural knowledge constitutes a key external resource for them – a fact which is directly transferable to international entrepreneurship and the idea that understanding of multiple cultural contexts gives rise to the identification of international opportunities (i.e. the capability of "institutional bridging" as advanced by Karra, Phillips and Tracey, 2008).

CASE STUDY

Ofo and the sharing economy: is bike ride sharing the next international entrepreneurial opportunity?

Manuel G. Serapio

The sharing economy has grown significantly during the past decade and created opportunities for new entrepreneurial ventures. Also known as "the access economy", "peer to peer economy", "collaborative consumption", the sharing economy uses "business models hosted in digital platforms that enable a more precise, real time measurement of spare capacity and the ability to dynamically connect the capacity with those who need it" (PricewaterhouseCoopers, 2015).

Estimates differ on the scale and growth rate of the sharing economy but all figures point to a significant rise. Ernst & Young estimates that the compounded annual growth rate globally of the sharing economy at over 130 per cent, increasing from US $3.5 billion in 2012 to US $115 billion in 2016 (Ernst & Young, 2015). Another projection forecasts that the sharing economy will reach global revenues of US $335 billion in 2025 from US $15 billion in 2015. This projected figure applies to just five key sharing sectors: travel, car sharing, finance, staffing, and music and video streaming (PricewaterhouseCoopers, 2015). Still, other sectors such as education, health, people/skills, and household goods are adopting the sharing economy model and exhibits promising opportunities for growth.

Among others, the surge in the use of mobile devices, the proliferation of mobile applications and digital platforms, increased connectivity through social media, and the growth in capacity from cloud-based computing have driven the momentum for the sharing economy. The sharing economy has facilitated the creation of economic activity in sectors where none existed before. It has spurred individual or micro entrepreneurs to participate as owners of goods or providers of services that they rent to customers on a short-term basis (Ernst & Young, 2015).

A prominent feature of the sharing economy is the speed, scope, and scale by which it has globalized. This has happened in two fronts. First, born global shared economy enterprises (BGSEE) have cross-borders at or close to inception. Popular examples include Uber which as of February 2015 operated in 250 cities worldwide. In just eight years, Airbnb reached 190 countries, 24,000 cities, and over 2 million homes. Second, the adoption and duplication of shared economy business models are taking place concurrently and rapidly in different markets. In the car ride share economy, for example, local and regional players have emerged to provide competitive business models and offerings, such as BlaBlaCar in Europe, Grab Taxi in Southeast Asia, and Didi Chuxing in China. As more shared economy models are developed and BGSEEs are established in local markets, these models and ventures are more than likely to cross-borders and be international.

CASE STUDY *(continued)*

China's share economy and the bike ride sharing industry

Growth in the sharing economy in China is happening in tandem with its expansion globally. However, this development is occurring in China at a massive scale. According to China's State Information Center, sharing economy transactions in China were worth more than $500 billion in 2016 involving about 600 million people and which could account for 10 per cent of China's GDP by 2020. As with other markets, the broad and rapid adoption of mobile technology has driven the growth in the sharing economy. Moreover, the explosion of non-cash transactions in China that have been facilitated by e-commerce giants, such as Alibaba (i.e. Alipay), Tencent (i.e. We Chat), and Baidu, have been distinctive factors influencing the rapid rise of shared consumption in China.

The sharing economy now pervades many aspects of Chinese life but none with a more iconic Chinese characteristic than bike ride sharing. After the Communist Revolution of 1949, the bicycle became the commuting tool of the Chinese people. In 1958 China was producing more than 1 million bicycles annually and by 1980 cycling accounted for about two-thirds of all travel in Beijing. In 1990 there was one bike for every two people in China (McCarthy, 2017).

Although cycling declined in the next two decades because of China's growing affluence and the population shifting to cars and mass transit as the preferred modes of commuting, the bike has made a comeback in recent years. Environmental considerations and gridlock traffic jams began to change people's attitudes to bicycles once again. In major cities, people were starting to use bicycles, especially for short commutes. City governments, such as Hangzhou, established policies and supporting infrastructure to facilitate the use of bicycles.

Ofo: China's pioneer in bike ride sharing

The bicycle's comeback inspired new business models that capitalized on the growth of the sharing economy. In 2015, ofo (pronounced as O-EFF-O and written in lower case letters), China's bike ride sharing pioneer, launched its first fleet of bicycles. The company was founded by Dai Wei, a graduate economics student at Peking University, who called on other students at Peking University to volunteer their bikes, let them be painted yellow, and be included as part of the campus bike ride share programme. This initial experience validated broad interest in a bike ride sharing scheme that served as the inspiration for Dai Wei to expand ofo (McCarthy, 2017).

The innovative model that Dai Wei pioneered combined the idea of a sharing economy plus smart appliances to solve the commute problems of the "last mile". Ofo created a bike sharing system that does not require the implementation of a docking station. A traditional public bicycle system requires a docking station, which not only occupies public space, but also makes it inconvenient for users to pick up and drop off bicycles. It also requires substantial funding from organizations including local governments to build and maintain the infrastructure system, which greatly hinders development.

CASE STUDY *(continued)*

In contrast, under the ofo model, users download the ofo app, key in the license plate of an ofo bicycle on the app, receive a code, and use the code to unlock the bicycle. The bicycle can be used whenever and wherever in need to take the user to his destination. Upon completing the ride, the user informs ofo via the phone app, locks the bike, and pays for the ride using a cashless mobile platform. Users can also share their own bicycles in the platform in exchange for the unlimited use of any ofo bicycles. Ofo users pay a refundable deposit of $14 to get the app and pay for the ride per hour (i.e. US $0.15 per hour; US $0.07/hour for students).

Dai Wei started ofo with a starting capital of 150,000 RMB or US $21,800. As previously noted, he piloted the business at Peking University with fellow schoolmates who signed up their 2,000 bikes for the initial programme. The business expanded quickly. At Peking University, 29,000 out of 40,000 students and staff use ofo with a daily turnover of 37,000 rides. Ofo is currently present in 200 universities and 34 cities in China. It currently has 1 million bikes and is the ninth largest Chinese company to surpass 1 million daily transactions.

Ofo has also been successful in attracting financing, most recently a $700 million Series E funding led by e-commerce giant Alibaba, Hony Capital and CITIC private equity. Earlier investors include Will Hunting Capital, dongfang, GSR Ventures, Matrix partners and others. The company is now valued at over US $2 billion.

On the other hand, competition has been quick to follow suit. Its largest competitor, Mobike, are red coloured bikes, uses a dockless system, and has incorporated GPS systems. Currently, there are over 30 bike ride sharing companies in China such that the companies have run out of colours to distinguish their bicycles to the public.

Ofo and bike ride sharing: the next major international entrepreneurial opportunity in the share economy?

Since its launch in 2015, ofo has become the largest bike sharing platform in the world. It currently has over 5 million registered users, providing more than 100 million rides in 34 cities in China. Its mission is to "make bicycles available to its users anytime and anywhere in the world". Instead of manufacturing more bicycles to meet the demand, its ultimate goal is to connect existing bicycles with people in demand so that people around the world can unlock any ofo bicycle via the platform to meet their need for a short trip.

Ofo's goal is to have 20 million registered users worldwide. The company has launched in London, Singapore, and selected cities in the US and is targeting 20 countries by year end 2017. Was it a wise decision for ofo to expand early and rapidly into international markets? Can it achieve the same level of success in market penetration, timing, and speed as companies like AirBnB, Uber, BlaBlaCar and others? Will the Chinese and ofo's bike ride sharing model of a dockless system work in other countries? Where should the company expand to meet its 20-market target and beyond? What routes to market should it take?

CASE STUDY *(continued)*

What challenges is ofo likely to face? How should it address these challenges? As the pioneering company in its space, ofo's success in addressing these questions will help determine whether ofo and bike ride sharing – Chinese style – represents the next international frontier for entrepreneurs in the sharing economy.

Note: Dr Manuel G. Serapio wrote this case with the assistance of Bijan Bewley. The information is from secondary resources. The case is intended for teaching purposes only.

Acknowledgment: CU Denver's Institute for International Business and Center for International Business Education and Research provided support for the preparation of this case.

Case references

Brennan, M. (2016). *China Bike Sharing Report: March 2017*. Chinachannel.com. Retrieved on 13 March 2018 from https://chinachannel.co/china-bike-sharing-report-march-2017/.
Ernst & Young. (2015). *The Rise of the Sharing Economy: The Indian Landscape*. India. Retrieved on 13 March 2018 from http://www.ey.com/Publication/vwLUAssets/ey-the-rise-of-the-sharing-economy/%24FILE/ey-the-rise-of-the-sharing-economy.pdf.
McCarthy, S. (2017). Bike sharing done right: A real Chinese innovation. *Supchina*. Retrieved on 13 March 2018 from http://supchina.com/2017/03/03/bike-sharing-real-chinese-innovation/.
Ming, C. (2017, 18 July). From bicycles to basketballs, everything's on loan in China's sharing economy. *CNBC (Consumer News and Business Channel)*. Retrieved on 13 March 2018 from https://www.cnbc.com/2017/07/18/from-bikes-to-basketballs-chinas-fast-growing-sharing-economy.html
PricewaterhouseCoopers. (2015). *Consumer Intelligence series "The Sharing Economy"*. PWC. Com/CIS sharing. Retrieved on 13 March 2018 from https://www.pwc.com/us/en/technology/publications/assets/pwc-consumer-intelligence-series-the-sharing-economy.pdf.
Yan, S. (2017, 17 April). Chinese bike sharing economy kicks into high gear. [Video] Consumer News and Business Channel, Squawk Box. Retrieved on 13 March 2018 from https://www.cnbc.com/video/2017/04/17/chinas-bike-sharing-economy-kicks-into-high-gear.html.
Yaraghi, N. and Ravi, S. (2017). *The Current and Future State of the Sharing Economy*. India: Government Studies in Brookings, Impact Series No. 032017. Retrieved on 13 March 2018 from https://www.brookings.edu/wp-content/uploads/2016/12/sharingeconomy_032017final.pdf.

NOTES

1 For the sake of convenience, we use here environment, context and institutions interchangeably. Although there are distinctions in terminology, i.e. legal, cognitive, normative or formal/informal institutions versus economic, political, legal, cultural environments, content-wise the subcategories are sufficiently similar and overlapping. For more detail please see North (1990).

2 EU (European Union), NAFTA (North American Free Trade Agreement), ASEAN (Association of Southeast Asian Nations), APEC (Asia Pacific Economic Cooperation).

3 The Global Entrepreneurship Monitor (GEM) research programme is an annual assessment of the national level of entrepreneurial activity. Initiated in 1999 with 10 countries, expanded to 21 in the year 2000 and over 60 countries in 2008, the programme covers both developed and developing countries.

4 Please see further readings and resources at the end of the chapter.

5 Here understood broadly in terms of convergence of society and markets.

6 As noted already with regard to externally determined influences, the analysis at the country (or societal) level, while having an impact on entrepreneurial organizations and actors, however is not sufficient to legitimize claims for all and for all types of differences.

7 At the macro-level this is related to trust in the functioning of legal, political and economic systems arising from laws, norms, and standards.

8 Locus of control is the degree to which people believe that they have control over the outcome of events in their lives, as opposed to external forces beyond their control. Individuals with a strong *internal locus of control* believe events in their life derive primarily from their own actions: for example, when receiving exam results, students with an internal locus of control tend to praise or blame themselves and their abilities. Students with a strong external locus of control tend to praise or blame external factors such as the teacher or the exam.

9 According to GEM Executive Reports.

10 Please see G. Hofstede (https://www.hofstede-insights.com/product/compare-countries/) or the GLOBE project (http://globeproject.com/) for more detail on cultural dimensions.

11 SE may be particularly informative with regard to institutional voids.

12 Social entrepreneurship as a context comparable to "industry" is the position advanced by Dacin, Dacin and Matear (2010).

 CHAPTER REFERENCES

Accenture. (2008). *Multi-Polar World 2: The Rise of the Emerging-Market Multinational*. Accenture, p. 4. Retrieved on 18 March 2018 from https://www.criticaleye.com/inspiring/insights-servfile.cfm?id=351.

Alvarez, S.A. and Barney, J.B. (2007). Discovery and creation: alternative theories of entrepreneurial action. *Strategic Entrepreneurship Journal, 1* (1–2), 11–26.

Andersson, S., Evers, N. and Kuivalainen, O. (2014). International new ventures: rapid internationalization across different industry contexts. *European Business Review, 26* (5), 390–405.

Austin, J., Stevenson, H. and Wei Skillern, J. (2006). Social and commercial entrepreneurship: same, different, or both? *Entrepreneurship Theory and Practice, 30* (1), 1–22.

Autio, E., Pathak, S. and Wennberg K. (2013). Consequences of cultural practices for entrepreneurial behaviors. *Journal of International Business Studies, 44* (4), 334–362.

Baker, T., Gedajlovic, E. and Lubatkin, M. (2005). A framework for comparing entrepreneurship processes across nations. *Journal of International Business Studies, 36*, 492–504.

Baumol, J. (1990). Entrepreneurship: productive, unproductive, and destructive. *Journal of Political Economy, 98* (5), 893–921.

Bell, J., McNaughton, R. and Young, S. (2001). "Born-again global" firms: an extension to the "born global" phenomenon. *Journal of International Management, 7* (3), 1–17.

Boter, H. and Holmquist, C. (1996). Industry characteristics and internationalization processes in small firms. *Journal of Business Venturing, 11*, 471–487.

Bowen, H.P. and De Clercq, D. (2008). Institutional context and the allocation of entrepreneurial effort. *Journal of International Business Studies, 39* (4), 747–767.

Bruton, D. and Ahlstrom, D. (2002). An institutional perspective on the role of culture in shaping strategic actions by technology-focused entrepreneurial firms in China. *Entrepreneurship Theory and Practice, 26* (4), 53–70.

Cannone, G. and Ughetto, E. (2014). Born globals: A cross-country survey on high-tech start-ups. *International Business Review, 23* (1), 272–283.

Covin, J.G. and Slevin, D.P. (1991). A conceptual model of entrepreneurship as firm behavior. *Entrepreneurship Theory and Practice, 16* (1), 7–25.

Dacin, P., Dacin, T. and Matear, M. (2010). Social entrepreneurship: why we don't need a new theory and how we move forward from here. *Academy of Management Perspectives, 24* (3), 37–57.

Daphne, K.A. (2016). *Top 10 Global Consumer Trends for 2017.* Euromonitor International. Retrieved on 13 March 2018 from http://go.euromonitor.com/white-paper-2017-top-10-global-consumer-trends-EN.html.

De Clercq, D., Hessels, J. and van Stel, A. (2008). Knowledge spillovers and new ventures' export orientation. *Small Business Economics, 31*, 283–303.

Desa, G. (2012). Resource mobilization in international social entrepreneurship: bricolage as a mechanism of institutional transformation. *Entrepreneurship Theory and Practice, 36* (4), 727–751.

Doing Business, http://www.doingbusiness.org/.

Gabrielsson, M., Kirpalani, M., Dimitratos, P. and Zucchella, A. (2008). Born globals: propositions to help advance the theory, *International Business Review, 17* (4), 385–401.

Gartner, W. (2004). Achieving "critical mess" in entrepreneurship scholarship. In J.A. Katz and D. Shepherd (eds) *Advances in Entrepreneurship, Firm Emergence and Growth* (Vol. 7, pp. 199–216). Greenwich, CT, USA: JAI Press.

Gassmann, O. and Keupp, M.M. (2007). The competitive advantage of early and rapidly internationalizing in the biotechnology industry: a knowledge-based view. *Journal of World Business, 42*, 350–366.

GEM (Global Entrepreneurship Monitor), http://www.gemconsortium.org/.

George, G. and Prabhu, G. (2000). Developmental financial institutions as catalysts of entrepreneurship in emerging economies. *Academy of Management Review, 25* (3), 620–629.

George, G. and Prabhu, G. (2003). Developmental financial institutions as technology policy instruments: implications for innovation and entrepreneurship in emerging economies. *Research Policy, 32* (1), 89–108.

Ghemawat, P. (2001). Distance still matters. *Harvard Business Review, 79* (8), 137–147.

GLOBE (Global leadership and organizational behavior effectiveness) http://globeproject.com/.

Hagen, B. and Zucchella, A. (2014). Born global or born to run? The long-term growth of born global firms. *Management International Review, 54* (4), 497–525.

Hannerz, U. (1990). Cosmopolitans and locals in world culture. *Theory, Culture & Society, 7*, 237–251.

Hymer, S. (1976). *The International Operations Of National Firms: A Study Of Direct Foreign Investment* (Vol. 14, pp. 139–155). Cambridge, MA: MIT Press.

Iakloveva, T., Kolvereid, L. and Stephan U. (2011). Entrepreneurial intentions in developing and developed countries. *Education & Training, 53* (5), 353–370.

Johanson, J. and Vahlne, J.E. (1977). The internationalization process of the firm: a model of knowledge development and increasing foreign market commitments. *Journal of International Business Studies, 8* (1), 23–32.

Johanson, J. and Vahlne, J.E. (2003). Business relationship learning and commitment in the internationalization process. *Journal of International Entrepreneurship, 1* (1), 83–101.

Johanson, J. and Vahlne, J.E. (2009). The Uppsala internationalization process model revisited: from liability of foreignness to liability of outsidership. *Journal of International Business Studies, 40* (9), 1411–1431.

Jones, M.V. and Coviello, N.E. (2005). Internationalisation: conceptualising an entrepreneurial process of behaviour in time. *Journal of International Business Studies, 36* (3), 284–303.

Jones, M., Coviello, N. and Tang, Y. (2011). International entrepreneurship research (1989–2009): a domain ontology and thematic analysis, *Journal of Business Venturing, 26,* 632–659.

Karra, N., Phillips, N. and Tracey, P. (2008). Building the born global firm: developing entrepreneurial capabilities for international new venture success. *Long Range Planning, 41* (4), 440–458.

Katz, J., Safranski, S. and Khan, O. (2003). Virtual instant global entrepreneurship. *Journal of International Entrepreneurship, 1* (1), 43–57.

Keupp, M. and Gassmann, O. (2009). The past and the future of international entrepreneurship: a review and suggestions for developing the field. *Journal of Management, 35* (3), 600–633.

Knight, G.A. and Cavusgil, S.T. (2004). Innovation, organizational capabilities, and the born-global firm. *Journal of International Business Studies, 35* (2), 124–141.

Knight, G.A. (2016). Theory development: appropriate and novel theories in International Entrepreneurship research. Second Odense Workshop on International Entrepreneurship, 20 May.

Lafuente, E., Vaillant, Y. and Rialp, J. (2007). Regional differences in the influence of role models: comparing the entrepreneurial process of rural Catalonia. *Regional Studies, 41* (6), 779–796.

Landier, A. (2005). Entrepreneurship and the stigma of failure. Retrieved on 19 March 2018 from https://ssrn.com/abstract=850446 or http://dx.doi.org/10.2139/ssrn.850446.

Lehdonvirta, V. and Ernkvist, M. (2011). *Converting the virtual economy into development potential: knowledge map of the virtual economy.* Washington, DC: infoDev/World Bank. Retrieved on 13 March 2018 from http://www.infodev.org/en/Publication.1056.html.

Levitt, T. (1983). The globalization of markets. *Harvard Business Review,* May/June, 92–102.

Loane, S. and Bell, J. (2006). Rapid internationalisation among entrepreneurial firms in Australia, Canada, Ireland and New Zealand: an extension to the network approach. *International Marketing Review, 23*(5), 467–485.

Lumpkin, G. and Dess, G. (1996). Clarifying the entrepreneurial orientation construct and linking it to performance. *Academy of Management Review, 21* (1), 135–172.

Mathews, J. and Zander, I. (2007). The international entrepreneurial dynamics of accelerated internationalisation. *Journal of International Business Studies, 38* (3), 387–403.

McClelland, D.C. (1961). *The Achieving Society.* Princeton, NJ: Van Nostrand.

McDougall, P.P. (1989). International versus domestic entrepreneurship: new venture strategic behavior and industry structure. *Journal of Business Venturing, 4* (6), 387–400.

McDougall-Covin, P., Jones, M.V. and Serapio, M.G. (2014). High-potential concepts, phenomena, and theories for the advancement of international entrepreneurship research. *Entrepreneurship Theory and Practice, 38* (1), 1–10.

Nelson, R. (1993). *National Innovation Systems: A Comparative Analysis.* New York, USA: Oxford University Press.

North, D. (1990). *Institutions, Institutional Change and Economic Performance.* Cambridge: Cambridge University Press.

Oviatt, B.M. and McDougall, P.P. (2005). Defining international entrepreneurship and modeling the speed of internationalization. *Entrepreneurship Theory and Practice, 29* (5), 537–554.

Peng, M.W. (2001). The resource-based view and international business. *Journal of Management, 27* (6), 803–829.

Perks, K.J. and Hughes, M. (2008). Entrepreneurial decision-making in internationalization: propositions from mid-size firms. *International Business Review, 17,* 310–330.

Prahalad, C. and Doz, Y. (1987). *The Multinational Mission: Balancing Local Demands and Global Vision*. New York, USA: Free Press.

Rennie, M. (1993). Born global. *The McKinsey Quarterly, 4*, 45–53.

Reynolds, P., Bygrave, W. and Autio, E. (2004). *GEM 2003 Executive Report*. Wellesley, MA: Babson College.

Rialp, A., Rialp, J. and Knight, G. (2005). The phenomenon of early internationalizing firms: what do we know after a decade (1993–2003) of scientific inquiry? *International Business Review, 14*, 147–166.

Sarasvathy, S.D. (2001). Causation and effectuation: toward a theoretical shift from economic inevitability to entrepreneurial contingency. *Academy of Management Review, 26* (2), 243–263.

Scheinberg, S. and MacMillan, I. C. (1988). An 11 country study of motivations to start a business. In B. Kirchoff, W. Long, W. McMullan, K.H. Vesper and W. Wetzel (eds) *Frontiers of Entrepreneurship Research* (pp. 669–687). Wellesley, MA: Babson College.

Scott, R. (1995) *Institutions and Organizations*. Thousand Oaks: Sage.

Shane, S. and Venkataraman, S. (2000). The promise of entrepreneurship as a field of research. *Academy of Management Review, 25* (1), 217–226.

Steensma, H.K., Marino, L. and Weaver, K.M. (2000). Attitudes toward cooperative strategies: a cross-cultural analysis of entrepreneurs. *Journal of International Business Studies, 31* (4), 591–609.

Strange, R. and Zucchella, A. (2017). Industry 4.0, global value chains and international business. *Multinational Business Review* (forthcoming).

Teece, D.J. (2014). A dynamic capabilities-based entrepreneurial theory of the multinational enterprise. *Journal of International Business Studies, 45* (1), 8–37.

Teece, D. J., Pisano, G. and Shuen, A. (1997). Dynamic capabilities and strategic management. *Strategic Management Journal, 18* (7), 509–533.

Terjesen S., Hessels, J. and Li, D. (2016). Comparative international entrepreneurship: a review and research agenda. *Journal of Management, 42* (1), 299–344.

The Economist. (2014). *A Cambrian Moment*. Special Report: Tech Startups. Retrieved on 13 March 2018 from http://www.economist.com/sites/default/files/20140118_tech_startups.pdf.

Thomas, A. and Mueller, S. (2000). A case for comparative entrepreneurship: assessing the relevance of culture. *Journal of International Business Studies, 31*, 287–301.

Van Stel, A., Carree, M. and Thurik, R. (2005). The effect of entrepreneurial activity on national economic growth. *Small Business Economics, 24* (3), 311–321.

Weber, M. (1930). *The Protestant Ethic And The Spirit Of Capitalism*. New York: Scribners.

Weerawardena, J., Mort, G.S., Liesch, P.W. and Knight, G. (2007). Conceptualizing accelerated internationalization in the born global firm: a dynamic capabilities perspective. *Journal of World Business, 42* (3), 294–306.

Westhead, P., Wright, M. and Ucbasaran, D. (2001). The internationalization of new and small firms: a resource-based view. *Journal of Business Venturing, 16* (4), 333–358.

World Bank. (2011). *World Development Indictors*. Washington, DC: World Bank.

Zaheer, S. (1995). Overcoming the liability of foreignness. *Academy of Management Journal, 38*(2), 341–363.

Zucchella, A. and Hagen, B. (2012). The international growth of e-commerce ventures. In S. Harris, O. Kuivalainen and V. Stoyanova (eds) *International Business: New Challenges, New Forms, New Perspectives* (pp. 137–154). London: Palgrave Macmillan.

Zucchella, A. and Magnani, G. (2016). *International Entrepreneurship*. London: Palgrave Macmillan.

2

International entrepreneurial organizations: characteristics and typologies

2.1 The characteristics of international entrepreneurial organizations (IEO): what do they have in common?

In Chapter 1 we introduced the concept of international entrepreneur and of the International Entrepreneurial Organization (IEO), an organization capable of exploring and exploiting opportunities in international markets.

International entrepreneurship can deal both with individuals pursuing international opportunities and with the organizations they establish. In this chapter we focus on the latter and provide first a synthesis of their characteristics (what they have in common), according to what we have learned in Chapter 1, and second an outline of their various typologies (what are their differences).

Chapter 1 provided a preliminary frame of commonalities among international entrepreneurial organizations, which we sum up below:

- The key role of entrepreneurs, characterized by similar attributes as their organizations, in terms of proactivity, risk taking and innovativeness;

- The central role of processes of exploration and exploitation of opportunities. International entrepreneurship happens when entrepreneurial opportunities across borders are either discovered or created and exploited;
- The pooling or resources and their orchestration to exploit opportunities. In literature much attention has been devoted to the creation of new firms for the exploitation of opportunities, though this is not the only way.

In framing commonalities among internationally oriented entrepreneurial organizations, we need to take the spatial (geographic) dimension of context particularly into account: the home and host environments come into play. The home environment can provide a stimulus to pursue foreign opportunities, for opposite reasons. For example, it can be a supportive environment, which encourages foreign growth or a hostile environment, which makes foreign countries more attractive in comparison with the domestic one. The same holds for foreign markets: an entrepreneurial organization may be attracted by foreign opportunities or create novel opportunities abroad, also arising from an apparently hostile context. Consequently, the second vector of international entrepreneurial action is represented by the processes of exploration and exploitation of opportunities that take place across these environments: this issue will be explored further in Chapter 3. Finally, a third vector is represented by the nature of entrepreneurial earnings (which is the ultimate goal why IEOs are established): are they pursuing profit or is their primary mission social?

Figure 2.1 outlines this triple E frame (Enabling/constraining Environment, Exploring/Exploiting processes, Entrepreneurial Earnings) and focuses on two key related issues for IE: the role of distance and foreignness. International opportunities arise across geographic boundaries and the IEO is subject – as mentioned – to the influence of the domestic and foreign environments. The latter are not only represented by countries, but also by smaller and larger geographic and institutional spaces. A high-tech entrepreneurial venture located in Silicon Valley, US, is at the same time affected by (and may also affect) a micro-regional environment (for example San Jose area), a US state (California), the US, the NAFTA region. In its activity of exploring and exploiting foreign and global opportunities it is affected (and may affect) similarly different levels of geographic and institutional spaces. Through these complex relationships with locations, opportunities can be discovered and created.

The concept of distance encompasses not only the geographic dimension, but also the economic, institutional and cultural ones. Distance is also a

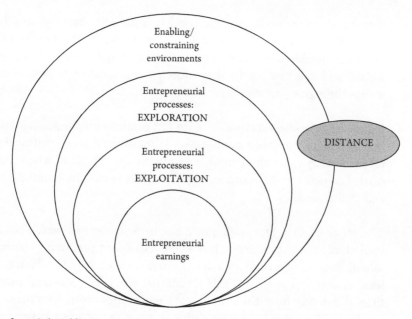

Source: Authors' elaboration.

Figure 2.1 The triple E framework

matter of individual perceptions: psychic distance refers to how distance is perceived by the firm decisions makers and represents an obstacle to internationalization, according to the gradual internationalization process literature (Johanson and Vahlne, 1977).

It is very important to underline that in IE distance is not necessarily a source of problems and costs. The mainstream international business literature builds on the assumption that doing business abroad has more disadvantages than doing business at home. This cost has two facets: doing business abroad is more costly from an economic point of view (cost of doing business abroad, CDBA) and it is also more costly from a social point of view (liability of foreignness, LoF). "Social costs arise from the unfamiliarity, relational, and discriminatory hazards that foreign firms face over and above those faced by local firms in the host country" (Eden and Miller, 2004, p. 187).

International entrepreneurship does not deny the role of distance and the consequent risks and costs of engaging in foreign markets, but it gives prominence to the opportunity seeking and risk-taking behaviour. In pursuing international opportunities IEOs have a proactive and uncertainty coping/risk-taking posture, instead of a risk averse one. In exploiting opportunities, they try to change environmental conditions at their advantage in a dynamic perspective, as opposed to the static one provided by the LoF and CDBA: firms can quickly learn how to overcome costs and risks of doing business abroad and can also try to shape foreign and apparently hostile environments, through entrepreneurial action.

Figure 2.1 thus suggests that distance can generate foreignness (in its different meanings), but this is not necessarily an obstacle to international growth for IEOs: they value opportunities and many opportunities arise in "distant" markets, thanks to the existence of differentials in culture, economic systems and institutions.

The story of Oca Sforzesca can describe a process in which distance is turned into a way to success. It is a very small firm producing Italian goose salami, located in a rural area in the north-west of Italy, in which there is a local cluster specialized in this traditional specialty (Mortara town). The firm, differently from the other local small competitors, who mainly focus on the local market (not even national, since the product is very regional and firms are very small) did not feel afraid of challenging distance. The young entrepreneurs targeted the Arab market, obtained halal certification and are now very successful there, providing Muslim consumers with a typical Italian specialty, salami-style, but without pork and produced under halal certification. The costs they had to bear in order to sell in distant (and very different) markets have been compensated by sales growth and higher profit margins. The product can at the same time comply with foreign needs and benefit from a strong country of origin effect. This case also provides insight about the role of different levels of the environment (local district, in which specialized competences are embedded, the country, the European Union) and about the capacity of small entrepreneurial ventures to modify home and host environments. For example, they now provide a benchmark for other small firms in the local system and more generally in the food industry. They also changed perceptions about salami in Muslim countries, allowing consumers to appreciate halal-compliant typical products.

Oca Sforzesca also confirms the triple O frame presented in Chapter 1: the entrepreneurs developed an international orientation and instilled it in their organization, they explored an opportunity that did not exist before or that others had overlooked, and in order to exploit it they had to find resources and develop capabilities around the new project. For example, obtaining the needed certifications required both financial resources and the development of capabilities, from manufacturing processes, to supply chain management to communication in different languages and new sales channels had to be found. Proactivity, innovativeness and risk-taking became the venture's DNA, which is now moving towards new challenges and novel opportunities to capture.

2.2 The different typologies of IEOs: international new ventures and born global firms

The IE field of research has its birth period between the end of the 1980s and the beginning of the 1990s. McDougall (1989) first highlighted the phenomenon of international entrepreneurship, and the following Oviatt and McDougall article (1994) is considered a milestone in the development of this field. Since then, much attention has been devoted to new and young firms, which early and quickly embrace international growth. From the early 1990s, two typologies of IEOs acquired increasing popularity: born global firms and international new ventures. In both cases, internationalization happens at the beginning or in the first years of life of the firm. According to Oviatt and McDougall (1994) the international business literature mainly focused on large multinationals. In addition, the internationalization process stream advanced the idea that foreign growth had to be late and slow. In Johanson and Vahlne's (1977) conceptualization, this is attributable to risk aversion of actors and to the psychic distance to foreign markets. Risk can be reduced through learning about foreign contexts, but this occurs through experience (experiential learning), which takes time. As a consequence, firms start operating abroad after consolidating the domestic market presence. They also initiate internationalization with modes which require lower commitment and lower risk, that is by exporting to "near" countries. Once they gain sufficient experience, they increase both commitment in each country and progressively extend their geographic scope to more "distant" countries.

International new ventures (INVs) are defined by Oviatt and McDougall (1994, p. 49) as "a business organization that, from inception, seeks to derive significant competitive advantage from the use of resources and the sale of outputs in multiple countries". These firms do not necessarily own assets abroad, for example foreign subsidiaries. According to Oviatt and McDougall "the definition of the international new venture is concerned with value added, not assets owned" (Oviatt and McDougall, 1994, p. 49). Another key aspect is that in both cases the use of resources and the sale of outputs are considered as dimensions of their international activity. In their conceptualization, Oviatt and McDougall also identify four types of INVs: the export/ import start-up, the multinational trader, the geographically focused start-up and the global start-up. The first two are also considered the new international market makers and share a limited number of activities in their value chain (notably logistics) coordinated respectively across a small or larger number of countries. The latter two share the coordination of a wider set of activities in the value chain across a few or many countries.

What are then born global firms? Knight (1996) defines them as follows:

> Born globals are companies that conduct international business at or near the founding of the firm. Despite the limited resources that usually characterize new businesses, born globals achieve substantial international sales from an early stage in their development, and are emerging in substantial numbers worldwide. The period from the firm's founding in its home country to initial foreign market entry is often three or fewer years.

In born global firms, it seems the focus is more on selling abroad and with a global scope. However, there are overlaps with the INV concept. The term was coined by Rennie (1993) in his study on Australian exporters: "Being born global means that exporting was the primary goal of the firm even upon its inception" (Rennie, 1993, p. 45).

The empirical investigation on born global firms has opened a number of questions about the time and space dimensions of the born global firm. Time refers to both precocity and speed of internationalization. A firm can be an early exporter, but then it may grow slowly and gradually in foreign markets. In this case we only have an early internationalizer or even an early global, who follows a slow international growth. Table 2.1 compares the two main schools of thought regarding the internationalization process: the late and slow Uppsala process and the born global/INV growth, characterized by precocity and speed. There are a number of "intermediate cases" that the literature in both fields has highlighted. For example, some firms can achieve

Table 2.1 Typologies of internationalization processes along time and space

Time and space in BGs	Regional scope	Global scope
Early	Early internationalizer	Early global
Fast	Fast internationalizer	Fast global (born-again global)
Early and fast	Born international	Born global
Late and slow	Traditional gradual internationalizers	

Source: Authors' elaboration.

fast global growth after some years from their foundation: this is the case of born-again global firms discussed by Bell, McNaughton and Young (2001). This happens when some critical event affects an otherwise scarcely or slowly internationalizing path. Also, the proponents of the gradual internationaliza-tion path *à la* Uppsala, acknowledge that some situations (hiring of knowl-edgeable staff, relationship with key customers/distributors abroad and so on) may speed and broaden the international growth of firms (Johanson and Vahlne, 1990 and 2009). Regarding the scope of the international growth, some authors have pointed out that a number of early and/or fast interna-tionalizers tend to focus on their region, and – as such – should be labelled "international" rather than "global" (Gabrielsson and Pelkonen, 2008).

The geographic scope can be approached in a more fine-grained approach, for example considering how many countries are involved and how dis-tant from the home base they are, along the different distance dimensions (geographic, economic, cultural/institutional). Also, a more fine-grained approach to the time variables (precocity and speed) could help in distin-guishing better the various categories. However, the purpose of Table 2.1 is to provide a preliminary approach to differentiated internationalization processes.

Another taxonomy of firms along their internationalization processes has been advanced by Servais, Zucchella and Palamara (2007) and includes the sourcing side of the international activity. The international sourcing and the internationalization of different activities along the value chain were already hypothesized in the above-mentioned Oviatt and McDougall (1994) defini-tion of INVs. However, since then the predominant attention of scholars has been on the selling side.

In their empirical work, Servais, Zucchella and Palamara (2007) found that a relevant percentage of firms (around 60 per cent) were both importers and exporters, either early and fast (25 per cent) or late and slow (35 per cent). Interestingly, some firms can be early international, but only on the sourcing side (born importer, 8 per cent).

Finally, a perspective of analysis can be also represented by the interna-tionalization path, after the beginning phase of the foreign growth. In fact, some authors (Vissak and Francioni, 2013) have invited to consider non-linearity of the path, because firms can be either slow and gradual internationalizers or early and fast, but after some time they may experience de-internationalization, re-internationalization and alternative ruptures and re-starts of the foreign expansion. More generally, there are calls for research on the longitudinal growth of born global firms after their first years (Almor, Tarba and Margalit, 2014): do they maintain distinctive features of internationalization or do they gravitate later on towards a slower and more gradual pattern? Hagen and Zucchella (2014) introduce the concept of "born to run" firms, in order to identify born global enterprises that continue in their fast global expansion along time and go through repeated renewals of their strategy and business model. Chapters 4 and 5 are devoted to exploring further this issue.

2.3   The different typologies of IEOs beyond international new ventures and born global firms

The first chapter and the first section of this chapter provide a frame for understanding international entrepreneurship that goes beyond international new ventures and born global firms, even though they represent its core cases. Any proactive, innovative and risk-taking organization exploring and exploiting international entrepreneurial opportunities can fall into the area of international entrepreneurship. For example, as mentioned already, some organizations pursuing primarily non-profit objectives can be considered as examples of international entrepreneurship. The next section is devoted to international social entrepreneurship, in order to understand better this issue, which represents an emerging and increasingly relevant field of study.

Established firms can be examples of international entrepreneurship, when they embrace fast global growth, even at a later stage in their life, as it happens for born-again global firms. Another case is represented by micro-multinationals, which pursue global opportunities through a variety of entry modes, including foreign subsidiaries and joint ventures, even if they have a small size. According to Dimitratos et al. (2003), micro-multinationals adopt a variety of entry modes and coordinate a number of activities of their value chains in diverse international markets. ATOM is a micro-multinational firm, mainly specialized in machinery for the cutting of leather for the footwear industry. They are based in an Italian luxury footwear district and from here they continually upgraded their manufacturing skills, becoming one of the leaders in their global market niche. They have exported in many different markets since their beginning in the early 1950s and in the last two decades they have invested in key world regions through manufacturing and sales subsidiaries and joint ventures, from China to Brazil. They still portray themselves as an internationally oriented entrepreneurial firm, always seeking for new business and experimenting new technologies (https://www.atom.it/en/).

Established small firms can pursue continually in their life entrepreneurial opportunities on a global scale, and consequently be included among the cases of international entrepreneurship. Small global firms (Dimitratos et al., 2010) are characterized by the capacity to sell their products in different and distant countries. Maintaining and continually nurturing this entrepreneurial growth across markets rests upon the possession of distinctive competences and unique products, usually targeted at a small number of global customers (niche strategy, Zucchella and Palamara, 2006). Moreschi manufactures luxury shoes in the same district in which ATOM is based and is approximately the same age and – like ATOM – is still a family business after two generations of entrepreneurs. Their value chains are very different because they chose to concentrate all the manufacturing activity in their home base and to export their shoes from there. Export represents 80 per cent of their sales and they started exporting very early in their life. They continually pursue growth in foreign markets and innovation in their products and distribution channels.

Ethnic entrepreneurship refers to firms created by immigrants and represents a growing area for studying how immigrants can develop organizations in the host country and from here explore and exploit global opportunities (Ilhan-Nas, Sahin and Cilingir, 2011). This stream focuses particularly on the entrepreneurs and their social networks. A related stream is represented by transnational entrepreneurship: "Transnational entrepreneurs (TEs) are individuals that migrate from one country to another, concurrently maintaining business related linkages with their former country of origin, and currently adopted countries and communities" (Drori, Honig and Wright, 2009, p. 1001). The same authors define ethnic entrepreneurs as "those individuals whose group membership is tied to a common cultural heritage or origin and are known to out-group members as having such traits" (Drori, Honig and Wright, 2009, p. 1004). In their contribution they suggest that firms founded by TEs are more prone to explore and exploit global opportunities, than the firms founded by ethnic entrepreneurs.

International entrepreneurship can also apply to the case of larger firms, when they act entrepreneurially in the formation and capture of global opportunities. For example, a subsidiary of a multinational firm (MNE) can behave entrepreneurially, provided it has an autonomous strategic mandate and the capacity to take risks and develop an innovative offer for its market. Birkinshaw (1997) was among the first analysing this perspective and suggesting that MNE subsidiaries can be examples of corporate entrepreneurship. For example, Philips' subsidiary in Canada created the company's first colour TV, while Philips Australia created the first stereo TV and finally Philips UK introduced the first TV with teletext capabilities. This happened because Philips' headquarters supported autonomy and innovation in their subsidiaries and developed a global network for sharing innovations in the group.

The IE concept can thus work also for an entire multinational group. A case, which has received attention in literature, is represented by multinationals from emerging economies, characterized by early and fast global growth. These Emerging Market Multinationals (EMMNE) – according to Luo and Tung (2007) – pursue aggressive/springboard international strategy or dizzying speed international expansion (Guillén and García-Canal, 2009). Denicolai, Strange and Zucchella (2015) report the case of the Taiwanese MNE Foxconn, which has experienced very fast global growth, establishing manufacturing facilities in different Asian countries and then in Brazil, Czech Republic, India, Hungary, Japan, Malaysia, Mexico, and Slovakia. Foxconn is a key supplier for lead firms in the electronics and in the smartphone industry, like Apple. The number of Foxconn employees rose exponentially from 9,000 in 1996 to 44,000 in 2000, to 603,000 in 2007, and over 1 million in 2011. Foxconn is a supplier with capacity to explore and exploit opportunities through technological innovation:

> These capabilities were well illustrated by Steve Jobs' demand for an unscratchable glass screen for the iPhone just weeks before the product launch in 2007, and by the subsequent willingness of Foxconn to assemble the products with the newly developed screens at very short notice (Duhigg and Bradsher, 2012). But the development of these capabilities has also enabled Foxconn to benefit from its own isolating mechanisms based on patents and its own firm-specific technical knowledge. (Denicolai, Strange and Zucchella, 2015, p. 357)

In this vein, there is room for extending the area of international entrepreneurship to proactive, innovative and risk-taking behaviour of large firms in international markets, as Zahra and George suggested (2002). Companies like Apple attracted the attention of entrepreneurship studies, for the capacity of the firm to be proactive, innovative and risk-taking repeatedly in their life. Google is another case of what is labelled (international) corporate entrepreneurship: "Since its founding in 1998, Google was one of the most innovative companies in the world. The company ranked at the top with other leading companies like Apple in the development of innovative products and technologies. Corporate entrepreneurship and innovation was the heart and soul of the company's success" (Finkle, 2012, p. 866).

Figure 2.2 provides a map of the different typologies of international entrepreneurial organizations, based on the literature streams briefly summarized

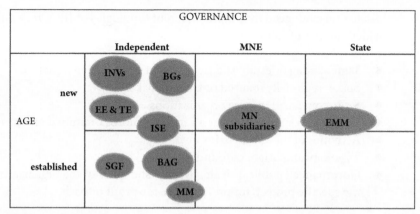

Legend:
INVs: International new ventures
BGs: Born global firms
BAG: Born-again global firms
EE&TE: Ethnic and transnational entrepreneurship
SGF: Small global firms
MM: Micro multinationals
ISE: International social entrepreneurship
MN subsidiaries: Subsidiaries of multinational firms
EMM: Emerging market multinationals

Source: Adapted from Zucchella and Magnani (2016).

Figure 2.2 A map of the typologies of international entrepreneurial organizations (IEOs)

above. Among the various perspectives of analysis, the figure focuses on the age of the organization and on its governance, distinguishing between independent, MNEs and state owned/state influenced firms, like a number of EMMNEs tend to be.

Figure 2.2 is not exhaustive of the variants of international entrepreneurship, but simply summarizes some key typologies, which correspond to the main streams that developed in the last three decades.

The notion of international entrepreneurial organization discussed in Chapter 1 can be a common umbrella for all these differentiated typologies of firms and organizations. It confirms the idea that "International Entrepreneurship has the potential to distinguish activities of all public and private organisations transcending national borders, regardless of age, size and industrial sector" (Dimitratos and Jones, 2005, p. 121).

Figure 2.2 selects some variables, which help in representing the field, notably the type of governance and the age of the firm. However, the above discussion evidenced that all the different typologies of IEOs may differ by a wider number of factors, viz.:

- Time: young or established, early or late internationalizers
- Space: regionally focused or truly global
- Size: from small to large organizations
- Entry modes: export versus a variety of more committed entry modes
- Activities of the value chains involved
- Typology and origin of founders
- Governance (public, private, hybrid) and goals of the organization or of the specific project, for profit or not-for-profit or both.

These dimensions of analysis all contribute to a richer perspective about international entrepreneurship, which is a fast expanding field, capable of encompassing very different types of organizations but also of their founders/ entrepreneurs. This book mostly focuses on the organizations set up by the latter, but we are aware that understanding better who the founders of these organizations are and what the characteristics of international entrepreneurs are is a very important piece of the IE puzzle.

Patagonia is a well-known outdoor clothing brand. It is an interesting case of international entrepreneurship, with many facets, in which the role of its founder and the organization are clearly intertwined. It is an example of entrepreneurship that crosses borders in different directions, from the sale of their products to the sourcing of materials and apparel. Their entire supply chains are traceable and working and environmental conditions at their overseas suppliers can be monitored by any customer through the Footprint Chronicle system.

They also "globalize" their ideals of sustainability, which are at the heart of the firm's mission:

> We believe the environmental crisis has reached a critical tipping point. Without commitments to reduce greenhouse gas emissions, defend clean water and air, and divest from dirty technologies, humankind as a whole will destroy our planet's ability to repair itself. At Patagonia, the protection and preservation of the environment isn't what we do after hours. It's the reason we're in business and every day's work. (http://www.patagonia.com/home/)

The firm goes beyond sustainability proclamations, they effectively act for change. They give 1 per cent of their sales to support environmental organizations around the world. They also took action against excessive consumption of goods and resources, through their ad on Black Friday in 2011 that read, "Don't Buy This Jacket". The organizations and the community projects they support are in different parts of the world.

The firm owes much to its visionary founder, Yvon Chouinard, and the capacity of the firm to continue also after his retirement to be entrepreneurial rests on how the entire organization has metabolized more than fifty years of being at the frontier of innovation and sustainability in the outdoor apparel.

The international orientation has been part of the company history since the beginning:

> During the late sixties, men did not wear bright, colourful clothes, not outside. "Active sportswear" consisted of basic grey sweatshirts and pants, and the standard issue for climbing in Yosemite was tan cut-off chinos and white dress shirts bought from the thrift store. On a winter climbing trip to Scotland in 1970, Chouinard bought a regulation team rugby shirt to wear rock climbing. Overbuilt to withstand the rigors of rugby, it had a collar that would keep the hardware slings from cutting into the neck. It was blue, with two red and one yellow centre stripe across the chest. Back in the States, Chouinard wore it around his climbing friends, who asked where they could get one.
>
> We ordered a few shirts from Umbro, in England, and they sold straight off. We couldn't keep them in stock, and soon began ordering shirts from New Zealand and Argentina as well. Other companies followed suit and we soon realized that we had introduced a minor fashion craze to the United States. We began to see clothing as a way to help support the marginally profitable hardware business, and by 1972 we were selling polyurethane rain cagoules and bivouac sacks from Scotland, boiled-wool gloves and mittens from Austria, and hand-knit reversible "schizo" hats from Boulder (http://www.patagonia.com/home/ http://www.patagonia.com/company-history.html).

The firm has shown characteristics of proactivity, innovativeness and risk taking since its foundation and along its life till now. One of the many examples is the decision to use only organic cotton in 1994:

> In the fall of 1994, we made the decision to take our cotton sportswear 100% organic by 1996. We had eighteen months to make the switch for 66 products – and only four months to line up the fabric. We found that there simply wasn't enough organic cotton commercially available to buy through brokers. We had to go direct to the few farmers who had gone back to organic methods. And then we had to go to the ginners and spinners and persuade them to clean their equipment after

running what would be for them very low quantities. We had to talk to the certifiers so that all the fiber could be traced back to the bale. We succeeded. Every Patagonia garment made of cotton in 1996 was organic, and has been ever since (http://www.patagonia.com/home/ http://www.patagonia.com/company-history.html).

Patagonia was the first Californian company to sign up for B certification, in January 2012, joining over 500 certified B Corporations in 60 different industries:

> To qualify as a B Corp, a firm must have an explicit social or environmental mission, and a legally binding fiduciary responsibility to take into account the interests of workers, the community and the environment as well as its sharehold-ers. A company must also amend its articles of incorporation to adopt B Lab's commitment to sustainability and treating workers well. In addition a B Corp must pay an annual fee based on revenues, biannually complete a B Impact Report (a lengthy questionnaire that measures social and environmental impact), meet B-Lab's comprehensive social and environmental performance standards and make that B Impact Report public, in order to receive the certification from B Lab (http://eu.patagonia.com/gb/en/b-lab.html).

"Patagonia is trying to build a company that could last 100 years", said founder Yvon Chouinard on the day Patagonia signed up. "Benefit corporation legislation creates the legal framework to enable mission-driven companies like Patagonia to stay mission-driven through succession, capital raises, and even changes in ownership, by institutionalizing the values, culture, processes, and high standards put in place by founding entrepreneurs" (http://eu.patagonia.com/gb/en/b-lab.html).

The case history of Patagonia shows many facets of an International Entrepreneurial Organization: the role of the founder, the early international orientation, the set-up of an innovative, proactive and risk-taking organization, the exploration and exploitation of opportunities at the global scale, the international entrepreneurship effort both in sourcing and in selling, both in generating revenues and profits and in investing in non-profit initiatives and in spreading globally the sustainability ideas. Finally, it is also exemplar of a hybrid governance model, the benefit company, and on how entrepreneurship can also extend to the organization's governance.

2.4 International social entrepreneurship

Social entrepreneurship (SE), and the new entrepreneurial model that comes with it, is gaining popularity – in practice, in scholarly research and in policy making. Social entrepreneurship signals a drive towards changing social conditions for the better, with long-lasting benefits to society at large. The field goes back to early 1980s, when some researchers focused attention on a dimension of classic commercial entrepreneurship highlighted by Schumpeter (1934) almost fifty years before, namely the impact of the firm's activity on social wealth and social value "allocation". Attention then moved from social value allocation to social value *creation*, and to how for-profit firms are able to create both financial value in terms of profits and social value for the people they serve.

Social entrepreneurship has become so inclusive now that almost all socially beneficial activities seem to fit into this "big tent" with the consequence of significantly different understandings of what makes for a social enterprise. Central and common elements in various definitions of social entrepreneurship focus on two aspects, that is, an "entrepreneurial" dimension and a "social" one. The entrepreneurial dimension, grounded in what we have said before, is that the entrepreneurs with their venture develop an innovative value proposition for a need of neglected, highly disadvantaged segments that lack financial means or welfare support. At the same time, though, social entrepreneurship gives centrality to the formation and exploitation of an opportunity with "mission-related impact" (Dees, Emerson and Economy, 2001) for a target population or society at large. The main aspect that differentiates social from for-profit entrepreneurship is the focus of the latter on economic goals and profit, while in social entrepreneurship the social mission is at the centre of the venture.[1] From our understanding, social ventures are run by entrepreneurs who create innovative solutions and business models in order to exploit a profitable (social) market opportunity and realize profits. At the same time, social entrepreneurs focus their primary concerns on social value creation rather than on value capture; they manage their business in order to entail the social mission and address the needs of a neglected fringe of people or nations, seeking proactively to leave a social impact on society.

Given these two central facets of social entrepreneurship, we can understand the hybrid nature of this kind of organization. They are a blend of for-profit enterprises and NGOs, sharing many aspects but at the same time being different from both forms. Social ventures have in common with for-profit companies the "entrepreneurial" push and the formation and exploitation of a promising and profitable market opportunity. They differ from commercial entrepreneurship with respect to their core of activity, the social mission, and that they proactively pursue the aim of changing and enhancing living conditions of a neglected part of the society. It is well-known that also for-profit firms, especially large MNCs, run Corporate Social Responsibility (CSR) programmes: nonetheless, also this kind of initiative is different from social ventures in the way they address social needs. CSR programmes are ancillary activities while the core focus of the firm is still related to "business as usual" and other traditional objectives and results. Maybe we could also say that CSR focuses on minimizing negative impact instead of maximizing positive impact as social enterprises do and that it is more based on the idea of doing good than on clear social purpose. NGOs, instead, allocate all their efforts and resources on alleviating a social disadvantage, but they do not necessarily run the activity in an entrepreneurial (innovative) sense. They generally aid the disadvantaged without a proactive engagement on changing the society but rather focusing on philanthropic activities. We are aware that such boundaries lead to a more restrictive view of social entrepreneurship, different from the "big tent" we mentioned at the beginning, but that it reflects the core of "true" social entrepreneurship.

We are now turning to the intersection of social and international entrepreneurship. In recent years, attention has been focused increasingly on understanding how social enterprises can form and exploit profitable opportunities in developing countries and, following the economic and social crises, increasingly also in many segments of developed countries. Calls to include social entrepreneurship in international entrepreneurship studies have been advanced and research has started to study the domains jointly. Zahra, Newey and Li (2014) for example propose to add social (and environmental) value creation in a definition of IE. The analysis of approaches and models adopted by social enterprises to enter a foreign market with the aim of addressing a social need and being financially successful at the same time is particularly interesting. It adds complexity to the already challenging tasks of entering multiple markets early and so allows to better understand innovative solutions and key determinants for running these (and other international) ventures successfully.

For example, the crucial role of networks and the embeddedness of social enterprises in the specific context has been stressed by scholars. The importance of networks has been underlined also in much IE and IB work but in the context of the social venture networks and the establishment of partnerships are constitutive elements. First, internationalization adds to the complexity of the SE and so increases the need of collaborative action – beyond the fact that many of the social issues *are* international (e.g. social action in response to ever more frequent natural disasters). Importantly, ISEs need an in-depth understanding of the local social context – being a foreigner, they require local partner knowledge and collaboration. Second, for an ISE, networks are particularly important to growing their impact and to coordinate actions better. Networks enable the flow of information and learning between the stakeholders through which collective intelligence increases which, in turn, helps to deliver impact more efficiently and more effectively. Third, the design of an effective business model that is built around the centrality of the social mission of the firm is a key aspect for the success of such ventures. Through a bottom-up approach and partnerships which take the particular sociocultural environment into account, social companies can come up with a broad variety of solutions and can exploit collective intelligence. SE also need mission-aligned partners on board for both the acquisition of resources and capabilities and for getting the addressed population's trust and legitimacy.

The story of TOMS reported in Box 2.1 illustrates the key elements we have discussed so far, that is, the opportunity seen by the entrepreneur and its exploitation through an innovative idea and business model; the importance of mission-aligned, locally embedded partners; entrepreneurial drive, empathy and continued focus on social value creation.

Partnerships are also helpful along the social venture's growth. When the venture scales up, complexity is increasing and organizational reshaping and separation may become vital. Organizational separation could consist of an internal separation of different tasks through the creation of autonomous business units but, due to the blended objective of the firm such internal complexity is already high. In this context, literature provides many examples where separation has been achieved through partnerships. Entering relationships that bring mutual multilateral advantages is therefore a way to delegate activities that concur to the fulfilment of the social aim but at the same time could divert excessively business attention from financial goals or simply help to extend and continually grow in social impact.

Another driver of IE that we have already mentioned is technology. Following the line of thought above, we may say that the potential of networking technologies for ISEs is enormous. More in general, digital technology and the Internet are particularly suited for social action as they can mobilize communities everywhere, facilitate sharing and help realize opportunity in innovative ways.

Two social enterprises, "Too Wheels" and "Disrupt Disability" are using the opportunities presented by technology to create cheaper and more

---

BOX 2.1

THE STORY OF TOMS

While travelling in Argentina in 2006, TOMS founder Blake Mycoskie, an avid traveller, witnessed the hardships faced by children growing up without shoes. His solution to the problem was to create a for-profit business that was sustainable and not reliant on donations. With every pair of shoes purchased, TOMS would help a person in need – one for one. From this idea, TOMS has evolved into a powerful business that helps address need and advance health, education and economic opportunity for children and their communities around the world. TOMS now gives shoes, sight, birth, clean water and protection against bullying – one for one – through offering a variety of footwear, eyewear, coffee and bags.

TOMS gives brand new, made-to-order shoes to meet the needs of the children in over 70 countries. "We've given over 60 million pairs of shoes to children in need, teaching us 60 million lessons – and it's leading to bigger and better things, like giving different types of shoes based on terrain and season, or creating local jobs by producing shoes in countries where we give."

TOMS Eyewear launched in 2011, has helped restore sight to over 400,000 people in need. "We give sight in 13 countries, providing prescription glasses, medical treatment and/or sight-saving surgery with each purchase of eyewear. Not only does a purchase help restore sight (through medical treatment, surgery or spectacles), it supports sustainable community-based eye care programmes, the creation of professional jobs (often for young women) and helps provide basic eye care training to local health volunteers and teachers."

Strong relations with their Giving Partners. Shoes, for example, are always given to children through humanitarian organizations (more than 90) who incorporate shoes into their community development programmes. For the Giving Partners they have defined the qualities they look for:

Sustainable – Giving Partners work with communities to address their needs in a way that will enable the community to meet its own needs in the future.

Local – We seek locally staffed and led organizations that have a long-term commitment to the regions where they work.

Need – TOMS' support furthers our Giving Partners' long-term goals and is integrated into their programmes.

Evolving – TOMS is committed to improving our Giving by continually evolving. We look for partners who can report back to us on how we can improve.

Neutral – TOMS products and services are provided to help people in need. Our partners do not distribute them with any religious or political affiliations.

➡

←

What started as a social enterprise has become a movement, including One Day Without Shoes and World Sight Day, annual days to raise awareness for the global issues of poverty and avoidable blindness and visual impairment.

Blake's unique approach to business yielded awards. For example, in 2009, Blake and TOMS received the Secretary of State's 2009 Award of Corporate Excellence and in 2011, Blake was named on *Fortune Magazine's* "40 Under 40" list, recognizing him as one of the top young businessmen in the world. Before TOMS, Blake started five businesses. He is passionate about inspiring young people to help make tomorrow better, encouraging them to include giving in everything they do as expressed in his book *Start Something*.

Source: http://www.toms.com/.

specialized solutions for people who need care living with disability. The two start-ups are examples of exploring opportunity in open-source projects which are each developing different types of wheelchairs that allow for user customization and radically lower prices of production.

The WHO estimates that over 65 million people worldwide need a wheelchair and yet 80 per cent of them, around 52 million, cannot afford a suitable wheelchair or one customized to their needs. Over the past healthcare spending has risen faster than economic growth in all OECD countries, putting much pressure on public expenditure on health and long-term care with ensuing pressure on individuals to self-manage and self-finance their care.

Although state funding in Italy, the founder Alessi's home nation, provides standard wheelchairs for disabled people, the more expensive wheelchairs required for playing sports are not covered. Fabrizio Alessi first started designing the DIY wheelchair as a student after spending time volunteering with a disability charity. Using Too Wheels, children and adults alike are able to play a host of games including basketball, tennis, softball or rugby. Too Wheels connects the ideals of open-source technology with the culture of making to provide a low-cost and adaptable DIY alternative to expensive ready-made sports wheelchairs. Makers are able to download the open-source wheelchair blueprint, adjust the design based on their unique measurements, and build the finished product from cheap and easily available materials such as plywood, metal tubing, and bicycle wheels. No special skills are required. If built correctly, for as little as €200 anyone across the world can own a sports wheelchair with the performance of a €2,000 premade alternative. Sports wheelchairs have been built using the Too Wheels open-source design in locations across the world. For example, a Too Wheels wheelchair was built in Ecuador's Fab Lab Yachay through a grant from the Fab Foundation. Elsewhere, students at India's Gujarat Technological University have built their own sports wheelchair (http://toowheels.org/).

With similar purpose and technology but a different model, Rachael Wallach started Disrupt Disability. One of the key experiences that inspired her for Disrupt Disability and the development of customized wheelchairs was her two months backpack travelling in South East Asia in her wheelchair. During her time there she had seen only two other wheelchair users, and they were not wheeling themselves – all of them were pushed (source: Stanford toowheels video on YouTube). That is where Rachael started to think about change and affordable, modular and fully customizable wheelchairs that are not only customized for form but also for function. Rachael launched a Hackathon where the key challenge was the question of how the nascent #HackOnWheels can make its vision a reality, beginning with building a digital design library for "anyone anywhere to freely use, adapt, develop and share" (http://toowheels.org/). In early 2017, 84 universities took part in the wheelchair design competition hosted by the Royal Society of Arts and sponsored by the Global Disability Innovation Hub where students were challenged to design visionary, customizable, user-centred wheelchairs for their library of open source designs.

The brief was as follows: (1) Want Your Wheels: Changing perceptions of wheelchairs and wheelchair users. How can a wheelchair be an extension of the body, an item of fashion, or wearable technology? How can wheelchairs be desirable, aspirational lifestyle products? (2) Wear Your Wheels: Designing a modular wheelchair. How can we develop a modular system of interchangeable customizable wheelchair parts that will give users maximum choice and control over their wheelchair? How can a modular system enable users to tailor their wheelchair to their body, lifestyle and environment?

The importance she gives to accessories and style for personalization reflect her wish to also disrupt perceptions: "We are proud of the wheels we wear – our wheels will be unique. As beautiful, fashionable and individual as we are" (Wallach, 2017). Rachael not only disrupts disability or perceptions of disabled – with her project she also disrupts manufacture, using 3D printing which allows fabrication of wheelchairs – similarly to Too Wheels – much more cheaply.

The difficulties that come with establishing and managing "blended" ventures internationally is illustrated well with examples in which companies have failed to accept and seek changes in their business concept and so failed in their social entrepreneurship activities. For example, Procter & Gamble did not succeed in bringing clean water to Indian villages. P&G worked with the Centres of Disease and Control to develop a powder that could purify large amounts of water at a really cheap price (US $0.10 per litre). Despite of that, the product was a flop: P&G did not take into account that different communities did not only long for clean water, they also wanted and were used to different and unique tastes. Since purified water has no taste, local communities refused to buy it. Moreover, villagers were sceptical towards unknown P&G managers that directly marketed the product in rural communities, fearing that the unknown powder put in the water by strangers was harmful. It is clear that in the P&G's approach to social entrepreneurship key critical aspects for the success of social ventures that we have mentioned earlier are missing. In particular, P&G adopted a managerial top-down approach, which has been proven to be inadequate in the field of social entrepreneurship, because of the crucial relevance of a close relationship with the target population and of the embeddedness in a social network to acquire capabilities and knowledge.

The comparison of small, just-born global firms with large and established ones is particularly interesting: while, generally, established international for-profit firms are more advantaged than smaller firms when entering a new foreign market, this is no more true in the field of social entrepreneurship. An in-depth empathy with the social problem and deep knowledge of the cultural, social and environmental context is crucial for the success of these kinds of ventures, as much as is for example, technical knowledge about the specific product or service offered. From this point of view, born global firms may more easily succeed since they are usually founded by a committed empathic entrepreneur and they can create a business model that includes and pursues the social mission from the very start. MNCs with ancillary social ventures who have a well-established reputation around the world instead may be confronted with issues of legitimacy when jumping into a market as social entrepreneurs, as they may not have all the required resources, capabilities and knowledge to approach a specific social problem and serve the real needs of a disadvantaged population. Moreover, they may be challenged by having to convince the local community of their social purposes, and by finding partners aligned with their new and unknown vision. Therefore, the embeddedness in a network with similar-minded organizations is even more crucial in the context of social ventures undertaken by MNCs, because through these partnerships large companies can get close to the population and reshape their established business model in order to include the social purpose. The examples above are useful to illustrate and discuss the different ways through which social entrepreneurs have been able to seize an opportunity internationally that others do not see or do not consider worth addressing. Through their unique and blended entrepreneurial and social posture ISEs drive change and change society to the better. The entrepreneurs of our examples have created innovative business models, which imply the embeddedness in a network of relationships with the local population and other, mission-aligned partners and, in many cases, the use of digital technology. In this way they have overcome the liability of newness and foreignness, have multiplied impact and managed to extend and grow their social objectives. In all the cases, the social value creation, has been given priority over the aim of financial success. This does not imply, as already discussed, that the firms are giving up profit; on the contrary, these companies have consciously chosen the market to achieve their goals, so that they can proactively change the current situation and bring social change by being self-sustained and not depending on donations.

A question which remains open is whether it is always possible for social ventures to give priority to the social mission and social value creation and how these companies behave in instances of economically critical situations and to what extent mission-driven goals prevail over financial success. In addition, it would be interesting to analyse in which way resources are allocated between different goals and provided to different countries, organizational divisions, or partners. Another question, related to the previous ones, concerns the way in which the international social enterprises measure performance and check whether social value has actually been created.

CASE STUDY

Nokero: growing an international social enterprise

Manuel G. Serapio

Steve Katsaros, founder and CEO of Nokero, admired the majestic Basilica of St. Peter. It was late Sunday afternoon in September 2017 and Steve was enjoying a well-deserved break from several weeks of intense work and preparation in Rome. Katsaros has come to Rome to participate as one of twelve semi-finalists in the Laudato Si' Startup Challenge (Laudato Si' Challenge, 2017). Inspired by His Holiness Pope Francis and supported by companies like Facebook, Instagram, Fresco Capital and others, the Laudato Si' Challenge is "a global initiative, an urgent call-to action that encourages early to mid stage startups to grow their breakthrough solutions to the world's boldest challenges" (Laudato Si' Challenge, 2017).

CASE STUDY *(continued)*

The challenge for 2017 was climate change and involuntary migration. Over 100 companies applied to compete for the challenge which was narrowed down to fifty companies after a preliminary selection process. This was followed by a rigorous, 60-day screening and interview process conducted by a panel of experts. From this process, twelve start-ups (semi-finalists) were selected to advance into an eight-week business accelerator in Rome to expand and scale their companies' solutions (Laudato Si' Challenge, 2017).

Each semi-finalist was assigned top business leaders as mentors to help them develop breakthrough solutions to take their social ventures to scalable, sustainable, and profitable levels. Each semi-finalist was also offered equity investments and ongoing support to "further define their products and services, with a goal of emerging as fully-investible enterprises". In December 2017, the Laudato Si' Challenge culminated with a grand ceremony and demonstration day inside Vatican City where six finalists presented their game-changing products and services to the world. The event also "memorialize[d] the 21st century standard of doing business: profitable, social, mission aligned and bankable" (Laudato Si' Challenge, 2017).

Katsaros viewed Nokero's selection as one of the twelve semi-finalists as auspicious. The Laudato Si' Challenge opportunity could not have come at a better time. While Katsaros was pleased with his company's growth from 2010 to 2015, the past two years have been challenging. Katsaros needed to find the right pathway to scale and sustain Nokero's business so that it could more meaningfully and broadly deliver on its mission of "eliminating kerosene lamps and bringing light to the energy poor so rural communities are safe, happy, healthy, and productive" (Nokero, 2017).

The Laudato Si' Challenge was a perfect opportunity for Katsaros to step away from the day-to-day operations of Nokero's business – to focus his mind and inspire his spirit. As Steve walked around and enjoyed St. Peter's Square, he thought of no better place to renew and reenergize himself and Nokero than the auspicious setting of the Laudato Si' Challenge in Rome.

Building an international social enterprise

Identifying the opportunity

Nokero was established by Steve Katsaros in 2010. Short for "No Kerosone", Nokero aimed to replace kerosene and diesel lanterns by "developing safe and environmentally friendly solar products that eliminated the need for harmful and polluting fuels used for light and heat around the world and that are affordable to customers around them" (Serapio, 2018, p. 512).

Over 1.3 billion people live without electricity including about 25 per cent of the population of all developing countries. Over 600 million people are in sub-Saharan Africa and more than 300 million people are in India alone (Lindeman, 2015). The majority of

CASE STUDY (continued)

these people use kerosene and diesel lanterns for their lighting which is a poor source of lighting, are detrimental to the environment, and pose serious health and safety hazards to users. For example, the World Bank estimates that 780 million women and children breathing kerosene fumes inhale the equivalent of smoke from two packs of cigarettes a day. The result is that two-thirds of the adult female lung cancer victims are non-smokers. In developing nations, about two million children suffer or die annually from debilitating respiratory problems, including acute respiratory infection, pneumonia, and influenza (Lights for Life, 2017).

Accidentally turned over lamps represent one of the major causes of fires in homes in poor communities. In India alone, 2.5 million people (350,000 of them children) suffer burns each year due to knocked over kerosene lamps. Kerosene lamps and other fuel-based lighting are a major source of CO_2 emissions, emitting 244 million tons of CO_2 emissions to the atmosphere each year (Lights for Life, 2017).

Kerosone is a poor source of lighting. It is not very bright and is highly inefficient. Most kerosene lanterns produce 2 to 4 lumens compared to 10–25 lumens produced by a solar bulb and 900 lumens by a 60-watt bulb (Lights for Life, 2017). Despite its risks and limitations, kerosene is still the common source of lighting for most people in poor communities because it is widely available for daily purchase in small quantities and at an affordable price. Most families in these communities also use kerosene for cooking.

"No kerosene for lighting in poor communities" is the world's bold challenge that Katsaros wanted to address when he first developed Nokero. This challenge now aligns with the Laudato Si' Challenge 2017's priority of addressing the impact of climate change on the world's poor.

Inventing the solution

Drawing the sketch of the product on a notepad, Katsaros invented the first Nokero light bulb (N100) in January 2010. Four days later, he filed a US patent on the N100 that was granted early the following year. Katsaros immediately signed up a factory in China to build the prototype. Six months later, in June 2010, the factory started commercial production of the N100. Since then, Katsaros has improved on the product and package replacing the N100 with the N200, N202, and a less expensive model, the N182. Nokero's latest model, the N233, was introduced in November 2016.

The Nokero 233 is a portable light, small and light weight, and is shaped like a light bulb for easy identification. Its brightness is 10 lumens on low illumination and 25 lumens on high illumination which is five times brighter than the kerosene lamp. Built to last five years, the N233 is shatter and rain proof.

The bulb can be put on an accompanying stand, hung on a rope, or laid on its side at night. It has a pivot feature that allows users to swivel the panel toward the sun for maximum charge. The same feature can be used to swivel the bulb to direct light where needed at night. The LED lights are enclosed in the shatter resistant bulb, do not get hot, and produce an even light (Serapio, 2018).

CASE STUDY *(continued)*

For orders of 1,000 solar bulbs or more, the N233 wholesales for about $8.00 (FOB China). Smaller quantity orders are priced between $15 and $20. The product is widely distributed online in e-commerce platforms like Amazon or directly from Nokero's website.

Building a born-global social enterprise

Katsaros has a strong international entrepreneurial orientation, solid engineering background, and rich experience as an inventor-entrepreneur. He comes from an immigrant family from Greece and has travelled extensively abroad. Katsaros' past entrepreneurial ventures include licensing inventions to sports companies (e.g. Dynastar Skis, K2 and Habervision) and developing RevoPower, a motorized wheel for bicycles that gets 200 miles per gallon at 20 miles per hour (Serapio, 2018).

He received his BS Mechanical Engineering degree from Purdue University, a Certificate in Entrepreneurship from the Jake Jabs Center for Entrepreneurship at the University of Colorado Denver and is a Collegiate Inventors Competition awardee. Katsaros is also a patent agent registered with the US Patent and Trademark Office which has issued him several patents for previous inventions and a Patent for Humanity Award. Katsaros has travelled all over the world to speak about Nokero's bold mission of eliminating kerosene; he is a frequent guest speaker at the Institute for International Business at the University of Colorado Denver, the United Nations, and other universities such as Yale University, Ohio State University, and Purdue University.

From the start, Nokero was a "born global social enterprise". Nokero's original legal entity, Nokero International, Ltd., has partners and investors from Hong Kong; Steve and Nokero's administrative team sits in Denver, Colorado; the company's supplier is located in Southern China; and its customers are spread out all over the world, including in some of the most remote locations in developing countries.

Nokero has received global coverage from both traditional and social media. In fact, its first major coverage by Al Velshi on the CNN programme, "The Big Eye", catapulted Nokero into the global scene. In July 2010, an influential London businessman offered support that led to the endorsement of soccer star Didier Drogba. This was quickly followed by coverage by other media outlets, namely *O'Globo* (Brazil), *The Washington Post, Sydney Times* (Australia), Air France, Sudwestrundfunk (Germany), *The Guardian*, Forbes, Inc., and others (Serapio, 2018).

Nokero's Laudato Si' Challenge

To date, Nokero has sold over 1.6 million solar bulbs. Its customers include social enterprises, government and international organizations, and the commercial channel. In regard to social enterprises, Nokero has partnered with Project C.U.R.E. (Commission on Urgent Relief and Equipment), whereby Nokero solar bulbs have been added to C.U.R.E. Kits for Kids (i.e. shoebox sized kits that contain everyday healthcare supplies, such as

CASE STUDY *(continued)*

mosquito/insect repellent and antibiotic ointments) and provided to parents who may not have access to an everyday medicine kit. In addition to Project C.U.R.E., Nokero has partnered with other social organizations, such as Shelterbox, Child Fund, Elephant Energy, and Power the World (Serapio, 2018).

Nokero aligns with the broad mission of many of these social enterprises, including alleviating global poverty, addressing climate change, promoting health and safety, and others. However, each of these social organizations have unique requirements (e.g. product acquisition, distribution and logistics protocols) that at times demand additional time and effort from Nokero. In addition, orders from these social enterprises tend to be opportunistic and difficult to predict.

While sales to government and international organizations may be large, they often involve long sales cycles and require specialized skills and networks in business development. Some governments that are contemplating large orders may also demand local content or assembly. Nonetheless, some of Nokero's largest quantity sales have come from government orders albeit these orders were "one and done" deals.

Nokero targets the commercial channel through direct web-based sales and licensed distributors. Since 2011, customers from more than 120 countries have ordered Nokero solar bulbs through the company's website (Serapio, 2018). Three major concerns for Katsaros regarding web-based sales is the company's inability to convert most of these orders to regular and frequent sales. In addition, web-based sales are not likely to reach Nokero's main target beneficiaries, namely users from poor communities and remote locations, unless these orders are made by people who turn around and donate the bulbs to them. Third, web-based sales started out strong for Nokero but have softened in recent years.

Collectively, Nokero's largest customers are distributors, associations and individuals that have ordered thousands of solar bulbs, including the South African Alternative Energy Association and major commercial distributors from India, Kenya, Ghana, Zambia, and Fiji (Serapio, 2018). With the exception of a few distributors, however, these partners have failed to meet their sales and performance targets consistently, thereby making it difficult for Nokero to scale its business.

Although posting sales of 1.6 million bulbs over six years is a respectable accomplishment for a company its size, Nokero has just barely scratched the surface of its addressable market of 1.3 billion people without access to electricity. How can Katsaros take the company to the next level of profitability, scalability and sustainability? Of major concern to Katsaros are the "one and done" orders and lack of consistency in Nokero's sales volume. How can Nokero avoid this "one and done" syndrome and create a more dependable customer base and consistent flow of orders? What should Nokero's "go to market" strategy be to allow the company to scale? Finally, how can Nokero emerge as a fully investible enterprise by investors who value the financial returns that the company can

CASE STUDY *(continued)*

generate, as well as the social dividends that it creates? Finding answers to these challenges is the outcome that Katsaros would like to take away from the Luadato Si' Challenge.

Note: Dr Manuel G. Serapio wrote this case based on (1) multiple interviews with and updates by Steve Katsaros and (2) secondary information on Nokero, the solar industry, and the Laudato Si' Challenge. The case draws from company information published in Manuel G. Serapio (2018). Nokero: lighting the world, in John Daniels, Lee Radebaugh, and Daniel Sullivan (eds) International Business Environment and Operations, *16th edition, 2018 (pp. 511–516). London: Pearson.*

Acknowledgement: CU Denver's Institute for International Business, Center for International Business Education and Research, and Jake Jabs Center for Entrepreneurship provided support for the preparation of this case.

Case references

Frieswick, K. (2015, April). The entrepreneur lighting up communities in need. *INC.* Retrieved on 13 March 2018 from https://www.inc.com/magazine/201504/kris-frieswick/let-it-shine.html.

Laudato Si' Challenge. (2017). About the Challenge. Retrieved on 13 March 2018 from http://www.laudatosichallenge.org/about.

Lights for Life. (2017, September). The impact of lighting poverty of children. *Lights for Life.* Retrieved on 13 March 2018 from lightforlifes.org.

Lindeman, T. (2015, 6 November). 1.3 billion are living in the dark. *The Washington Post.* Retrieved on 13 March 2018 from https://www.washingtonpost.com/graphics/world/world-without-power/.

Nokero. (2017, September). Solar lights are changing lives. *Nokero.* Retrieved on 13 March 2018 from https://www.nokero.com/.

Rudolf, J.C. (2010, 25 June). A solar bulb may light the way. *The New York Times.* Retrieved on 13 March 2018 from https://green.blogs.nytimes.com/2010/06/25/a-solar-bulb-may-light-the-way/.

Serapio, M.G. (2018). Nokero: lighting the world, in John Daniels, Lee Radebaugh, and Daniel Sullivan (eds), *International Business Environment and Operations,* 16th edition (pp. 511–516). London: Pearson.

Steele, T. (2014, 27 June). Nokero introduces world's most affordable solar light bulb. *AltEnergyMag.com.* Retrieved on 13 March 2018 from https://www.altenergymag.com/article/2014/07/nokero-introduces-worlds-most-affordable-solar-light-bulb/1455/.

NOTE

1 Of note, not all scholars place the social enterprises among for-profit organizations. Bacq and Janssen (2011) argue that the main school in Europe posits that these companies should not make any profit, and concentrate only on their social mission; the "entrepreneurial" aspect of the venture then can be seen just in terms of the innovativeness of solutions. American researchers undoubtedly place social enterprises among for-profit firms instead: depending on the affinity with different schools of thought, social firms have positive profit, but it is just a means to financial self-sustainability; profits must be reinvested in the social mission of the venture.

We embrace and support the latter position, as we consider it more effective in describing social enterprises' behaviour; additionally, it furthers our understanding of the other key aspect of social entrepreneurship, namely its "entrepreneurial" dimension.

 CHAPTER REFERENCES

Almor, T., Tarba, S.Y. and Margalit, A. (2014). Maturing, technology-based, born-global companies: surviving through mergers and acquisitions. *Management International Review, 54* (4), 421–444.

ATOM. Retrieved on 13 March 2018 from https://www.atom.it/.

Bacq, S. and Janssen, F. (2011). The multiple faces of social entrepreneurship: a review of definitional issues based on geographical and thematic criteria. *Entrepreneurship and Regional Development, 23* (5–6), 373–403.

Bell, J., McNaughton, R. and Young, S. (2001). "Born-again global" firms: an extension to the "born global" phenomenon. *Journal of International Management, 7* (3), 173–189.

Birkinshaw, J. (1997). Entrepreneurship in multinational corporations: the characteristics of subsidiary initiatives. *Strategic Management Journal, 18* (3), 207–229.

Dees, J., Emerson, L. and Economy, P. (2001), *Enterprising Nonprofits: A Toolkit for Social Entrepreneurs.* London: John Wiley & Sons.

Denicolai, S., Strange, R. and Zucchella, A. (2015). The dynamics of the outsourcing relationship. In R.V. Tulder, A. Verbeke and R. Drogendijk (eds) *The Future Of Global Organizing (Progress in International Business Research, Volume 10)* (pp. 341–364). London: Emerald Group Publishing.

Dimitratos, P., and Jones, M. V. (2005). Future directions for international entrepreneurship research. *International Business Review, 14* (2), 119–128.

Dimitratos, P., Johnson, J., Slow, J. and Young, S. (2003). Micromultinationals: new types of firms for the global competitive landscape. *European Management Journal, 21* (2), 164–174.

Dimitratos, P., Plakoyiannaki, E., Pitsoulaki, A. and Tüselmann, H.J. (2010). The global smaller firm in international entrepreneurship. *International Business Review, 19* (6), 589–606.

Disrupt Disability. Retrieved on 13 March 2018 from https://www.disruptdisability.org/ and YouTube.

Drori, I., Honig, B. and Wright, M. (2009). Transnational entrepreneurship: an emergent field of study. *Entrepreneurship: Theory and Practice, 33* (5), 1001–1022.

Duhigg, C. and Bradsher, K. (2012, 21 January). How the US lost out on iPhone work. *The New York Times.* Retrieved on 13 March 2018 from http://www.nytimes.com/2012/01/22/business/apple-america-and-a-squeezed-middle-class.html.

Eden, L. and Miller, S.R. (2004). Distance matters: liability of foreignness, institutional distance and ownership strategy. *Advances in International Management, 16* (04), 187–221.

Finkle, T.A. (2012). Corporate entrepreneurship and innovation in Silicon Valley: the case of Google, Inc. *Entrepreneurship: Theory and Practice*, 36 (4), 863–884.

Gabrielsson, M. and Pelkonen, T. (2008). Born internationals: market expansion and business operation mode strategies in the digital media field. *Journal of International Entrepreneurship*, 6 (2), 49–71.

Guillén, M.F. and García-Canal, E. (2009). The American model of the multinational firm and the "new" multinationals from emerging economies. *The Academy of Management Perspectives*, 23 (2), 23–35.

Hagen, B. and Zucchella, A. (2014). Born global or born to run? The long-term growth of born global firms. *Management International Review*, 54 (4), 497–525.

Ilhan-Nas, T., Sahin, K. and Cilingir, Z. (2011). International ethnic entrepreneurship: antecedents, outcomes and environmental context. *International Business Review*, 20 (6), 614–626.

Johanson, J. and Vahlne, J.E. (1977). The internationalization process of the firm: a model of knowledge development and increasing foreign market commitments. *Journal of International Business Studies*, 8 (1), 23–32.

Johanson, J. and Vahlne, J.E. (1990). The mechanism of internationalisation. *International Marketing Review*, 7 (4), 11–24.

Johanson, J. and Vahlne, J.E. (2009). The Uppsala internationalization process model revisited: from liability of foreignness to liability of outsidership. *Journal of International Business Studies*, 40 (9), 1411–1431.

Knight, G. (1996). Born global. *Wiley International Encyclopedia of Marketing*. London: Wiley.

Luo, Y. and Tung, R.L. (2007). International expansion of emerging market enterprises: a springboard perspective. *Journal of International Business Studies*, 38 (4), 481–498.

McDougall, P.P. (1989). International versus domestic entrepreneurship: new venture strategic behavior and industry structure. *Journal of Business Venturing*, 4 (6), 387–400.

Oviatt, B.M. and McDougall, P.P. (1994). Toward a theory of international new ventures. *Journal of International Business Studies*, 25 (1), 45–64.

Patagonia. Retrieved on 13 March 2018 from http://www.patagonia.com/home/.

Rennie, M.W. (1993). Born global. *The McKinsey Quarterly*, 4, 45–53.

Schumpeter, J.A. (1934). *Capitalism, Socialism and Democracy*. New York: Harper, reprinted in 1975.

Servais, P., Zucchella, A. and Palamara, G. (2007). International entrepreneurship and sourcing: international value chain of small firms. *Journal of Euromarketing*, 16 (1–2), 105–117.

TOMS. Retrieved on 13 March 2018 from http://www.toms.com/.

Too Wheels. Retrieved on 13 March 2018 from http://toowheels.org/.

Vissak, T. and Francioni, B. (2013). Serial nonlinear internationalization in practice: a case study. *International Business Review*, 22 (6), 951–962.

Wallach, R. (2017, 1 June). Disrupting disability. [Video]. Retrieved on 19 March 2018 from https://www.youtube.com/watch?v=t5RSxqOTXTI.

Weerawardena, J., Mort, G.S., Liesch, P.W. and Knight, G. (2007). Conceptualizing accelerated internationalization in the born global firm: a dynamic capabilities perspective. *Journal of World Business*, 42 (3), 294–306.

Zahra, S.A. and George, G. (2002). Absorptive capacity: a review, reconceptualization, and extension. *Academy of Management Review*, 27 (2), 185–203.

Zahra, S.A., Newey, L.R. and Li, Y. (2014). On the frontiers: implications of social entrepreneurship for international entrepreneurship. *Entrepreneurship: Theory and Practice*, 38 (1), 137–158.

Zucchella, A. and Magnani, G. (2016). *International Entrepreneurship*. London: Palgrave Macmillan.

Zucchella, A. and Palamara, G. (2006). Niche strategy and export performance. In A. Rialp and J. Rialp (eds) *International Marketing Research* (pp. 63–87). London: Emerald Group Publishing.

3

Sensing, seizing and transforming international entrepreneurial opportunities

3.1 IE as a process of sensing, seizing and transforming opportunities across borders

The emerging literature on international entrepreneurship (IE) has provided wide acceptance of the view of international entrepreneurs as "discovering, enacting, evaluating, and exploiting opportunities across borders to create future goods and services" (Oviatt and McDougall, 2005; McDougall-Covin,

Jones and Serapio, 2014, p. 2). This popular definition views IE as involving a three-step entrepreneurial process of (1) identifying and forming opportunities across borders (sensing); (2) mobilizing resources globally to exploit and capitalize on the opportunities (seizing); and (3) building and renewing an enterprise around the opportunities to create goods and services (transforming). The identification and exploitation of opportunities, the proactivity and innovativeness of entrepreneurs and organizations which accompany opportunity identification and formation, and the matching of resources with opportunities across borders are central elements of IE (Oviatt and McDougall, 2005; Zucchella and Scabini, 2007).

In this chapter, we address the process of opportunity identification, formation, and exploitation which is the typical starting point of IE. We also briefly touch on enterprise building and transforming around opportunities (this topic is discussed in more detail in Chapters 4 and 5). The chapter begins with a definition of opportunity, a comparative discussion and examples of discovered versus created opportunities, and an examination of opportunity from an international entrepreneurial context. Next, we draw from the dynamic capabilities framework and address IE from the three-step entrepreneurial process, mentioned above, namely: (1) Sensing: Identification and assessment of opportunities at home and abroad; (2) Seizing: Mobilizing of resources globally to address opportunities and capture value from doing so; and (3) Transforming: Continued renewal (Al-Aali and Teece, 2014; Teece, 2007). How entrepreneurs approach opportunities using the theoretical frameworks of causation and effectuation is also discussed. We conclude the chapter with a case study on Wonderbly, a UK-based, born-global company whose founders sensed, seized, and transformed an opportunity with a spirited start-up idea of developing a best-selling picture book for children entitled, *Little Boy/Girl Who Lost His/Her Name.*

3.2   What is an opportunity?

There is strong agreement among entrepreneurship scholars that opportunity exists when product or factor markets are imperfect (Venkataraman, 1997; Alvarez, Barney and Anderson, 2013), thereby providing an opening for individual entrepreneurs or firms to capitalize on these imperfections in order to generate economic wealth. This definition of opportunity has three noteworthy features.

First, opportunities arise from conditions of market imperfections. This view reflects the neoclassical economic perspective which posits that under conditions of perfect market competition, economic agents do not have opportunities to exploit in order to realize economic benefits.

Second, while the presence of imperfect market competition is a necessary condition for an opportunity, it is not sufficient (Alvarez, Barney and Anderson, 2013). Based on the definition proposed here, to comprise an opportunity an economic agent must sense the opening that such imperfections provide and capitalize on it. Under this situation, the entrepreneur is an active economic agent and always alert to imperfections in product or factor markets.

Third, the above definition features a key goal of entrepreneurship, that is, the goal of *pursuing* economic wealth. Some scholars argue that an opportunity is only an opportunity if it leads to the creation of economic wealth. This chapter's proposed definition of opportunity does not embrace this narrow view. The realization of economic wealth is not what makes an opportunity an opportunity. Instead, it is the potential of realizing economic wealth that defines an opportunity and which leads entrepreneurs to pursue it. In addition, our definition recognizes that the potential may or may not be realized despite an entrepreneur's best efforts (Alvarez, Barney and Anderson, 2013).

Other scholars have also argued that the goal of pursuing opportunities should not be confined to the pursuit of financial gains but includes more broadly the realization of blended values. From this perspective, opportunities represent an opening for the entrepreneur to pursue a blended value of financial, social, and environmental gains (Zahra, Newey and Li, 2014). Wealth creation is viewed not just in terms of gains that entrepreneurs earn but also gains that they contribute. In this vein, IE has been defined more broadly as "the recognition, formation, evaluation, and exploitation of opportunities across national borders to create new businesses, models, and solutions for value creation, including financial, social, and environmental" (Zahra and George, 2002; Zahra, Newey and Li, 2014, p. 138). The proposed definition of opportunity here embraces the broad definition of value generation to include financial, social, and environmental gains.

3.3 Discovered versus created opportunities: theoretical perspectives

As noted above, the goal of entrepreneurship is to form and exploit opportunities in order to generate value. Two theories have been proposed to explain how entrepreneurial opportunities are formed, namely discovery theory

Table 3.1   Discovered versus created opportunities

	Discovered Opportunities	Created Opportunities
Nature of Opportunities	Opportunities exist as objective phenomena and independent of entrepreneurs.	Opportunities do not exist by themselves; they are dependent on the actions of entrepreneurs.
Nature and Role of Entrepreneurs	*Ex ante* differences between entrepreneurs and non-entrepreneurs. Entrepreneurs search and discover opportunities.	*Ex post* differences between entrepreneurs and non-entrepreneurs. Entrepreneurs shape and form opportunities.
Nature of Decision Making Context	Risky: outcome probabilities are known.	Uncertain: outcome probabilities are not known.

Source: Adapted from Alvarez and Barney (2007).

and creation theory. While both theories agree that opportunities arise from market and product imperfections, they differ in their analysis of the origin of these imperfections, the nature and role of entrepreneurs, and nature of the decision-making context in forming these opportunities (Alvarez and Barney, 2007). Table 3.1 and the following discussion shed light on these differences.

3.3.1   Discovered opportunities

In discovery theory, competitive imperfections arise from exogenous factors. These factors may include shifts in consumer preferences, demographic changes, technological advancements, regulatory changes, political disruptions, and others. Because the emphases in discovery theory are exogenous forces shaping opportunities, the implication is that of opportunities as objective phenomena. In other words, these opportunities exist and are waiting to be discovered, and the role of the entrepreneur under this situation is to scan the environment and search for these opportunities.

Despite the objective presence of opportunities, not everyone is able to successfully and in a timely manner discover them. As shown in Table 3.1., there is an *ex-ante* difference between entrepreneurs who discover the opportunities and non-entrepreneurs who do not. Discovery theory assumes significant differences between the two, either in terms of their ability to sense these opportunities or capacity to seize and exploit them (Kirzner, 1973; Shane, 2003).

"Alertness" has been one of the key concepts used to explain these differences. While these opportunities may be objective phenomena, they are not as apparent to everyone. Among others, some individuals are more alert to opportunities than others because of cognitive phenomena, differing risk preferences, and disposition towards problem-solving. In many cases, the opportunities that await discovery are formed not by one exogenous shock but a combination of external forces. In fact, a key trait that describes entrepreneurs that have successfully "discovered" opportunities is the alertness to identify various external shocks, connect the dots, and correctly interpret how these could lead to new opportunities.

The experience of Intuitive Surgical provides an interesting case in point. In early 2000, a young start-up called Intuitive Surgical discovered an opportunity to manufacture robotic surgical systems, most notably the Da Vinci Surgical System, by capitalizing on the following technological, market, and competitive developments.

First, significant advances were being made in robotics and telemedicine technologies that would make it more feasible to use robotic surgical systems in certain key surgery procedures. The founders of Intuitive Surgical eventually developed, licensed, or acquired these technologies which became the company's main intellectual property.

Second, the shortage of surgeons in the United States and the growing competition among hospitals led to more hospitals demanding the latest technologies to assist surgeons perform various procedures. Soon, ownership of the Da Vinci Surgical System became a differentiating factor for hospitals in attracting both surgeons and patients.

Third, the regulatory environment was turning more supportive towards the use of robotic surgical systems with the US Food and Drug Administration eventually approving the Da Vinci System for use in general laparoscopic and thoracoscopic surgery, as well as cardiac, prostate, and gynaecologic procedures. Since Intuitive Surgical's founding, more than 3 million surgical procedures have been done using the company's surgical robotic systems (https://www.intuitivesurgical.com/).

In discovery opportunity, entrepreneurs form and exploit opportunities under conditions of risk. Unlike in uncertainty conditions where probabilities are not known, risky conditions mean that the entrepreneur is able to assess the risk–reward profile associated with the decision. However, not all individuals may have access to data and resources that will inform such assessment. This information asymmetry explains why some individuals are able to identify opportunities better and exploit them faster than others. For example, Rocket Internet, a Berlin-based incubator and investment company, has developed a business out of discovering opportunities in different products and markets by systematically scanning the environment for new trends and developments in the online space.

3.3.2 Created opportunities

In contrast to discovered opportunities, created opportunities are shaped and created endogenously by entrepreneurs. Entrepreneurs form and exploit these opportunities through their actions and reactions to produce new products and services where none existed before. In creation theory, entrepreneurs do not wait for exogenous factors to form opportunities. These entrepreneurs act and their actions lead to the creation of the opportunity.

The development of the iPad offers one of the most famous examples of a created opportunity. Steve Jobs was the principal architect of the iPad. It was his pet project. In many ways, Jobs went against the prevailing wisdom as to what the market needed at that time and what technology allowed, namely a cheaper netbook instead of a tablet; using high performance Intel chips rather than the all-in-one chip based on ARM architecture; incorporating a keyboard and/or stylus in the tablet rather than using a multi-touch device and so on. In fact, the night after Jobs announced the iPad, he was annoyed and depressed by the reviews that the iPad received from critics (Isaacson, 2011). In fact, some analysts even predicted that the iPad would be irrelevant in a few years.

However, as more customers got to use the iPad, they realized why Jobs and his colleagues at Apple designed the product the way they did. As one commentator put it:

> My first thought as I watched Jobs run through his demo, was that it seemed like no big deal . . . Then I got a chance to use an iPad, and it hit me. I want one. (Jobs) has an uncanny ability to cook up gadgets that we did not know we needed, but then suddenly can't live without. (Isaacson, 2011, p. 496)

In creation theory, entrepreneurs are considered to be no different, *ex ante*, than non-entrepreneurs in regards to identifying and forming opportunities. However, differences may emerge or be more evident *ex post*. Individuals who take a more entrepreneurial path with current or past opportunities may, over time, develop cognitive abilities that make them more perceptive of opportunities and more confident towards operating under conditions of uncertainty (Shane, 2000). Such was the case with Jobs who had multiple experiences creating opportunities prior to launching the iPad (e.g. Mac computers, iPhone, iPod and so on).

Finally, as noted above and in Table 3.1., entrepreneurs create opportunities under conditions of uncertainty. This implies that entrepreneurs who work in uncertain conditions have no, or at best, poor visibility regarding the risk–reward profile of opportunities. Nonetheless, these entrepreneurs proceed in creating the opportunity as the process of creation itself gives them improving visibility regarding the potential outcomes from the opportunity.

3.4 Discovered versus created opportunities: practice perspectives and selected examples

In the literature, there has been an ongoing debate on what entrepreneurial opportunities exactly are and an even livelier discussion on whether opportunities are discovered or created (Ramoglou and Tsang, 2016; Alvarez et al., 2017). For the most part, the debate has addressed the question of whether opportunities are discovered or created primarily from theoretical or philosophical perspectives. The following discussion attempts to link theory to practice, and provides examples of discovered and created opportunities.

Most entrepreneurs will agree with the definition in the literature about what differentiates discovered versus created opportunities. To put it in a more pragmatic perspective, the former is about "filling gaps" while the latter pertains to "creating gaps". For example, in the lodging industry, CitizenM created its hotel chain to fill a gap in the industry: a hotel for mobile customers (i.e. the M in CitizenM) who are looking for affordable luxury in exciting cities in the world (see www.CitizenM.com). In contrast, AirBnB created a completely different business model in the lodging industry based on "booking unique homes and experiencing a city like a local resident" (see www.airbnb.com). The latter has been a major disruptive force and created a completely new business paradigm in the lodging industry.

Although created opportunities like AirBnB often gets the spotlight in the business press, entrepreneurs often point to the fact that the lion's share of opportunities in entrepreneurship and international entrepreneurship are discovered opportunities. In fact, one could argue that even with created opportunities, once a gap has been created and the opportunity matures, new gaps are likely to emerge but within the same space for entrepreneurs to discover and fill. For example, Grab Taxi soon followed Uber's lead and identified a space to fill in car ride sharing in Southeast Asia. Grab differentiated its offering by engaging taxi owners and drivers, instead of just car owners, as partners. Other ride sharing companies that have emerged in different parts of the world are 99 Taxis (Brazil), Easy Taxi (Latin America), Tappsi (Colombia), Didi Kuadi (China), BlaBlaCar (Europe), Hailo (UK), Ants (Denmark, Norway), Get Taxi (Israel), and TaxiDiali (Africa).

On the other hand, creation opportunities can arise from and follow discovered opportunities. Netflix's entrepreneurial journey provides an interesting example of this relationship. Netflix entered the movie rental business to fill an important gap that it had discovered. Revenues from late return fees was an important income stream for movie rental companies which many of them (i.e. Blockbuster) naturally were not willing to give up despite it being a major sore point for their customers. Netflix identified this as a major gap and filled it with a "no-late-fee" offering. Also, in lieu of renting a movie CD, video, or game from a brick and mortar store, Netflix offered a mail-in service only model for renting and returning. This arrangement proved more convenient to renters. This plus the "no late fee" offer drew more renters to Netflix.

After Netflix had switched from mail-in to broadband delivery of its movies, the company created a major gap by capitalizing on the opportunity to produce its own content (e.g. House of Cards). Reed Hastings and Netflix cooked up this model initially in response to the company being squeezed by content providers for licensing fees. It was also an attempt on the part of Netflix to bring back customers that it had lost after the company increased its subscription fees, as well as to create more sticky customers. This proved to be a novel and brilliant move by Hastings which forced Netflix's competitors, including cable companies and TV networks, to follow suit (Liedtke, 2015).

3.5 Opportunities in an international entrepreneurial context

The types of opportunities that this chapter will focus on are international entrepreneurial opportunities. As noted briefly in Chapter 1, international entrepreneurial opportunities are opportunities that are formed and exploited across national borders. The direction by which these opportunities are exploited across national borders may vary: it can be outbound, inbound, or cross-border. Outbound refers to the exploitation of opportunities from a home market to a target market abroad. Halal Guys is an example of an outbound exploitation of an international entrepreneurial opportunity from its home market in the United States. Halal Guys are pioneers of American Halal food whose food cart became New York City's "most famous open-air dining operation, the # 1 Most Yelped business in NYC, and one of the top 3 Most Yelped businesses in the United States" ("The greasy competition among NYC's halal's street carts", 2014; https://thehalalguys.com/). After remaining a predominantly US entrepreneurial company (i.e. a food truck) since its founding in 1990, Halal Guys decided in 2014 to exploit its famous brand by opening franchises in Kuala Lumpur, Toronto, Manila, Jakarta, and other foreign locations (Serapio, forthcoming).

Outbound exploitation of opportunities often involves the replication of entrepreneurial businesses in foreign markets. The impetus for such exploitation originates from the home market and is championed and "pushed" by the entrepreneur from the home market. In contrast, the inbound exploitation of opportunities is "pulled" by an entrepreneur from a target country who sources an entrepreneurial idea from abroad and seizes it by importing the opportunity into his home country. For example, the Rustan's Group, a major conglomerate retailer in the Philippines, has formed SSI, a corporate entrepreneurial venture that is tasked with sourcing retail ideas and brands from abroad for transfer back to the Philippines. Such inbound forms of entrepreneurial opportunity exploitation are popular in several industries, such as media/TV programming, where successful entrepreneurial concepts are sourced abroad and licensed or replicated by producers in local markets. Two prominent examples are the successful reality shows "The Voice" (Holland) and "MasterChef" (UK). The majority of these opportunities are discovered opportunities (Serapio, forthcoming).

Tutor Vista provides an example of an international entrepreneurial opportunity that Krishnan and Meena Ganesh, a husband and wife entrepreneurial team from India, "created" in a cross-border fashion. The company's founders exploited an opportunity to provide quality tutorial services online to students across the world at an affordable price. Tutor Vista matched a promising opportunity, namely the growing need for tutorial services (e.g. among K-12 students in the United States) with available resources (i.e. highly qualified tutors in India and other countries). Additionally, the founders capitalized on advances in broadband technologies, enabling Tutor Vista to deliver personal tutorial services at rates of about $100 per month, much lower than traditional rates for live tutoring of $40 per hour in the United States. Moreover, the company leveraged a younger generation's increasing preference for online learning (Serapio, forthcoming).

3.6 Dynamic capabilities: sensing, seizing and transforming opportunities

We noted at the beginning of this chapter that the presence of market imperfections is a necessary but not a sufficient condition for an opportunity. To comprise an opportunity, an economic agent must be alert to the imperfections in product and factor markets, and be able to capitalize on it. In this section we address the capacities which an economic agent (i.e. the entrepreneur) needs to sense opportunities, seize it, and transform an enterprise around opportunities.

The Dynamic Capabilities framework provides a useful lens for understanding opportunity identification, exploitation, and formation. As defined by Teece (2007, p. 1319), "Dynamic Capabilities enable business enterprises to create, deploy, and protect the intangible assets that support long-run business performance." Similarly, Eisenhardt and Martin (2000, p. 1107) define Dynamic Capabilities as "the firms' processes that use resources – specifically the process to integrate, reinforce, gain, and release resources-to match and even create market change . . . Dynamic Capabilities thus are the organization and strategic routines by which firms achieve new resource configuration as markets emerge, collide, split, evolve, and die."

Companies with strong dynamic capabilities are entrepreneurial (Teece, 2007). Specifically, they have strong capacities in three key areas: (1) Sensing: identification and assessment of opportunities at home and abroad; (2) Seizing: mobilizing of resources globally to address opportunities and capture value from doing so; and (3) Transforming: continued renewal (Al-Aali and Teece, 2014, p. 107; Teece, 2007). The following discussion highlights each of these capacities and links them to international entrepreneurship.

3.6.1 Sensing

Sensing involves exploring technological possibilities, probing markets, listening to customers and scanning the environment (Al-Aali and Teece, 2014, p. 107). As noted previously, entrepreneurs tend to be better than non-entrepreneurs in sensing and exploiting opportunities. However, even among entrepreneurs, some individuals stand out from their peers in sensing (and seizing) opportunities. Steve Wynn, a pioneer entrepreneur in the casino industry in the United States, is one of the most notable examples. In the 1980s, Wynn sensed a threat and an opportunity with the growing legalization of gaming in other states. The threat was that if gambling was the reason to come to Las Vegas, fewer people would likely do so since casinos were already available in their home or neighbouring states. On the other hand, Wynn saw an opportunity to make Las Vegas a more exciting destination and attract not just gamblers but more conventioneers and vacationers to the city.

Wynn envisioned Las Vegas as an entertainment and recreation centre. In 1989, Wynn opened the Mirage, a $660 million plus mega resort. The hotel featured an iconic show (Siegfried and Roy); an erupting volcano, a novel and free entertainment for guests and spectators; and a collection of fine restaurants. This proved to be a winning formula that Wynn followed up on with even bigger projects, namely the Treasure Island and the Bellagio in the 1990s. Wynn's competitors, such as Las Vegas Sands, Harrahs, and Caesar's Palace, rushed to copy him. For this reason, Wynn is often credited with changing the face of the Las Vegas strip and transforming it into one of the world's major entertainment capitals (Munk, 2014).

Fifteen years after launching the Mirage, Wynn followed up on his success by developing the "Wynn" and "Encore" to cater to a more affluent crowd, as well as the growing millennial customer segment. Likewise, Wynn saw the huge potential of Macau with the opening of China and was one of the first gaming developers to commit to building similar and bigger casino resorts there.

Scholars have cautioned that a company's over reliance on a visionary founder-leader like Wynn for opportunity identification is fraught with risks. In fact, this has recently become a major issue with the Wynn enterprise given the personal controversies surrounding Steve Wynn and which may have led him to resign from the company. Indeed, if successful entrepreneurial ventures were to sustain its success, the venture would have to formalize and codify its process of ideation and opportunity exploration.

The process of sensing typically starts with scanning the environment for ideas, gaps, and innovation possibilities. In many cases, the entrepreneur does not start looking for business ideas but simply solutions to a personal need or interest. For example, frustrated with his experience in Germany of not easily finding ice to chill drinks, Matthew Meredith, an American working in Germany, launched Ice Age Ice to market and distribute ice cubes in Europe (Bourdette, 2003). Similarly, Lara Merriken started LaraBar when she could not find energy bars that were both delicious and nutritious to take with her to hikes and sporting activities (Diner, 2007; Merriken, 2007). These two businesses started from their founders' experience searching for solutions to personal needs and emerged as international entrepreneurial ventures.

Unlike the above-mentioned examples of "environmental search leading to entrepreneurial ideas", "environmental search looking for entrepreneurial ideas", is a systematic effort to scan the environment for entrepreneurial opportunities. For example, a considerable amount of search is currently taking place among Chinese entrepreneurs aspiring to come up with the latest app and business model to leverage the explosion of the sharing economy in China. Ofo, a bike sharing entrepreneurial venture, featured in Chapter 1, is a case in point.

Organizations and clubs have emerged all over the world to facilitate the ideation process. House of Genius is a global network of entrepreneurs and collaborators that meet once a week in different parts of the world to discuss innovation and entrepreneurial ideas. Companies and government-led organizations have created "listening posts" to scan the environment for new technologies, new applications and new markets. Industry–academia collaborations have been established and strengthened for the purpose of tapping into leading edge faculty and university basic and applied research (e.g. Deep learning and artificial intelligence research at the University of Toronto; Computing at the University of Illinois at Urbana Champaign; Cross-border e-commerce at Zhejiang Gongshang University and so on).

Customers and suppliers comprise important sources of information in opportunity sensing and identification, particularly in international intrapreneurship. AECOM, the global design firm, noted that feedback from customers has caused them to switch their "design thinking" from developing specialized industrial and commercial spaces to simply "creating work spaces" (Chow, 2017). Suppliers could inform customers about the latest technologies and market trends that may help the latter develop new products and services, as well as create new business models. For example, 3D printing suppliers are enabling their medical device customers to reconfigure their product delivery systems where the latter are able to print parts (e.g. artificial joints) more closely to specifications and delivering them just in time and on site.

Finally, entrepreneurs sense opportunities from customers' moves. Alibaba's Singles Day on 11-11 each year is the largest shopping day in the world ($18 billion in 2016), far greater than Black Friday and Cyber Monday in the United States combined. This unique innovation, which started as an anti-Valentine's Day event, has taught retailers in different parts of the world various lessons about opportunity creation related to e-commerce, special events marketing, social media and so on. When Amazon.com launched its own version of Amazon Prime Day, some observers noted that "Amazon might have learned from Alibaba's Singles Day success . . . Alibaba is a little bit more progressed. They have celebrities; there's a whole online kickoff. They have made it a pretty big affair" (Gernon, 2017).

3.6.2 Seizing

After opportunities have been sensed, they need to be seized. What "seizing" means here is for the entrepreneur to focus attention or intellect on opportunities. According to Al-Aali and Teece (2014, p. 107), among the capabilities behind seizing are "identifying, establishing control and influence over, and coordinating complementary assets to take advantage of the opportunity".

There are two critical elements to seizing as an international entrepreneurial action. The first and perhaps the most important element is timing. When to seize an opportunity is often key to entrepreneurial success. Risks related to timing are two-tailed, that is, an entrepreneur can be too early in acting on the opportunity or he can be too late. For example, the timing dimension is particularly critical to global commercial warehouse developers (i.e. ProLogis) who must correctly time when to buy and develop land in different parts of the world. Being too early meant sitting on real estate way before it could be viably developed commercially resulting in significant carrying costs; being too late carries the risk of having to overpay for the land.

In some cases, an entrepreneur would have to predict whether the opportunity is short-lived or long-lasting. Short lived opportunities, such as fads, compel the entrepreneur to move early (and fast); longer lasting opportunities, such as fashions, provide the entrepreneur greater degrees of freedom for later (and slower) entry.

A second element relates to the pathway for entrepreneurial action. Eisenhardt and Martin (2000) described the pattern of seizing (as well as sensing and transforming) in dynamic capabilities as being dependent on market dynamism. In moderately dynamic markets where change occurs frequently but roughly in predictable and linear paths, entrepreneurs plan and organize their actions in a fairly ordered fashion. Citing Pisano (1994) and Fredrickson (1984), Eisenhardt and Martin (2000) described the pattern of dynamic capabilities as orderly, predictable, and relatively stable in moderately dynamic markets. The seizing process, using Pisano's term (Pisano, 1994), is described in terms of "learning before doing" where the entrepreneur (or manager) first analyses the situation and comes up with the appropriate approach for seizing the opportunity (Eisenhardt and Martin, 2000).

In contrast, in high-velocity markets where change is rapid and less predictable, dynamic capabilities in general and the process of seizing in particular often involves a "learn by doing approach". This involves a more experimental approach of hypothesis formulation, testing, and reformulation (Eisenhardt and Martin, 2000; see also Chapter 5 this volume). Entrepreneurs tend to rely a great deal on the prototyping of products and processes in high-velocity markets. As described in the case for Chapter 1, the founder of ofo in China prototyped and tested his bike ride sharing idea with the help of schoolmates at the University of Peking. Next, he rolled the business out in other campuses in China before doing a full market launch in major Chinese cities.

3.6.3 Transforming

The transformation process entails developing business and execution models, and renewing it as opportunities demand. It is rarely the case that the original idea or opportunity which an entrepreneur sets out to seize is exactly how the entrepreneurial venture unfolds. As noted above, there is a significant amount of hypothesis formulation, testing, and reformulation that takes place along the way, particularly in high velocity markets, and an entrepreneurial organization with strong dynamic capabilities is able to "learn by doing" and make strategic adjustments along the way.

Andrew Mason started Groupon as a social group buying enterprise. Mason's entrepreneurial idea was to get commitments for social causes and the ones that got a critical mass of votes ended up as the ventures getting the company's support. From this initial experience, Mason realized the power and potential of group buying on the one hand but difficulties of implementing it for social projects on the other hand. This led Mason to pivot; he kept the original plan to capitalize on group buying but applied it to a commercial context, namely to get customer sign-ons for discount programmes offered by companies and only implement the ones that gain a critical mass of support from the buying public. Groupon, the e-commerce marketplace that Mason eventually created reflects this transformed business model (Carlson, 2011).

Mistakes can play a key role in influencing the transformation process in dynamic capabilities. As explained by Eisenhardt and Martin (2000, p. 1114):

> [S]mall losses, more than either successes or major failures contribute to effective learning. Success often fails to engage managers' (or entrepreneurs') attention

sufficiently so that they learn from experience. Major failures raise defenses that block learning. In contrast, small failures provide the greatest motivation to learn as such failures cause individuals to pay greater attention to the process, but do not create defensiveness that impedes learning.

An important dividend of learning from small mistakes is that it informs the development of rules to more effectively deal with future opportunities, which Eisenhardt and Martin (2000) called "simple rules". For example, learning from previous mistakes, a global beer company instituted two simple rules for market selection and entry for its traditional and craft beer offerings. First, it would not enter a country where routes to market for on-premise (e.g. bars, restaurants) beer sales are blocked by local competitors. Second, and conversely, it would strongly consider entering a market where there are domestic partners outside of the beer business that could help them build their brand and gain fast market entry for off-premise (e.g. supermarkets, retail store) sales.

The process of building an enterprise around opportunities, such as securing funding, assembling a top management team, staffing for operations and so on are discussed in more detail in the following chapters. In the Nine Dragons example that follows below, we tie-in all three of the capacities of dynamic capabilities to illustrate the successful sensing, seizing, and transforming of international entrepreneurial opportunities.

3.7 Causation and effectuation in international entrepreneurial opportunity identification

The preceding discussion focused on the importance of sensing, seizing, and transforming as key capacities in exploiting and forming opportunities in international entrepreneurship. In this section, we address a more fundamental question, namely: "How do entrepreneurs form opportunities?"

The theoretical framework of causation and effectuation offers a rich perspective to examine this question. Drawing on the foundational work of Sarasvathy (2001), the causation perspective takes the view that entrepreneurs discover and form opportunities by expertly "predicting the future so as to control it". In contrast, effectuation views entrepreneurs as shaping opportunities by "controlling the future so as not to have to predict it". The former focuses on the "predictable aspects of an uncertain future", the latter on the "controllable aspects of an unpredictable future".

BOX 3.1

NINE DRAGONS: EXPLOITING AND FORMING INTERNATIONAL OPPORTUNITIES

Zhang Yin identified and exploited an opportunity in the waste paper business and made it into one of China's most successful entrepreneurial companies. The company that Zhang established was Nine Dragons Paper (Holdings) Ltd., an entrepreneurial venture which grew to become the biggest paper manufacturing and trading company in China and one of the largest in the world.[1]

Zhang's entrepreneurial journey started in the early 1980s when she moved to the southern coastal city of Shenzhen, one of China's first Special Economic Zones. There Zhang started working for a foreign-Chinese joint venture paper trading company.[2] This initial experience exposed her to an exciting opportunity that she would capitalize on for over two decades, namely, China's significant and growing demand for recyclable paper. Sensing the opportunity and heeding the advice of an elderly man who told her that "Wastepaper is like a forest, paper recycles itself, generation after generation", Zhang moved to Hong Kong to form at age 28 her first start-up company.[3] The company "shipped waste paper up the coast to Chinese paper mills".[4]

The timing for launching her company could not have been better since Chinese manufacturers were ramping up exports to the United States and Europe. With the explosive growth in Chinese exports, Zhang knew that companies in China would have an insatiable demand for paper to make packaging materials. Her company sold whatever it could produce to customers in China. However, Zhang realized that sourcing paper primarily from China set a limit to her company's ability to grow. Paper products from China were of poor quality, often made from grass, bamboo or rice stalks, and not ideal for recycling. In contrast, paper made in the United States was derived from wood pulp.[5] Paper scraps were also in more abundant supply in the United States. As Zhang explained, "The US had rich resources, and if I stayed in Hong Kong I could not satisfy (the) demand in China".[6]

Zhang moved to Los Angeles in 1990 and married for the second time, to Liu Ming Chung, who was born in Taiwan, grew up in Brazil, and is fluent in English. Together, they formed America Chung Nam to trade and export paper scraps from the US to China.[7] The company quickly made deals with companies and scrap yards in the US to haul their garbage for a modest fee. Zhang also observed that "Ships from China were arriving in California fully loaded, only to head home with expensive vacancies".[8] She negotiated discounted deals with the freight companies to load her scrap paper into their containers and to ship them to China. With these lucrative deals from scrap suppliers and shippers in hand, it did not take long for America Chung Nam to become the largest exporter by volume from the US to China.

In 1995, Zhang (who also goes by her Hong Kong name, Cheung Yan) returned to China to found Nine Dragons Paper (Holdings) Ltd., opening her first paper-making facility in

←

Dongguan in China's Pearl River Delta region. She assumed the title of Chairwoman and Liu became Chief Executive Officer. A decade later, in 2005, the company had 11 giant paper making machines in various plants in China, more than 5,000 employees, $1 billion in annual revenues, and over $150 million in profits.[9] In 2006, the company listed in the Hong Kong Stock Exchange. With this listing, Zhang became one of the wealthiest entrepreneurs in China with a net worth exceeding US $1.5 billion.

3.7.1 Causation

This chapter featured several entrepreneurs that have demonstrated excellent capacities to identify or predict external shocks and anticipate how these could potentially translate into opportunities. For example, Zhang Yin projected in the 1980s that it was only a matter of time before China became the manufacturing platform of the world. Looking for a business to get into, Zhang made the correct decision to focus on packaging materials since this was the one product that every Chinese exporter would need as China becomes the world's factory.

Entrepreneurs that use a causal approach share several common aspects in their approach to opportunity exploration and formation. First, they are highly capable in predicting the future. In a related vein, the futures that these entrepreneurs anticipate are often not just about a single development but several developments which combine to form opportunities. Second, these entrepreneurs do not wait for opportunities to play out; they act. Third, these entrepreneurs put themselves in an advantageous position so that they are in the right place at the right time to explore and exploit opportunities.

An entrepreneur's expert ability at prediction has been attributed to cognitive phenomena. Entrepreneurs that are excellent at forecasting the future are often described as having great intuition. As Wayne Gretzky, one of professional hockey's greatest players, once said, "I skate to where the puck is going to be and not where it has been". However, as great a hockey player as Gretzky is, some observers would contend that practice played an important role in the development of his great "intuition for prediction". Similarly, an entrepreneur's predictive capabilities and alertness to opportunities are enhanced by repeated practice. As Eisenhardt and Martin (2000, p. 1114) noted, "Repeated practice are an important learning mechanism for the development of dynamic capabilities (i.e., including sensing capacities)".

In today's world of Big Data, analytics have taken centre stage in opportunity exploration and formation. The terms, "environmental scanning" and "future mapping", have given way to new constructs and practices like "predictive analytics" and "data driven decision-making". Among others, the proliferation of data provides important insights on trends and developments in consumer, product, and factor markets. In international entrepreneurship, companies utilize big data to learn about current trends in cross-border e-commerce and to project future trends. For example, Alibaba.com has recently reconfigured its business model, calling it the "Five News". In essence, the model centres on "New Technology" (i.e. big data, cloud computing and so on) driving "New Retail", "New Finance", "New Energy", and "New Manufacturing" (Srivastav, 2017).

3.7.2 Effectuation

Despite the proliferation of data and analytical tools that help entrepreneurs predict the future, opportunity exploration and formation based on prediction continues to be a challenging endeavour for most international entrepreneurs. As discussed in this chapter, entrepreneurship is already characterized by a great deal of risk and uncertainty; the addition of an international dimension adds more layers of complexity to opportunity exploration and formation. These additional complexities include differences attributable to cultural and geographic distance, as well as to unique dimensions of risks (e.g. political risks).

Effectuation offers a different approach to opportunity discovery and creation that helps address the additional risks and complexities in international entrepreneurship. According to Sarasvathy et al. (2014, p. 72) "Effectuation posits a theoretical framework describing how expert entrepreneurs utilize resources within their control in conjunction with commitments and constraints from self-selected stakeholders to fabricate new artifacts such as ventures, products, opportunities, and markets". In other words, effectuation does not rely on an accurate prediction of the future in order to control it. Instead, it emphasizes using effectual principles to enable international entrepreneurs to control the future so as not to have to predict it. These principles include Bird in Hand, Lemonade, Affordable Loss, Crazy Quilt, and Pilot in the Plane.

Bird in hand

This effectual principle emphasizes the various categories of means available to the entrepreneur, namely: identity (who I am), knowledge (what I know), and networks (whom I know). In the context of opportunity exploitation and formation, the entrepreneur focuses on the central question: "What can I do?" instead of "What should I do?" By framing the entrepreneurial action of opportunity exploration and formation on the former rather than the latter question, the entrepreneur discounts the importance of prediction and focuses more on her capabilities (Sarasvathy et al., 2014).

Jollibee Foods Corporation (Jollibee), a Philippine-based fast-food company, is an avid practitioner of the Bird in Hand principle. Ranked in 2016 as the ninth largest fast-food retailer in the world in terms of market capitalization, Jollibee has attained success with its entrepreneurial expansion into international markets by doing what it does best (i.e. best in class fast-food, retail, and supply chain operations), serving the customers that it knows best (i.e. the 7 million plus Filipino diaspora in the United States and abroad), and leveraging its strong identity with Filipino customers abroad (Minana, 2016).

Lemonade

This effectual principle embraces surprises as part of the opportunity exploration and formation process. As noted earlier in this chapter, the process of opportunity discovery does not always follow a linear and predictable process. Surprise discoveries may present themselves and the effectual entrepreneur must make "lemonade from the lemons" that s/he discovers. South Korean K-Pop star, Psy, was a virtual unknown until his video, Gangnam Style, became a viral hit on YouTube. Although the scale and speed of his success may have come as a surprise even to Psy, he was nonetheless quick to embrace (and monetize) the opportunity. Psy turned himself into a one-man, born global, music sensation, and in the process earned him multi-million dollars from Gangnam Style (McIntyre, 2014).

Affordable loss

An opportunity formation process that is based on prediction typically seeks to calculate the maximum returns that one can gain from exploiting or creating opportunities. For many aspiring entrepreneurs, however, calculating a maximum number is elusive and usually leads to an "analysis-paralysis" syndrome. In contrast, the effectual principle of affordable loss focuses only on what an entrepreneur could afford to lose, thereby giving her an objective number to use in deciding whether to exploit an opportunity or not. Earlier in this chapter, we highlighted LaraBar, a maker of high-quality energy bars. Lara Merriken launched LaraBar using mostly resources that she could afford to lose. In particular, Merriken spent over a year working at Whole Foods in order to learn the trade, establish networks, and better understand her customers. Looking back, Merriken credits her decision to work at Whole Foods as one of the smartest moves that she made for LaraBar. If things did not work out, her loss was the time that she spent working at Whole Foods for low pay. However, the upside was that she gained tremendous knowledge about the food retail business; experience that gave her the confidence to launch LaraBar (Merriken, 2007; Diner, 2007).

Crazy quilt

Because entrepreneurs expand into international markets with very limited resources, they typically rely on other individuals and organizations to partner with. The latter self-select and invest resources in the entrepreneur's business because they see opportunity in co-creating the venture with the entrepreneur. This process of engaging self-selecting partners who put "skin in the game" is the crazy quilt principle of effectuation (Sarasvathy et al., 2014, p. 74). Nokero International, the case featured in Chapter 2, attracted a good number of partners early in its development. These partners believed in Steve Katsaros' mission of alleviating global poverty by providing light to the un-electrified and promoting a healthier life by replacing kerosene with solar lighting. Among others, these self-selecting partners bought lights, promoted Nokero in social and traditional media, provided capital, and assisted the company to sell and distribute its solar bulbs.

Pilot in the plane

Best explained by Sarasvathy et al. (2014, pp. 74–75), the Pilot in the Plane principle of effectuation:

> [E]mphasizes the role of human beings in determining the shape of things to come . . . and is a rejection of inevitable trends. Faced with a highly uncertain event space, effectual entrepreneurs seek to learn more about it not with a view of updating their probability estimates, but with a view of intervening in the event space itself to transform and reshape it . . . Effectual entrepreneurs do not see history running on autopilot but rather consider themselves one of the many who copilot the course of history.

The four effectual principles of bird in hand, lemonade, affordable loss, and crazy quilt, noted above, are embodied in this fifth effectuation principle of pilot in the plane. All five principles view the entrepreneur's role as actively shaping and forming opportunities.

In this chapter, we identified a number of very capable entrepreneurs who seized and formed opportunities. These include Reed Hastings at Netflix; Apple's Steve Jobs, and Zhang Yin at Nine Dragons. All of these entrepreneurs rejected the inevitability of trends, and through creativity, innovation, and persistence, piloted their respective companies to success.

CASE STUDY

Wonderbly: sensing, seizing and transforming an international entrepreneurial opportunity

Manuel G. Serapio

Wonderbly is an innovative international new venture that has achieved impressive growth since its founding in 2013. The company's name, "Wonderbly" is a combination of "wonderful" and "impossibly", reflecting the company's purpose "to help make impossibly personalized books that bring wonder into children's lives" (Cowdrey, 2017). The company's first book was called *Little Boy/Girl Who Lost His/Her Name*. In a short span of four years, this title alone has sold more than 2.5 million books in over 130 countries, making it the best-selling picture book in the UK, Australia and Canada, and the highest grossing book in six markets including the United States ("Meet the Founders of Lost My Name", 2016).

Unlike any other children's picture book, *Little Boy/Girl Who Lost His/Her Name* uses technology and creativity to customize the story around a child's name. Customers order the book from the company's website and enter the child's first name. Using a special algorithm, Wonderbly customizes the story line, which features a hero or heroine finding the lost letters of the chosen name while meeting a host of other characters (Serapio, forthcoming).

The following tells the story of Wonderbly: (1) How the founders *sensed* an opportunity and came up with their spirited start-up idea; (2) How they *seized* the opportunity by developing an amazing picture book that became an international business seller, and (3) How they *transformed* the opportunity and built a successful international entrepreneurial venture. It also explores the opportunities and challenges that Wonderbly is likely to face as it grows the business, broaden its product line, and increase its global footprint. Will the company be able to build on the success of its inaugural book and continue to develop "impossibly wonderful" children's picture books? How can Wonderbly duplicate its phenomenal success in the United Kingdom in other international markets? What factors have driven the company's fast paced internationalization and will the company be able to sustain it?

CASE STUDY *(continued)*

Sensing the opportunity

The idea for *Little Boy/Girl Who Lost His/Her Name* came from Asi Sharabi, who was underwhelmed by a book which his 3-year old daughter received as a gift. "At first I got the warm, fuzzy feeling of seeing my daughter's name on some of the pages. But it lasted exactly one second" (Platts, 2017). He thought that the book and others in the market were "too gimmicky and commercial". The authors just slapped a child's name in the photo book without incorporating serious and exciting content. According to Sharabi, "these books were not written by serious authors, the photos were not created by great illustrators, and there simply was no leveraging of technology" (Platts, 2017).

"A proper, well-conceived and beautifully written and illustrated book just did not exist in the market – it was dominated by tacky, inferior products, so we decided to do something about it", said Sharabi (Platts, 2017). Sharabi thought that he could do better by improving the creative and technological aspects of the book. To this end, he called several of his friends consisting of creative writer David Cadji-Newby, illustrator Pedro Serapicos, and technologist Tal Oron, and the four of them set out to develop a personalized book that was superior to what was available in the market ("Meet the Founders of Lost My Name", 2016).

The four friends were known as "dadpreneurs", as there were three dads and an uncle in the group (Dredge, 2014). To test their idea, the friends started a pilot project. Cadji-Newby wrote the stories. Once that was underway, Pedro started drawing. The technical part which Sharabi and Oron worked on came afterwards and took the longest time. As the founders noted, "the process happened fairly slowly which required a huge time commitment . . . We knew we had success on our hands after our first (sales in) Christmas 2013 and that gave us the courage to leave our full-time jobs in March 2014" ("Meet the Founders of Lost My Name", 2016).

Seizing the opportunity

And so the *Little Boy/Girl Who Lost His/Her Name* picture book was born. The child's personal experience in finding his name is unique and filled with excitement and adventure throughout the journey. The child meets different characters during his journey who gives the child the first letter of their own name to help the child find theirs.

The company's mission is "to make stories that'll blow kids socks off while still doing crazy things with technology" (Cowdrey, 2017). What's magical about the book is how it resonates with the child and captures her attention. Among others, the book helps the child discover her identity while learning about many things: words, animals, fun creatures and so on. It creates a heart-popping moment of discovery with the child that the book "is about me". Additionally, it makes the parent (or reader) a master story teller and each can add their personal message to the child that lives with the child for a lifetime (https://www.wonderbly.com/).

CASE STUDY *(continued)*

From the start, the founders described their venture as a "full stack" technology start-up rather than a book publisher. The company creates the stories and illustrations in-house and develops its own technology to customize the book (Dredge, 2014; Serapio, forthcoming). The company exists online and only on its own website. All books are print to order.

Lady luck smiled on the company when the founders pitched on "Dragon's Den", a popular programme for entrepreneurs in the United Kingdom. The founders' decision to pitch in "Dragon's Den" was simply for exposure and investment. According to them:

> Word-of-mouth was already working wonders for us and we wanted to attract investors that could add value to (our company) beyond their funding . . . Being on Dragon's Den was, from a business standpoint, a perfect way to place our vision in front of the right people – not just the dragons, but the viewing public, some of whom were press and others who were likely to be interested in the product (Ramesh, 2015).

The founders quickly won over the assembled dragons who served as potential judges and investors. One top dragon in particular, Piers Linney, owner of Outsourcery, an IT and communications firm, invested £100,000 for a 4 per cent equity in the company. The founders pitch was that the company combined "the power of traditional storytelling with the possibilities of innovative technology" which resonated well with Linney (Ramesh, 2015).

"Dragon's Den" gave *Little Boy/Girl Who Lost His/Her Name* tremendous exposure, and 60,000 people flocked to the company's website in 24 hours. This was followed by a lot of "word of mouth" endorsements from customers and fans that gave the company even wider recognition beyond the United Kingdom (Serapio, forthcoming). Since the company launched the book and sold 22,000 copies in the very first month, sales have not looked back. As noted previously, sales grew exponentially to more than 2.5 million books in over 130 countries. Following its appearance in "Dragon's Den", the company was reported to have attracted investment offers from other ventures, including Google Ventures, Greycroft Partners, Chernin Group, and Allen & Company (Serapio, forthcoming; Neely, 2017).

Transforming the business

Sharabi and his colleagues had to make several important decisions in building and transforming their company and it seems that they made some pretty wise choices. First is their choice of Hackney in London as the place to base their headquarters. By locating in Hackney which is London's artistic nucleus, the company was able to attract the best talent and network with other artistic companies. In addition to Tal Oron, one of the cofounders who lived in Hackney, many of the company's employees were also Hackney residents. In addition, the company found excellent warehouse space nearby in the vibrant Broadway market ("Meet the Founders of Lost My Name", 2016).

CASE STUDY *(continued)*

Second and perhaps the biggest move that the company had to make was the decision to rebrand. When the company first launched, it was called "Lost My Name", after the company's first picture book title. As the founders explained in a blog:

> The months and years went by, and we grew, and we made more books. Books about children's homes and their first birthday, and their favorite foods. Extraordinarily personalized, rather wonderful books, about all kinds of things. . .Which got us thinking. We realized that the name "Lost My Name" did not really reflect the books we have been creating. And we didn't want people to just think we only made one book, since we were rather pleased with the other ones, too. So we decided to change our name to Wonderbly. It felt right. It made us smile. It's different, and fun, like us (we hope) (Cowdrey, 2017).

Today, Wonderbly creates several personalized books, including: *The Journey Home Book* which depicts a child's intergalactic journey home; *Kingdom of You* is about a child's favourite things, and *The Birthday Thief*, a story that magically changes based on the child's birth date. All these books employ Wonderbly's formula of combining creative stories and illustration with innovative technology (https://www.wonderbly.com/).

A third set of decisions had to do with the choice of partners for the company. These include funders and marketing partners. Successful start-ups like Wonderbly that demonstrate strong performance from launch tend to attract considerable interest from venture capitalists and other financial partners. Wonderbly's choice of funders for their Series A and B funding reflect its strong preference for strategic venture partners who could provide investment capital, as well as complementary support and expertise to the company. For example, Wonderbly's Series A investment included funding from Project A Ventures, a Berlin-based investor that assist companies accelerate growth in e-commerce and marketplaces. Ravensburger, a leading publisher of games, puzzles, and children's books led Wonderbly's Series B funding of $8.5 million (O'hear, 2017; Cowdrey, 2017).

In August 2016, the company decided to use Smartly.io as its Facebook marketing partner. Smartly, an ad optimization solutions provider for performance marketers, was instrumental in helping Wonderbly reduce their cost per order and automate a number of marketing processes which gave the marketing team more time to manage more markets (Neely, 2017). Most recently, Wonderbly agreed to partner with the Roald Dahl Estate, owners of valuable IPs, such as Willy Wonka's Chocolate Factory, after the latter sought them out as a creative partner (Cowdrey, 2017). As a result of this partnership, Wonderbly's latest picture book release is entitled *My Golden Ticket*, a personalized book that transports any child to Willy Wonka's chocolate factory (https://www.wonderbly.com/).

Opportunities and challenges in international markets

Because Wonderbly's books are all print to order and customers place their orders using the company's website, it has been possible for the company to internationalize early and fulfil

CASE STUDY *(continued)*

orders from most customers abroad. Wonderbly creates and prints their books in the UK and ships them from their London warehouse. The company's bigger internationalization decisions focused more on the language(s) of offer for their books and the countries they should concentrate their marketing efforts on.

The company initially focused its efforts on English-speaking countries, namely the UK, Australia, Canada and the United States. Shortly thereafter, the books were published in other languages, including German, Spanish, French, Dutch, Italian, Portuguese, Swedish, Danish, Chinese, and Japanese (https://www.wonderbly.com).

Some countries posed cultural challenges as well. For example, several Western children's book publishers have tried and failed to make inroads into China. As Sharabi explained, "it takes more than a new set of characters; it means leaping into a whole new set of cultural expectations and traditions" ("How Lost My Name reinvented its product for Chinese customers", 2016). Chinese parents still expect children's books to be functional and educational, and could altogether resist Wonderbly's approach of creative and fun storytelling. Besides, there is not a tradition of reading bedtime stories to kids. The company was also unsure how effective their approach will be using Chinese names and characters ("How Lost My Name reinvented its product for Chinese customers", 2016).

The success of *Little Boy/Girl Who Lost His/Her Name* has attracted copycat offerings from other book publishers which are sold through third party e-commerce platforms. Of greater concern are counterfeit books that could pose as a Wonderbly book. The risk of counterfeits may increase as Wonderbly transfers some of its printing operations outside of the United Kingdom. For now, Sharabi is confident that Wonderbly's combination of creative and technological elements will be difficult for others to copy ("How Lost My Name reinvented its product for Chinese customers", 2016).

Will Wonderbly be able to replicate its success in other international markets? Could it sustain the company's fast-paced growth and international expansion? What other opportunities are in store for the company as it expands its global footprint? These are some of the questions that Sharabi and his colleagues would have to address as they write the next chapter in Wonderbly's amazing story.

Note: Dr Manuel G. Serapio wrote this case using secondary information on Wonderbly and Lost My Name. It is intended for teaching purposes only.

Acknowledgement: CU Denver's Institute for International Business and Center for International Business Education and Research provided support for the preparation of this case.

Case references

Cowdrey, K. (2017, 28 July). Lost My Name becomes "Wonderbly". *The Bookseller*. Retrieved on 13 March 2018 from https://www.thebookseller.com/news/lost-my-name-loses-its-name-become-wonderbly-603681.

CASE STUDY *(continued)*

Dann, K. (2014, 1 September). Securing investment: how our small business set a record on Dragon's Den. *The Guardian*. Retrieved on 13 March 2018 from https://www.theguardian.com/small-business-network/2014/sep/01/dragons-den-record-investment-lost-my-name.

Dredge, S. (2014, 30 January). Nosy Crow talks fairytales, reluctant readers and game like apps for kids. *The Guardian*. Retrieved on 13 March 2018 from https://www.theguardian.com/technology/2014/jan/30/nosy-crow-fairytale-apps-kids.

Dredge, S. (2015, 25 June). British children's stories startup Lost My Name tells a $9 million funding tale. *The Guardian*. Retrieved on 13 March 2018 from https://www.theguardian.com/technology/2015/jun/25/lost-my-name-funding-google-ventures.

Eyre, C. (2015, 28 January). Children's book start-up Lost My Name plans global expansion. *The Bookseller*. Retrieved on 13 March 2018 from https://www.thebookseller.com/news/childrens-book-start-lost-my-name-plans-global-expansion.

Gillette, F. (2015, 7–8 July) Lost My Name creates a personalized children's book seller (how four sleep deprived dads rewrote the future of kid's books). *Bloomberg*. Retrieved on 13 March 2018 from https://www.bloomberg.com/news/articles/2015-07-08/lost-my-name-book-hints-at-future-of-kids-entertainment.

How Lost My Name reinvented its product for Chinese customers. (2016, 5 November). *Courier*. Retrieved on 13 March 2018 from http://www.courierpaper.com/workshop/lost-name-reinvented-product-chinese-customers/.

Meet the Founders of Lost My Name. (2016, 28 January). *Access London*. Retrieved on 13 March 2018 from https://www.keatons.com/access-london/meet-the-founders-of-lost-my-name/.

Nawilis, C. (2015, August). International entrepreneur profile: Lost My Name. University of Hawaii, Shidler College of Business Administration. Honolulu: Hawaii.

Neely, A. (2017, 24 April). How data catapulted the personalized children's book. *DMNews*. Retrieved on 13 March 2018 from http://www.dmnews.com/dataanalytics/how-data-catapulted-the-personalized-childrens-book/article/652509/.

O'hear, S. (2017, 31 July). Lost My Name, the tech driven book publisher, raises $8.5 million and partners with Roald Dahl Estate. *Tech Crunch*. Retrieved on 13 March 2018 from https://techcrunch.com/2017/07/31/wonderbly/.

Platts, E. (2017, 6 September). Asi Sharabi, Wonderbly: The Power of Story Telling [Video]. Retrieved on 13 March 2018 from https://www.youtube.com/watch?v=JQolvcPwXo8.

Ramesh, J. (2015, 15 June). In-depth: Depesh Mandalia, marketing and growth at Lost My Name. *Figaro Digital*. Retrieved on 13 March 2018 from http://figarodigital.co.uk/article/in-depth-depesh-mandalia-marketing-growth-at-lost-my-name/.

Reid, C. (2015, 10 July). Lost My Name transforms customized kids' books. *Publishers Weekly*. Retrieved on 13 March 2018 from https://www.publishersweekly.com/pw/by-topic/childrens/childrens-industry-news/article/67470-lost-my-name-transforms-customized-kids-books.html.

CASE STUDY *(continued)*

Salter, C. (2015, 6 July). The picture book that parents worldwide and Google Ventures can't put down. *Fastcompany*. Retrieved on 13 March 2018 from https://www.fastcomp any.com/3048158/the-picture-book-that-parents-worldwide-and-google-ventures-cant -put-down.
Serapio, M.G. (forthcoming). Speed and timing of entrepreneurial internationalization: entrepreneurial company focus (Lost My Name). International Entrepreneurship (course-ware) by Serapio M. Retrieved on 13 March 2018 from http://www.venturehighway.com. https://www.wonderbly.com.

NOTES

1 Written by M.G. Serapio from secondary sources including Barboza, D. (2007, 15 January). China's "Queen of Trash" finds riches in wastepaper, *International Herald Tribune-New York Times*; Flannery, R. (2006, 2 November). Dragon lady: a look at Yan Cheung, China's richest woman and chairman of Nine Dragons, *Forbes*; Osnos, E. (2009, 30 March). Wastepaper queen, *The New Yorker*; Cheng, A. (2007, January). Chinese woman's fortune rests on cardboard, *Seattle Times*; Correa, L. et al. (2012). Nine Dragons, case study report, University of Colorado Denver, Fall; and Read, S. and Dew, N. (2015, September). 9 Dragons: a profit from waste, society for effectual action. Adapted from Serapio, M. (forthcoming) *International Entrepreneurship*. Module 4. Retrieved from http://www.venturehighway.com.
2 Barboza, D. (2007, 15 January). China's "Queen of Trash" finds riches in wastepaper. *International Herald Tribune-New York Times*. Retrieved on 13 March 2018 from http://www.nytimes.com/2007/01/15/business/worldbusiness/15iht-trash.4211783.html.
3 Osnos, E. (2009, 30 March). Wastepaper queen. *The New Yorker*. Retrieved on 13 March 2018 from https://www.newyorker.com/magazine/2009/03/30/wastepaper-queen.
4 Osnos, E. (2009, 30 March). Wastepaper queen. *The New Yorker*. Retrieved on 30 March 2018 from https://www.newyorker.com/magazine/2009/03/30/wastepaper-queen.
5 Barboza, D. (2007, 15 January). China's "Queen of Trash" finds riches in wastepaper. *International Herald Tribune-New York Times*. Retrieved on 13 March 2018 from http://www.nytimes.com/2007/01/15/busi ness/worldbusiness/15iht-trash.4211783.html.
6 Flannery, R. (2006, 2 November). Dragon lady: a look at Yan Cheung, China's richest woman and chairman of Nine Dragons. *Forbes*. Retrieved on 13 March 2018 from https://www.forbes.com.
7 Barboza, D. (2007, 15 January). China's "Queen of Trash" finds riches in wastepaper. *International Herald Tribune-New York Times*. Retrieved on 13 March 2018 from http://www.nytimes.com/2007/01/15/busi ness/worldbusiness/15iht-trash.4211783.html.
8 Osnos, E. (2009, 30 March). Wastepaper queen. *The New Yorker*. Retrieved on 13 March 2018 from https://www.newyorker.com/magazine/2009/03/30/wastepaper-queen.
9 Barboza, D. (2007, 15 January). China's "Queen of Trash" finds riches in wastepaper. *International Herald Tribune-New York Times*. Retrieved on 13 March 2018 from http://www.nytimes.com/2007/01/15/busi ness/worldbusiness/15iht-trash.4211783.html.

 ### CHAPTER REFERENCES

Al-Aali, A. and Teece, D. (2014). International entrepreneurship and the theory of the (long-lived) international firm: a capabilities perspective. *Entrepreneurship Theory and Practice, 38* (1), 95–116.

Alvarez, S. and Barney, J. (2007). Discovery and creation: alternative theories of entrepreneurial action. *Strategic Entrepreneurship Journal, 1* (1–2), 11–26.

Alvarez, S., Barney, J. and Anderson, P. (2013). Forming and exploiting opportunities: the implications of discovery and creation process for entrepreneurial and organizational research. *Organization Science, 24* (1), 301–317.

Alvarez, S., Barney, J., McBride, R. and Wuebker, R. (2017). On opportunities: philosophical and empirical implications. *Academy of Management Review, 42* (4), 726–730.

Augier, M. and Teece, D. (2007). Dynamic capabilities and multinational enterprise: Penrosean insights and omissions. *Management International Review, 47* (2), 175–192.

Bourdette, N. (2003, 19 August). An American pushes Europe to embrace a modern ice age. *Wall Street Journal*, New York, Retrieved on 13 March 2018 from https://www.wsj.com.

Carlson, N. (2011, 31 October). Inside Groupon: the truth about the world's most controversial company. *Business Insider*. Retrieved on 13 March 2018 from http://www.businessinsider.com/inside-groupon-the-truth-about-the-worlds-most-controversial-company-2011-10?IR=T.

Chow, A. (2017, 18 September). Global experiences in clean energy development, 2017 China Mass Entrepreneurship and Innovation Week, Sino-US Green Innovation Forum. Shanghai: China.

Diner, P.J. (2007). *Larabar: Making a Name in a Crowded Sector: Who Says a Nutrition Bar Can't Taste Good?*, University of Colorado Denver, Institute for International Business and Center for International Business Education and Research: Global Executive Forum, Fall.

Eisenhardt, K. and Martin, J. (2000). Dynamic capabilities: what are they? *Strategic Management Journal, 21* (10/11), 1105–1121.

Fredrickson, J. (1984). The comprehensiveness of strategic decision processes: extension, observations, future directions. *Academy of Management Journal,* 27(3), 445–467.

Gernon, D. (2017, 10 July). Alibaba's Singles Day is Amazon's Prime Day – on steroids. *Consumer News and Business Channel*. Retrieved on 13 March 2018 from https://www.cnbc.com/2017/07/10/alibabas-singles-day-is-amazons-prime-day--on-steroids.html.

Intuitive Surgical, https://www.intuitivesurgical.com. Frequently Asked Questions. Accessed 22 August 2017; 3 October 2017.

Isaacson, W. (2011). *Steve Jobs*. New York, NY: Simon & Schuster.

Kirzner, I. (1973). *Competition and Entrepreneurship*. Chicago, IL and London: University of Chicago Press.

Kirzner, I. (1997). Entrepreneurial discovery and the competitive market process: an Austrian approach. *Journal of Economic Literature,* 35(1), 60–85.

Lessard, D., Teece, D. and Leih, S. (2016). The dynamic capabilities of meta-multinationals. *Global Strategy Journal, 6,* 211–224.

Liedtke, M. (2015, 27 February). How Netflix's $100 million bet on House of Cards paid off. *Huffington Post*. Retrieved on 13 March 2018 from http://www.huffingtonpost.ca/2015/02/27/netflixs-risky-bet-on-h_n_6766788.html.

Luo, Y. (2000). Dynamic capabilities in international expansion. *Journal of World Business, 35* (4), 355–378.

McDougall-Covin, P., Jones, M. and Serapio, M.G. (2014). High potential concepts, phenomena and theories for the advancement of international entrepreneurship research. *Entrepreneurship Theory and Practice, 38* (1), 1–10.

McIntyre, H. (2014, 16 June). At 2 billion views "Gangnam Style" has made Psy a very rich man, *Forbes*. Retrieved on 13 March 2018 from https://www.forbes.com/sites/hughmcintyre/2014/06/16/at-2-billion-views-gangnam-style-has-made-psy-a-very-rich-man/#2428f1e13fdb.

Merriken, L. (2007, June). Perspectives on international entrepreneurship: the experience of LaraBar. Faculty Development in International Entrepreneurship Program, University of

Colorado Denver, Institute for International Business and Center for International Business Education and Research. Denver, CO: USA.

Minana, J. (2016, November). Jollibee: US and international expansion. Jollibee Foods Corporation. Robert Reynolds Distinguished Lecture. University of Colorado Denver, Institute for International Business and Center for International Business Education and Research. Denver, CO: USA.

Munk, N. (2014, 24 April). Steve Wynn's Biggest Gamble. *Vanity Fair.* Retrieved on 13 March 2018 from https://www.vanityfair.com/news/2005/06/steve-wynn-las-vegas-resort.

Oviatt, B. and McDougall, P. (1994). Towards a theory of international new ventures. *Journal of International Business Studies, 25* (1), 45–64.

Oviatt, B.M. and McDougall, P.P. (2005). Defining international entrepreneurship and modeling the speed of internationalization. *Entrepreneurship Theory and Practice, 29* (5), 537–553.

Pisano, G.P. (1994). Knowledge, integration, and the locus of learning: an empirical analysis of process development. *Strategic Management Journal, 15* (S1), 85–100.

Pitelis, C. and Teece, D. (2010). Cross-border market co-creation, dynamic capabilities and the entrepreneurial theory of the multinational enterprise. *Industrial and Corporate Change, 19* (4), 1247–1270.

Prange, C. and Verdier, S. (2011). Dynamic capabilities, internationalization process and performance. *Journal of World Business, 46* (1), 126–133.

Ramoglou, S. and Tsang, E. (2016). A realist perspective of entrepreneurship: opportunities as propensities. *Academy of Management Review, 41* (3), 410–434.

Sarasvathy, S. (2001). Toward a theoretical shift from economic inevitability to entrepreneurial contingency. *Academy of Management Review, 26* (2), 243–263.

Sarasvathy, S., Kumar, K., York, J. and Bhagavatula, S. (2014). An effectual approach to international entrepreneurship: overlaps, challenges and practice possibilities. *Entrepreneurship Theory and Practice, 38* (1), 71–94.

Serapio, M. (forthcoming). *International Entrepreneurship.* Retrieved on 13 March 2018 from http://www.venturehighway.com.

Shane, S. (2000). Prior knowledge and the discovery of entrepreneurial opportunities. *Organization Science, 11* (4), 448–469.

Shane, S. (2003). *A General Theory of Entrepreneurship. The Individual–Opportunity Nexus.* Cheltenham, UK and Northampton, MA, USA: Edward Elgar Publishing.

Shane, S. and Venkataraman, S. (2000). The promise of entrepreneurship as a field of research. *Academy of Management Review, 25* (1), 217–226.

Srivastav, T. (2017, 17 October). Jack Ma outlines new strategy to develop "Alibaba Economy". *The Drum.* Retrieved on 13 March 2018 from http://www.thedrum.com/news/2017/10/17/jack-ma-outlines-new-strategy-develop-alibaba-economy.

Teece, D. (2007). Explicating dynamic capabilities: the nature and micro foundations of (sustainable) enterprise performance. *Strategic Management Journal, 28* (13), 1319–1350.

Teece, D., Pisano, G. and Shuen, A. (1997). Dynamic capabilities and strategic management. *Strategic Management Journal, 18* (7), 509–533.

The greasy competition among NYC's halal's street carts. (2014, 16 August). *New York Post.* Retrieved on 13 March 2018 from http://nypost.com/2014/08/16/the-greasy-competition-among-nycs-halal-street-carts/.

The Halal Guys, https://thehalalguys.com. Accessed 8 August 2014; 3 October 2017.

Venkataraman S. (1997), The distinctive domain of entrepreneurship research: an editor's perspective. In J. Katz and R. Brockhaus (eds) *Advances in Entrepreneurship, Firm Emergence, and Growth* (vol. 3, pp. 119–138), Greenwich, CT: JAI Press.

Wan, D. (2017). Briefing and Visit to Alibaba. Hangzhou, China, 22 September.

Weerawardena, J., Mort, G.S., Liesch, P. and Knight, G. (2007). Conceptualizing accelerated internationalization in the born global firm: a dynamic capabilities perspective. *Journal of World Business*, 42 (3), 294–306.

Winter, S. (2003). Understanding dynamic capabilities. *Strategic Management Journal*, 24 (10), 991–995.

Zahra, S.A. and George, G. (2002). International entrepreneurship: the current status of the field and future research agenda. In M.A. Hitt, R.D. Ireland, D.I. Sexton and M. Camps (eds) *Strategic Entrepreneurship: Creating An Integrated Mindset* (pp. 255–288). Malden, MA: Blackwell Publishers.

Zahra, S., Newey, L. and Li, Y. (2014), On the frontiers: the implications of social entrepreneurship for international entrepreneurship. *Entrepreneurship Theory and Practice*, 38 (1), 137–158.

Zucchella, A. and Magnani, G. (2016). *International Entrepreneurship: Theoretical Foundations and Practice*. New York, NY: Palgrave Macmillan.

Zucchella, A. and Scabini, P. (2007). *International Entrepreneurship: Theoretical Foundations and Practices*. New York, NY: Palgrave Macmillan.

4

Processes of building and managing the international entrepreneurial firm

4.1 Building and sustaining competitive advantage

The concepts of strategy and competitive advantage are at the very heart of business success. These concepts help to understand why some companies appear to have little difficulty in growing and changing while other companies decline and even collapse; why some new ventures internationalize early, fast, intensively and on a global scale while many of their counterparts are active only on their home markets or do internationalize later in their life and slowly, "like rings in the water" (i.e. Uppsala model, Johanson and Vahlne, 1977). Companies that grow internationally and change quickly in order to shape or adapt to their dynamic environment are firms that know how to build strategies that secure and sustain competitive advantage.

Competitive advantage is included in one of the key definitions of Oviatt and McDougall (1994, p. 49), where the authors define "an international new venture as a business organization that, from inception, seeks to derive significant competitive advantage from the use of resources and the sale of outputs in multiple countries". The key point in this context – a bit overlooked in current research in IE – therefore is how these firms derive competitive advantage from *being* international.

First, a more intensive competition or the presence of sophisticated customers in foreign markets forces companies to improve both products and processes and thus remain competitive. Second, there is the possibility of "learning by exporting (being international)". Being exposed to superior but also to diverse foreign knowledge and technology fosters innovation, from product to process to marketing and management innovation. Presence on foreign markets helps to form alliances and networks which may be a means for accessing or accumulating lacking resources. Finally, a scale effect may be important. Internationalization extends the market and since many costs, for example, R&D are largely fixed, such investments are recouped quicker and over larger sales volumes. This helps again productivity and profitability and again creates incentives to invest in R&D and innovation which in turn sustains competitiveness.

The fact that internationalization extends the market is especially important for nichers, usually small firms, which are able to exploit a global segment in different countries. They do not only enhance their revenue and profit potential, internationalization here may be the only way to implement a sustainable business where the domestic market may simply be too small.

In summary, the readiness to identify and exploit opportunity everywhere may initiate a virtuous circle in building and reinforcing the competitive advantage of the firm. Not all entrepreneurs and not all businesses are equally well equipped to address the global scale and convert it into economies of scale and scope; address the just right level of adaptation; optimize the choice of location for the different activities; foster knowledge sharing, and anticipate and dialogue with the international environment.

How to address the international scale and which "ingredients" are necessary to do so is a question of the founders/teams, governance issues, finance and business models and strategic design – topics we will explore in the following sections.

4.2 Choosing the right people and governance

4.2.1 Entrepreneurs and their teams

Especially in the case of the international new venture, the women and men who are starting and running it, as well as the outside parties providing key services or important resources[1] for it are key. Resources in the new, that is, young, small and resource-constrained, venture are mainly residing in the human (social) capital of the start-up. At an early stage, it is the entrepreneur(s) and their wider social and business network which provide the unique, valuable, difficult to imitate resources that can provide the basis for new ventures' competitive advantages (Barney, 1991) and enable the new ventures to form and exploit opportunities, strategize, and acquire additional resources.

The founders of early internationalizing firms

Characteristics and competencies that have been found to differentiate the founders in INVs and born globals from their domestic counterparts point to a global mindset, an international entrepreneurial orientation, a strong learning capability and an institutional bridging capability.

Founders of international new ventures have been reported to see the world as their marketplace when designing their business and strategies rather than being focused on their domestic markets or customer segment. Combined with entrepreneurial orientation (Covin and Slevin, 1991; Lumpkin and Dess, 1996), a composite of proactive, innovative and risk-taking behaviour, the global view makes these entrepreneurs alert to international opportunities and, at the same time, ready to exploit them. A global mindset or international orientation comes with international experience, business- or education-wise. Staying abroad not only "opens" the mind and fosters knowledge of different institutional and cultural environments, it also helps to form social and business networks which can be used and built upon during internationalization. Ganotakis and Love (2012) recently showed that human capital gained though experience has an effect through the decision to become an exporter, while human capital gained through education operates principally through enhancing export performance (i.e. makes the firm more export intensive). In the case of the decision to become international, attitudes and perceptions of the risks and costs associated with exporting are among the main determinants behind a strategic decision to become an exporter: experiential learning, or in different words, international experience, significantly reduces negative attitudes and perceptions towards the risks of operating abroad. By contrast, human capital gained through education fosters problem solving and assists entrepreneurs to develop appropriate management and operational practices necessary for reaching higher levels of export performance once the initial exporting decision is made (Ganotakis and Love, 2012).

In general, we may conclude, it is a more sophisticated – international – knowledge base combined with a strong entrepreneurial posture which helps to innovate and recombine and add resources conducive to entering and competing in the international arena.

The entrepreneurial team composition

New ventures, however, are rarely the product of a solitary entrepreneur. Most new ventures are created by an entrepreneurial team, defined as a "group of individuals that is chiefly responsible for the strategic decision making and ongoing operations of a new venture" (Klotz et al., 2014, p. 227) and which operates "with a common goal which can only be achieved by appropriate combinations of individual entrepreneurial actions" (Harper, 2008, p. 617).

Cooper and Daily (1997, p. 144) suggest that "entrepreneurial teams are at the heart of any new venture" and several studies claim that firms founded by entrepreneurial teams are more likely to survive and to achieve faster growth than ventures started by individual entrepreneurs (e.g. Cooper and Bruno, 1977; Bird, 1989; Roberts, 1991; Eisenhardt and Schoonhoven, 1990).

Up to now, the focus in IE research has been on the single entrepreneur but research on entrepreneurial teams is emerging: early work of McDougall, Shane and Oviatt (1994), demonstrated that firms that were international from inception were, typically, founded by teams and research by Bloodgood, Sapienza and Almeida (1996) and Reuber and Fischer (1997, 2002), posited – in line with the work on characteristics of the solo entrepreneur – that the international experience of the top management team was related to greater firm internationalization and enhanced performance.

Work that digs deeper into team characteristics of INVs is limited. However, in line with Ensley, Pearson and Amason (2002) we propose that entrepreneurial teams may be considered the first Top Management Team (TMT) of the venture and argue that – similar to findings for TMTs in established companies – entrepreneurial teams and their characteristics may predict their performance and internationalization trajectories. The assumption is that firms are "reflections of their managers" (Hambrick and Mason, 1984) and that their human capital, that is, the sum or the mix in terms of education, experience, knowledge and skills and so on, is likely to affect new venture performance. Work originating from Upper Echelons (UE) research on TMTs shows that the size, the composition, and the dynamics of the team greatly influence their companies' culture, innovation, internationalization and general performance outcomes.

Denicolai, Hagen and Pisoni (2015) for example found clear differences in innovation and internationalization outcomes across four types of entrepreneurial teams in SMEs as described by their team size, composition, and characteristics (e.g. prior experience of various types, education, and age of their team members). Under the same UE perspective, a very recent meta-analysis of new venture teams shows for instance that heterogeneous teams allow more latitude of action because their set of strategic choices is broader (Jin et al., 2016). Heterogeneous teams possess a broader range of task-relevant knowledge, skills and abilities because their members have different opinions and perspectives and so establish a more diverse pool of resources that may be helpful in dealing with non-routine problems and reaching higher quality, more creative, and innovative outcomes (van Knippenberg and Schippers, 2007). It is not only the benefit of new ideas through different viewpoints, the mere presence of diversity in a group creates awkwardness, and the need to diffuse this tension leads to better group problem solving through more careful information processing (Kellogg School of Management at Northwestern University, Kellogg Insight, 2009). Confirming this view, research also indicates that the diversity of characteristics, such as functional background and education, is beneficial for team performance (Jackson and Joshi, 2011). While homogenous groups feel more confident in their performance and group interactions, it is the diverse groups that are more successful in completing their tasks. Diverse teams also overperform in terms of growth and negative cash flow (Ensley and Hmieleski, 2005). Also findings from research on funding mirror benefits of heterogeneity: here task oriented-diversity (e.g. education, functional experience) is positively related to the willingness of respondents to provide capital and the same applies for relations-oriented diversity (e.g. age, nationality). The overall quality of the founding team is often the main reason for awarding funding, more than the quality of the project itself. This is referred to as "backing the jockey rather than the horse" in venture capital circles and the requirement of track records of individuals and founding teams.

Moving from benefits of diversity to benefits of size, Kozlowski and Bell (2003) argue that larger teams provide more resources, such as time, energy, money, and expertise, which are particularly beneficial for completing difficult tasks in complex and uncertain environments, exactly the conditions under which INVs and born global firms operate. Additionally, complex and uncertain environments confront entrepreneurial teams often with non-routine problems where more heterogeneity should be more beneficial.

Overall, therefore, we know from the general entrepreneurship and management research that social capital of an entrepreneurial team matters to a great extent on strategic choice, funding opportunities and performance in general. While the importance of TMTs in the formation and development of new ventures is well recognized, their impact on the rapid internationalization remains relatively underresearched. Surprisingly little research is available given the fact that the complexity of conditions under which early internationalizers operate is often exacerbated by an absence of organizational learning within the newly created firm and a lack of precedence upon which they might rely (Loane, Bell and McNaughton, 2007). Such conditions demand diverse capabilities, knowledge and skills within the team of decision makers and insight into team composition therefore would be of great value to founding teams and TMTs in any kind of IEOs.

One of the few studies which explicitly focuses on entrepreneurial teams in INVs is Loane, Bell and McNaughton (2007) who present a cross-national study conducted in Australia, Canada, Ireland and New Zealand. Around 73 per cent of all firms were team formations which typically had internationalized more rapidly with higher levels of export revenue than those founded by individual entrepreneurs. They also tended to be active in more export markets. Collectively, the founding teams had significant prior international experience with individual members having either worked or studied abroad (56 per cent) or having worked in an international firm in the domestic market (55 per cent). Around 55 per cent had relevant industry or sector experience. Typical configurations involved one or more individuals with relevant technical skills, one with financial acumen and one with business skills. Hagen and Zucchella (2014), in the context of born global firms, find that international experience is a baseline characteristic of born global firms and show that the sustainable, fast growing "born-to-run" firms differentiate from their born global counterparts in their growth orientation, the willingness and ability of founders to decentralize power and responsibility, the diversity and the openness of the team to outside advice. This posture corresponds to a frequently mentioned learning capability and the learning from different sources which is stressed as one of the most important capabilities of the early internationalizing firm (Weerawardena et al., 2007; Zahra, Ireland and Hitt, 2000).

Loane, Bell and McNaughton (2007) and Hagen and Zucchella (2014) also demonstrate the significant impact that such teams have in creating the core internal capabilities and leveraging the external resources required for rapid and dedicated internationalization. They stress the need to augment the management team in order to address key resource or knowledge gaps and/or to expand international networks. Evident in many of the companies is the impact of changes in team structures on business strategy (see also born again global companies, Chapter 2). More in detail, Loane, Bell and McNaughton (2007) report that over time team diversity increased in response to the changing needs of the firm. Founder(s) often recognized that nascent firms had skills gaps, and deliberately sought to engage the right people to compensate for these gaps, a finding which is confirmed by Hagen and Zucchella (2014) for those born global firms which were growing exponentially over time. They find that the firms which extend their teams and look for outside advice strategically prepare for growth, especially in the international arena.

Changes in teams through 'buying in' new members to improve firms' capabilities were not the only reason for changes in founding team structure, also the introduction of new equity partners forced changes in the structure of management teams or exits of founding team members (Loane, Bell and McNaughton, 2007; Loane, Bell and Cunningham, 2014). Buying in a 'diversity' of skills, networks, and knowledge, was done not for the sake of heterogeneity per se, but rather, to add specific missing resources to the firm's resource base. Beyond acquiring resources and capability through buying in, Hagen and Zucchella (2014) also note a proactive posture of the team in terms of networking and alliance building as a means to build additional resources for continued international growth.

We conclude that the team who is running the firm is of great impact not only during the (pre-) foundation and early stages of the business, it also determines the path the ventures take on the long run. The mechanisms of transiting from individual and team characteristics and resources to building capabilities at firm level is yet to be understood. Firm-level research however shows that an entrepreneurial posture, a mindset for action, experimentation and innovation, must be cultivated and that a maintained firm-wide learning capability from different sources (diverse teams and networks included) is key. Being international, a priori, builds a formidable basis for learning from different sources and exploring opportunities – market- and partner-wise.

4.2.2 Alternative governance models

Oviatt and McDougall in their seminal 1994 article argue that INVs rely on alternative structures and modes of mobilizing resources and controlling their vital assets in order to address a "triple liability". Three liabilities, that is, the liability of newness, smallness and foreignness, limit the ventures' ability to access different types and adequate amounts of resources and their ability to develop appropriate governance mechanisms for resource exchange.

Due to their lack of resources, INVs own a comparably small percentage of the resources which are essential to their survival and international expansion. Alternative structures, such as licensing or franchising, may constitute reasonable ways to maintain control of valuable assets in exchange of resources where the partners share complementary assets to their mutual benefit (Oviatt and McDougall, 1994) (see Chapter 5, section 5.3 this volume for a more detailed discussion). However, such partnerships require elaborate contracts and entail the risk of expropriation of the new ventures' assets through their partners. Blomqvist et al. (2008) for instance, emphasize the fact that contracting is costly and time-consuming, as different laws and business practices in different countries, as well as the need to revise contracts, increase the required effort.

An even more powerful way therefore to generate resources and an alternative to internalization for the early internationalizing firm is the network (Oviatt and McDougall, 1994).

WHAT IS A NETWORK? "Networks encompass a firm's set of relationships, both horizontal and vertical, with other organizations – be they suppliers, customers, competitors, or other entities – including relationships across industries and countries" (Gulati, Nohria and Zaheer, 2000, p. 203).

Interpersonal and inter-organizational relationships are viewed as the media through which entrepreneurs and their firms gain access to a variety of resources held by others. A plethora of studies confirm the important and varied role that networks play in influencing entrepreneurial processes and outcomes. Most studies, with some exceptions on the role of capital, concentrate on intangible resources. A key benefit of networks described in this context is the access to information and advice which is conducive to identifying and exploitation of opportunities, especially in the early stages of the venture's life. Foreign market knowledge (e.g. Lamb and Liesch 2002; Coviello and Munro, 1995) for example is particularly relevant in our context of international start-ups. Also, networking ability has been found to help develop products for global markets (Mort and Weerawardena, 2006). Relationships have also reputational effects which are crucial, especially under conditions of uncertain and dynamic environments and the liability of foreignness. Such reputational or signaling effects concern investors but also potential employees, suppliers or foreign customers who take known and reputable partners as a surrogate for the venture's "quality" and so facilitate any kind of resource or other exchange.

Networks, in terms of governance, depend on the social, that is, informal, control of behaviour through trust and moral obligation, instead of formal contracts. Mutual trust between partners, rather than legal enforcement, is the governance mechanism and the critical factor which in turn influences the quality of the resources exchanged. Especially because of its positive impact on information flows, trust is cited as a key driver of innovation through interfirm collaboration. Opportunistic behaviour in networks is avoided because partners do not put their business and personal reputations at stake as they are well aware of negative consequences in current and future transactions. Such a governance mode based on trust and cooperation can create cost advantages in comparison to market transactions because costly contracting, monitoring or (re)negotiating is not needed.

Also the ventures' network size and position, for example, the quantity of weak and strong ties and its centrality in the network, has a direct impact on the flow of resources. Especially with regard to internationalization, these elements need to be stressed. Extant research has found that entrepreneurs who had network ties abroad at the time of foundation were more likely to internationalize. Johanson and Vahlne (2009) go a step further: they define insidership in relevant network(s) as a key explanatory variable for successful internationalization and introduce the liability of outsidership. A second precondition for internationalization, according to these authors, is the learning which ensues from trusted and committed networking.

Although most research on networks point to positive effects on the entrepreneurial process and outcomes, in some studies no effect, equivocal or even negative results are supported. The "dark" side of networks may be summarized with dependence and lock-in, negative spill-overs in terms of reputation and the like.

Also, a quantitative study by Aspelund and Moen (2012) fails to identify any differences between born global firms' and traditional international SMEs' international governance structures. The authors comment that their results oppose a lot of qualitative work over the past decade and that their results also imply that INVs are strategic in deciding their governance structures, regardless of their resource situation.

In summary, the huge body of research on network speaks to a positive impact on entrepreneurial processes and outcomes through mobilization of resources in all stages of the INVs life cycle – from pre-foundation to start-up and post-internationalization.

4.3 International entrepreneurial finance

Finance is the lifeblood of every company but for international entrepreneurial ventures, funding is particularly critical. Along with decisions related to choosing the right people and governance, mentioned above, making the right financial decisions is critical to the development, growth, and sustained competitive advantage of the new venture.

Entrepreneurs face various financial decisions in developing, growing, and internationalizing the entrepreneurial venture. These decisions include the determination and sizing of funding requirements, mobilizing resources, and selection of the appropriate types and sources of funding to support the venture's development and growth. In this section, we will address the choice between debt financing and venture capital in new enterprise creation; compare three major types of equity financing of entrepreneurial ventures (e.g. angel investors, venture capital, corporate partners) and discuss the role of two new sources of funding support for new ventures (e.g. crowdfunding or peer-to-peer lending and incubators/accelerators). Funding considerations in entrepreneurial internationalization will also be examined. We conclude with a discussion of Supercell, a born global entrepreneurial venture that has successfully mobilized financial resources in launching and growing a leading global enterprise in the social gaming industry.

4.3.1 Debt versus venture capital

In a 2014 survey of the 5,000 fastest growing companies in the United States listed by *Inc.* magazine, the Kauffman Foundation found that debt financing accounted for the majority share of entrepreneurial finance, with bank loans dominating among other forms of debt. About 40 per cent of the initial start-up capitals in a new venture are loans from banks. Also relying on the so-called three Fs (i.e. family, friends and fools) is a common way to get started: friends may be willing to invest and family may feel obliged to invest in the start-up – one more reason why cultivating a network is important to entrepreneurs. The advantages of love money are manifold: low rates, lenient credit standards and the opportunity for the FF-investor to participate in the new venture success.

Equity financing, particularly angel investor and venture capital financing, or smart money, amounted to less than 3 per cent and 1 per cent of new firm financing, respectively (Wiens and Bell-Masterson, 2015). However, the role of venture capital in financing entrepreneurial firms has grown in significance and scale in recent years, particularly in high-technology industries, such as software development, Internet technologies, social media, global e-commerce, marketplace platforms, biotechnology, and others.

The pros and cons of bank finance versus venture capital have been widely addressed in the literature. For example, Bettignies and Brander (2007, p. 809) noted that bank loans dominate venture capital as a source of entrepreneurial finance because "debt contracts (offered by banks) have superior incentive properties for the entrepreneur relative to equity-based venture capital finance . . . Bank financing leaves the entrepreneur with full ownership of the firm, avoiding dilution of entrepreneurial effort and loss of entrepreneurial control."

On the other hand, the desirability of venture capital financing over bank debt lies in the additional value that the venture capitalist provides to the entrepreneurial venture in the form of high-value managerial input. Because a venture capitalist has an equity stake in the venture that could lead to a contingent financial payoff (i.e. a highly successful venture could lead to an attractive payoff), the venture capitalist has an appropriate incentive to contribute useful advice and meaningful involvement in the venture. Further, Bettignies and Brander (2007, p. 826) have maintained that "venture capital is most useful when the entrepreneurial venture lies within the venture capitalist's area of managerial expertise". The same authors also contend that providing the venture capitalist a higher equity than necessary to attract venture capital finance is advantageous to the entrepreneurial company as it provides important incentives for the venture capitalist to contribute to the entrepreneurial venture.

While entrepreneurial ventures generally prefer bank financing over venture capital financing, most ventures at the start-up stage cannot access them because they do not have assets or cash flows to back their borrowing. For example, in a large-scale study of over 2,000 entrepreneurial firms in the United Kingdom, Cosh, Cumming and Hughes (2009, p. 1497) found that:

> Banks are more likely to provide the desired amount of capital to larger firms with more assets. Leasing firms, factor/discounting/invoicing firms, trade customers/suppliers and partners/working shareholders are more likely to provide the desired capital to firms with higher profit margins. Profit margins are not statistically relevant to venture capital funds and private individual investors; smaller firms are more likely to obtain finance from private individuals; while young innovative firms seek external capital from venture capital funds.

Although the challenge of funding is common to all new ventures, regional gaps in the development of the risk capital market make financing in Europe more difficult than in the US (e.g. Cotta Ramusino, 2018). For example, venture capital investments in the US account for around 54 per cent of the global VC investment. In the US, from 2007 to 2016, venture capitalists invested a total of around $500 billion a year, with an annual investment of around $48 billion (National Venture Capital Association, 2016). The European annual VC investment is only 10 per cent of the American investment, that is, around $4 billion per year (InvestEurope, 2016).

Beyond the regional gap, research also continually confirms a gender gap and finds that women entrepreneurs raise smaller amounts of capital than men to finance their firms, and are more reliant on personal rather than external sources of financing. Within the context of growth-oriented entrepreneurship, this distinction is important because growth-oriented firms typically require substantial amounts of external capital in the form of both debt and equity. If women entrepreneurs do not seek, or if they are not able to obtain, external capital, their prospects for growing their firms are diminished considerably (e.g. Greene et al., 2010).

4.3.2 Equity financing

Angel investors

Angel or private investors are typically wealthy individuals that invest in entrepreneurial start-ups, with the aim of obtaining venture capital financing (Cumming and Zhang, 2016). Angels invest money in exchange for convertible debt or equity. Some of these private investors, often called Super Angels, invest in a portfolio of start-ups and are willing to lead or participate in multiple rounds, usually starting with a seed round. Film celebrity Ashton Kutcher and Reid Hoffman, LinkedIn founder are names often mentioned in this category.

Angel investors may bring additional benefits of connecting entrepreneurs with key resources, such as venture capitalists, industry experts, and professional managers. Successful entrepreneurs turned angel investors may be able to offer high value input to the entrepreneur, although most private investors do not possess the expertise or time to advise the entrepreneur (Stevenson and Roberts, [2002]2006). Some investors may tend to micro-manage and demand a great deal of time from the entrepreneur. With the exception of Super Angels, most private investors are less likely to invest additional funds, if required, particularly if the venture is successful and requires significant additional rounds of investments (Stevenson and Roberts, [2002]2006). Some angels also require a disproportionate return on their investments.

Venture capital

Venture capital is a professionally managed pool of equity capital. In exchange for managing a pool of equity capital, the general partners of the venture are paid a management fee and a percentage of the gain on investments. Endowments and pension funds make up the larger share of funds invested in the venture capital, although wealthy individuals may invest in the venture capital as limited partners.

As noted above, a key benefit of financing a start-up with venture capital is the high value expertise and contribution that venture capitalists could offer to the entrepreneur, including helping the entrepreneurial company bring on board capable management team members and positioning the venture for strategic exits (e.g. buyouts or IPOs). Venture capital firms usually possess specialized expertise in terms of subject/industry area of investments, geographic focus, and funding rounds (e.g. early, mid, late stage) that could be beneficial to the entrepreneurial venture. In addition, venture capital firms may engage other venture companies in syndicating a large investment, particularly in subsequent or later rounds of financing. On the other hand, venture capital firms demand a high return on their investments, typically a hurdle rate of 40 per cent compound annual rate of return of ten times of original investment in five years. Some may even impose demanding requirements on the entrepreneurial venture that could lead to a possible dilution of entrepreneurial effort and loss of entrepreneurial control.

Corporate/strategic partners

A growing number of corporations have established funding units or investment vehicles to take equity positions in entrepreneurial ventures. In general, corporations seldom fund an early stage start-up but most do so in a later round when there is more visibility in the potential of the enterprise. Among others, these corporations seek equity participation in ventures that it could potentially acquire down the road or start-ups that possess promising business models or technologies. Corporate funders may offer a longer-term horizon and provide strategic assistance to entrepreneurial ventures in key areas that are critical for the latter's growth, such as branding and channel development. The corporate investor may even serve as a major client for the new venture. Unilever Ventures provides a case in point of a major corporate investor in new ventures. The company invests in promising new ventures in personal care and provides them with strategic assistance to take the enterprise to the next level of growth.

4.3.3 Non-traditional channels for new venture financing

Bellavitis, Filatotchev and Kamuriwo (2017, p. 2) have observed the emergence of new sources of finance, particularly for science and technology start-ups that "can raise financing from numerous sources, such as accelerators and incubators, proof of concept centers, university based seed funds, crowdfunding platforms, and IP-backed financial instruments". Similarly, the Kauffman report (Wiens and Bell-Masterson, 2015), noted above, has observed a growing trend among new ventures to use non-traditional channels to raise capital. According to the report, "crowdfunding, in particular, has garnered much attention, and with good reason – online platforms are growing at astronomical rates, and in the first half of 2014, more than 20 percent of startups applying for loans did so through an online lender."

Also referred to as peer-to-peer lending or investing, crowdfunding can be a loan, investment, pre-order, or contributions from individuals acting at the same time. Crowdfunding platforms, such as Kickstarter.com, IndieGogo, Quirky, RocketHub, Companisto, CrowdCube, FundedbyMe and others, connect communities of small investors to entrepreneurial ventures and business owners looking for funding. Crowdfunding could be in the form of debt crowdfunding (peer-to-peer lending) where participants extend loans to a start-up project or idea that they believe in; equity crowdfunding where participants make investments in exchange for a small equity in the venture; donation crowdfunding where participants donate funds to social causes; and reward-based crowdfunding where prospective consumers assist ventures to ramp up production by buying products from the venture.

A notable example of the power and reach of crowdfunding in assisting entrepreneurs secure funding from non-traditional sources is Pebble, the entrepreneurial venture that has run three out of the four highest-funded projects on the Kickstarter platform. In April 2012, Pebble turned to Kickstarter to raise $100,000 for its Pebble e-paper watch. Within 28 hours, the company had raised more than $1 million, a figure that grew to over $10.2 million from more than 68,000 people one month later. The company's subsequent campaign for Pebble Time, a colour e-paper smartwatch with up to seven days of battery, and a new timeline interface that highlights important events in the user's day, raised more than $12 million from 67,000 people (Ferrua Villanueva, 2016).

Peer-to-peer (P2P) lending developed after the financial crisis and the following period of recession when most loan opportunities for small businesses disappeared. Some of the immediate benefits of a P2P loan is that no collateral is required. Also, lower interest rates tend to be available, depending on credit score, loan amount and loan term, because the peer-to-peer lenders operate with low overheads. Since it is an online lending environment, ventures also enjoy faster approval and less paperwork except for a few online forms and a digital signature. Once repaid, there is also the opportunity to continue using the P2P lending connection to tap additional funds later on whenever additional capital is required. That accessibility can help to develop the venture more quickly rather than requiring time pounding the pavement for funds. Examples include Funding Circle, Lending Club, Street Shares and SoFi, among other P2P lenders, well-known tried and trusted P2P platforms. For example, Lending Club offers business loans up to $300,000 without collateral for loans or lines under $100, business plan or projections, visits of business and costly appraisals or title insurance. Overall, since 2007, more than $31 billion have been borrowed, and it counts more than 1.5 million customers (source: Lending Club website).

Crowdfunding is growing significantly and is forecasted to surpass venture capital funding soon. According to Forbes (2015), the practice itself is more than doubling, every year. In 2015, $34.4 billion was raised across the different crowdfunding models that include rewards, donation, equity and P2P lending. Europe, in 2015, is the third largest market valued at $3.26 billion, with Asia being slightly ahead at $3.4 billion.

Globally, incubators/accelerators – organizations that speed up the development and growth of early stage companies – have increased in number and significance. These incubators/accelerators (referred to here in general as accelerators) provide support, mentoring, business introductions to start-up companies, and physical space – with a view that early and focused attention increases the odds for future round funding. As Natty Zola, Managing Director of TechStars observed: accelerators have become "a proven way to quickly grow a startup by learning from experts, finding great mentorship, and connecting to a powerful network. They provide resources that reduce the cost of starting a company and the early capital a team needs to get their venture off the ground to achieve key early milestones" (Gust.com, 2015).

In exchange for the value that they provide, most accelerators require equity stakes (e.g. 7–10 per cent) in the start-ups that they support, as well as charge them a modest fee for office space and other services. The larger payoff for these accelerators comes with the increase in the value of their equity positions in their supported start-ups with subsequent funding rounds or strategic exits by these companies. Private organizations; national, state, and local governments; and academic institutions in different parts of the world have established or contributed to accelerators of different types, size, industry focus, and business models. Since YCombinator, the pioneer accelerator, launched in the mid-2000s, the number of accelerators have grown all over the world. Prominent examples are Plug N Play, Startup 500, Techstars (USA); Seed Rocket, Barclays Accelerator, H-Camp (Europe); and Chinaccelarator, Magic, Business World Accelerator (Asia).

4.3.4 Funding considerations and entrepreneurial internationalization

As noted earlier in this chapter, the Top Management Team (TMT) plays a vital role in the internationalization decision-making process of entrepreneurial ventures. However, an equally important voice in this process are the people and organizations that fund the entrepreneurial venture, particularly venture capitalists who provide strategic input to the company. Funding decisions, particularly the choice of funding partner, could influence an entrepreneurial company's ability to internationalize, as well as impact the timing, speed, and scope of its internationalization.

To this end, the founder and TMT of an entrepreneurial venture would have to address a number of funding questions as it relates to the company's internationalization, including: What funding levels are required to support internationalization? What funding sources are most likely to be supportive of internationalization? What is the risk profile and orientation of funding partners (i.e. angel investors, venture capitalists) towards internationalization? How can funding partners benefit the venture's internationalization, not just in terms of financing but access to networks, markets, and other resources?

The relationship between funding decisions and entrepreneurial internationalization may revolve around the following dynamics. The first dynamic is the additional risk and complexity that internationalization may bring to the venture. Some venture capitalists shun international expansion, particularly at early stages of a company's development, and prefer that the entrepreneur focus on the domestic market. The same triple liabilities – liability of newness, smallness, and foreignness – surrounding governance, noted above, may be of primary concern to the venture capitalist. A related dynamic to this is a venture capitalist's strong preference for monitoring and control, which is implemented more easily if the venture is in close proximity to the investor's base of operations.

Conversely, a third dynamic relates to valuation targets. Some venture capitalists may favour internationalization, including accelerated and broad internationalization, because it could demonstrate a venture's potential opportunity not just as a domestic concern but a global enterprise. All other things equal, a global opportunity could fetch a higher valuation and better premium than a purely domestic opportunity.

Finally, entrepreneurial internationalization may be attractive to some venture capitalists because it could enhance a venture's access to a broader base of capital, networks, distribution channels, and other resources that could be critical to the venture's success. The experience of Wonderbly (see case in Chapter 3) attests to this dynamic. The funding pathway that Wonderbly pursued included initial funding from influential UK angel investor Piers Linney of Outsourcery, followed by Berlin-based Project A ventures which specializes in accelerating e-commerce and marketplace businesses; and culminated in a Series B corporate investment from Ravensburger, a leading publisher of children's books. All these funders paved the way for Wonderbly's rapid growth by broadening its reach to an international audience.

4.3.5 Supercell: leveraging funding for competitive advantage

It is important that an entrepreneurial venture and its funders are aligned in regard to their goals, including the development and implementation of its internationalization strategy. The phenomenal journey of Supercell demonstrates the critical importance of aligning structure with strategy, as well as matching funding and governance with a company's strong culture.

Supercell is a game development company founded in Finland in 2010. Among its highly successful games are Hay Day, Clash of Clans, and Clash Royale. Supercell attracts 100 million daily players worldwide, generating more than $6 million in revenues per day. The immense popularity of its games could be attributed to the company's formula of (1) focusing on the mobile platform (phones and tablets); (2) developing games that are simple and fun, games that could be enjoyed by novice and experienced players alike; and (3) building a social element that provides a glue for players to play, compete, and communicate with each other (Kerr, Jones and Brownell, 2016).

From the start, Supercell has embraced a philosophy of "Get big by thinking small." It has emphasized a culture of total independence for its game teams. The company goes into great lengths to recruit the best game developers from all over the world and has organized these developers into high-performance, autonomous "cells" (that is, "Supercells"). The fact that the company has managed to keep a headcount (including game developers) to only about two hundred people from 30 countries, despite the company growing revenues from €78 million in 2012 to more than €2 billion in 2015 (Kerr, Jones and Brownell, 2016), reflects the company's selectivity and the game developer cells' incredible productivity.

Supercell's high standards is embodied in its funding decisions, that is, (1) to keep Supercell well-capitalized so that the company could think long-term and create games for the long haul; (2) select partners that share in the company's vision and mission; and (3) structure financing deals that allowed Supercell to maintain its autonomy and strong culture. The company was initially funded from the founders' savings and a €400,000 loan from the Finnish government's funding agency for technology and innovation (Tekes). This was followed by a seed funding, a larger Series A of $12 million from Accel Partners, and secondary financing with a valuation of $770 million. Illka Paanen, Supercell's founder, remarked that the two things the company did well in its formative years, despite not having developed a hit game yet, was to raise funds and recruit the world's best game developers. These two things will prove later to be the key drivers for Supercell's success (Kerr, Jones and Brownell, 2016).

In 2013 SoftBank acquired 51 per cent of Supercell stock for $2.1 billion. Two years later, SoftBank acquired another 22.7 per cent of the company (Lin, 2016). Despite having a large majority position in the company, SoftBank maintained a hands-off approach to Supercell. Paanen and his team continued to lead and run the company and the game developers cells maintained their autonomy to choose the games to develop, drop, or bring to market.

In June 2016, Supercell sold 84.3 per cent of its shares (including all of SoftBank's shares) to Tencent for $8.6 billion or a company valuation of over $10 billion (Osawa and Needleman, 2016; Lin, 2016). One of the three companies that comprise "BAT" (China's top Internet and e-commerce companies which includes Baidu, Alibaba and Tencent), Tencent has revenues in excess of $30 billion and is the developer of China's popular messaging app called WeChat. This move will boost Supercell's popularity in Asia, which already accounts for 25 per cent of mobile gaming revenues in the world. As with the deal with SoftBank, Tencent would allow Supercell to retain its autonomy. The company's headquarters will remain in Finland; Paanen and the current leadership will continue to run the company; and Supercell will maintain its culture of a company that "Gets big by thinking small" (Kerr, Jones and Brownell, 2016).

CASE STUDY

FacilityLive: tying venture finance with venture creation and growth

Birgit Hagen and Antonella Zucchella

Gianpiero Lotito and Mariuccia Teroni, the co-founders of FacilityLive, have great news. Behind closed doors, the first report of the European Union Tech Study Tour (European Parliament, 2017) was presented to the IT Directorate Generals of the three main EU Institutions, that is, the European Parliament, the European Commission and the Council of the European Union. In the report, the FacilityLive founders' "Small Valley" idea, their venture and their vision of the digital economy in Europe are featured prominently.

The report describes the policy route to establishing a European ecosystem conducive to improve the maturity of the EU's tech industries, to drive the innovation capacity of tech companies and to boost their partnering activities. About FacilityLive and their vision, the report says:

> Lotito gave a very insightful overview of the recent history of the ICT industry, as well as his vision on the industry's future. In his view, Europe cannot simply copy the Silicon Valley model of doing things. Instead Europe should strive to set up a "network of Small Valleys", connecting medium size creative cities built around a historical university (such as Pavia, Leuven, Cambridge, Salamanca, Uppsala etc.), with efficient communication links, and with businesses tightly woven into the local fabric. According to Lotito, one should be looking for places where the university, the city hall, and a start up cluster are all within walking distance from one another. Such places offer the opportunity to experiment with new technology using the local community as a testing ground, especially if local authorities have an open mind set on regulating innovation . . . It appears that a locally rooted, "Small Valley" model could define the EU ICT landscape of the future. (European Parliament, 2017)

Since 2014 the entrepreneurs have both been ambassadors of prestigious initiatives of the European Commission linked to the promotion of digital skills and the modernization of Europe's industry. Not only at the European level, also in Italy their commitment and contribution to fostering technology innovation is widely recognized: for example, Teroni was nominated in 2015 Successful Woman Web Entrepreneur by a project of the European Commission, Lotito was the 2016 Innovative Entrepreneur chosen by the Italian Ministry of Economic Development to represent Italy at the EU Council for Competitiveness in Amsterdam, and also the their hometown, Pavia, a small city close to Milan in Italy, in 2015 awarded its historical Gold medal to the entrepreneurs.

Notwithstanding widespread recognition, for sceptics FacilityLive took wrong decisions from the outset. Instead of staying in Europe (even worse, in a small Italian city), investing in a European ecosystem, and looking for long-term partnerships to start and finance

CASE STUDY *(continued)*

growth, FacilityLive should have taken the "traditional" road to Silicon Valley, a well-developed ecosystem offering huge opportunities for venture finance and development to digital start-ups with the potential to become a unicorn.

It is only four years back, in September 2010, that FacilityLive, after a prototyping phase, was co-founded by Lotito and Teroni who had previously partnered for a long time in entrepreneurial digital projects in the publishing industry. The two are highly complementary in terms of skills and background: Teroni graduated in management and Lotito has a background as a technologist. Seven years later, in October 2017, FacilityLive has patents granted in 44 countries across the world and operates offices in Pavia, Brussels and London with 80 employees. It has raised €32 million of capital from 89 private investors and reached a company valuation of €225 million. Venturebeat positions it together with Spotify, BlaBlaCar and others among the most highly valuated start-ups in Europe (Rociola, 2017).

Horizontal, inclusive and agile

FacilityLive revolutionizes search. It has been described as the David who challenges Goliath, that is, Google (CNBC, 2016), because it has solved a problem which Eric Schmidt, Google's Chairman, described in 2014 like this:

> Try a query like "show me flights under €300 for places where it's hot in December and I can snorkel". That's kind of complicated. Google needs to know about flights under €300; warm destinations in winter; and what places are near the water, with cool fish to see. That's basically three separate searches that have to be cross-referenced to get to the right answer. *Sadly, we can't solve that for you today. But we are working on it.* (London Stock Exchange's ELITE Programme page about FacilityLive)

The BBC World News TV (2016) in a live interview with Lotito defined FacilityLive as the Italian start-up trying to change web searching. Lotito adds to this and cites the movie on J. Edgar Hoover (Leonardo di Caprio) and the scene where Hoover illustrates his new approach in speeding up the retrieval of books in the huge Congress Library. Instead of adding people to improve and accelerate the retrieval, he introduced the use of catalographic tags which decreased the search time for a book from many days to less than two minutes. The analogy between "adding people" (i.e. adding massive computation and computing power) and the "catalographic tags" (i.e. a truly intelligent and innovative technology that uses a new way of organizing, managing and searching information) simply explains the main difference between the current applications and FacilityLive's search paradigm. Their search engine is the core component of a "horizontal platform",[2] a platform of platforms, which can generate many vertical platforms. It is thus different from existing (vertical) platforms where one dominant layer (i.e. booking) relates to a multitude of smaller players (i.e. hotels).

Also, their strategic vision is "horizontal": they depart with a system-level vision where their approach benefits all stakeholders involved and value is created with and for all partners.

CASE STUDY *(continued)*

Their horizontal idea finds potential application in very different industries and contexts, from a utility to a public administration to an entire local ecosystem where FacilityLive can create a truly "horizontal platform" that can generate many services through different "vertical platforms". In the case of a city, for example, a territorial horizontal platform may include transportations platforms, citizens services platforms, tourism platforms and so on. The approach is flexible and easily adaptable to the needs of a wide range of potential businesses, partners and systems of partnerships, which makes it also geographically scalable.

When presenting FacilityLive's models and projects, Lotito emphasizes the system view, referring to value partners instead of speaking of customers or suppliers. To this end FacilityLive has developed the "FacilityLive Labs" concept in which the co-creation with partners, from joint project design and experimentation to the exploitation stage are key to their business which is, under their view, a network or a system-level strategy which must benefit all stakeholders, that is, the Small Valleys (trademark[3]), involved. Enabled by the FacilityLive platform, the traditional relationship between a supplier and a customer is transformed into more inclusive and innovative relationships among business partners. The presence of the platform in Cloud enables FacilityLive to provide faster services and deliveries as well as multiple possible business and pricing models (i.e. subscriptions plus revenue sharing). In the medium to long-term this approach will allow FacilityLive to deliver also B2C services, giving individuals the possibility to organize their contents and information inside their personal devices.

A beyond-market strategy

Beyond disruptive technology and innovative business models, FacilityLive is also pioneering an innovative and potentially disruptive model of non-market strategy (see Table 4.1). Traditionally this concept has been associated with cultivating close relationships with regulatory bodies and policy makers, in order to defend and promote corporate interests. In FacilityLive they prefer to interpret the non-market strategy as "strategy beyond market" (SBM) (de Figueiredo et al., 2016) because it aims at developing legitimation and reputation for the firm and, at the same time, at creating economic and social value for the ecosystems involved (both local and national/supranational), ranging from universities to governments and to people. The first aim enables fast international growth: as Lotito says "We have reached these growth goals also building on our beyond-market strategy, and especially the legitimation and the reputation that resulted from it" (Lotito, 2017). For example, one of their key ideas, the creation of a number of interlinked "Small Valleys" throughout Europe aims at the sustainability of firms in their natural place in the EU, an idea which is very different from the big (Silicon) valley and the big global players of the digital economy. Lotito and Teroni believe firmly that the European response to the digital challenge rests on leveraging and combining some strengths of the European heritage and culture, like a system of prestigious historical universities and their local milieus. Lotito is promoting this idea and ensuing projects, like the creation of a digital corridor from southern Italy to

CASE STUDY (continued)

Table 4.1 FacilityLive milestones at a glance

2010	(29 September) – FacilityLive is founded by Gianpiero Lotito and Mariuccia Teroni
2011	In parallel with the code compilation, FacilityLive starts the market test
2012	Patents granted in Europe and South Africa. From 2012 to 2014 FacilityLive obtains patents in 42 countries, including the US and main countries in the EU
2013	FacilityLive decides to stay in Pavia instead of moving the company to the Silicon Valley, in order to contribute to the creation of a new technology industry "Made in Europe"
2014	FacilityLive is the first non-UK company to be admitted to the ELITE Programme of the London Stock Exchange in London
	FacilityLive becomes Gartner Cool Vendor for CRM Customer Service and Support and enters in their official list of the major global software vendors for enterprise search
	FacilityLive is the only European start-up listed in the panel of the European Internet Forum (EIF), the official body for the development of digital technology trends in Europe
	Italia Startup and Milan Politecnico appoint FacilityLive as "the most invested Italian tech startup" having raised more than €10 million in private capital
	London office established; beginning of a permanent presence in Brussels
2015	During the market test phase FacilityLive realizes projects for blue chips such as Vodafone, Unicredit, Accenture etc.
	FacilityLive obtains patents in 44 countries of the world
	Gartner consecrates FacilityLive as a "disruptive technology" by inserting the company in four of its prestigious Global Software Vendor List (Enterprise Search; Knowledge Management; Point Based Solutions; Cool Vendor 2014 for CRM)
	FacilityLive is the only start-up invited to the European Business Summit in Brussels, the annual event bringing together all European industrial associations
	FacilityLive is one of the five founding members of EUTA (European Tech Alliance), the first association of Made in Europe companies aimed at supporting the development of European start-ups
	FacilityLive raises €20 million in private capital and achieves €225 million of company evaluation
	FacilityLive closes business agreements with major multinational companies and consolidates important partnerships with global system integrators
2016	FacilityLive's CEO is the Innovative Entrepreneur chosen by the Italian Minister of Economic Development to represent Italy at the European Council for Competitiveness in Amsterdam

CASE STUDY *(continued)*

Table 4.1 (continued)

2016	FacilityLive is raising almost €30 million of private capital at a company valuation of €225 million
	FacilityLive's technology is adopted by Vodafone Italy for a system able to collect via search all the company information used by their 7,000 call centre operators to answer faster and better to any customer questions
2017	FacilityLive's platform has more than 1 million of written lines of code
	The European Commission (DG Grow) asks FacilityLive to design the possible future unique portal of the European Public Administration starting from the 28 national portals. The study is released in June 2017
	FacilityLive's technology is adopted by STFC – the primary European Scientific Council – for a reporting tool driven by search and by major public administrations including the European Commission
	FacilityLive is chosen by the G7 Italian Presidency to realise the official Web App and the Search experience of the G7 Italy 2017 public website to allow delegates and journalists from all over the world to obtain organized and pertinent information about their participation in the Taormina Summit
	FacilityLive officializes its presence in the Belgian capital opening a representative office in Brussels
	End of validation period
	Start of FacilityLive's Cloud delivery, FacilityLive's Labs and FacilityLive's Territorial Projects
	The Small Valley concept starts being communicated

Source: FacilityLive, https://www.facilitylive.com/media/.

the north of Europe, in different countries and he is convincing an increasing number of policy makers. The corridor passes through key nodes (represented by the "Small Valleys" and their innovative ecosystems) where each node can develop its own vocation, in terms of industries and audience/users, from innovative promotion and fruition of tourism to healthcare technologies. In Liverpool, for example, they are launching a project with Liverpool City Region on the creation of a digital ecosystem involving diverse industries.

FacilityLive SBM encompasses a number of other actions. They are among the five founding members of the European Tech Alliance, which comprises tech companies that have been built in Europe and are focused on the issues of scaling in the EU so that they can continue to grow and compete globally. On the local level in Pavia, the FacilityLive Coding4Kids project, is a good example of community engagement and an illustration of value creation through the contribution to a digital culture and a culture of innovation. FacilityLive conceived this innovative idea to teach coding to kids in the primary schools of Pavia. The kids are hosted at FacilityLive's Headquarters, in the tech hub of the town,

CASE STUDY *(continued)*

and get in touch with what a firm is, what innovation means, and learn coding directly from FacilityLive's developers at the same time. Teroni, who leads the entire project, says "coding is more a process of thinking than just the act of writing software": therefore, the project in its next edition will include teachers, who have approached FacilityLive to be part of the project, parents, entrepreneurs and policy makers. Education, and thus mutual benefit for the partners involved, is also visible in the relations with one of FacilityLive's local stakeholders, the University of Pavia. Among other initiatives, they jointly run a joint master's programme in Digital Management at the University of Pavia, cooperate in FacilityLive's graduate programme and in the above-mentioned FacilityLive's Labs with industrial and institutional partners to ensure cross-fertilization.

Traditional non-market strategy is about defending and appropriating value, "our SBM is giving back to the community what we received when we were here as students and as young entrepreneurs. It is about gratitude, it is about engagement". In the end, promoting a digital culture and innovation culture creates a fertile ground for developing talents and developing their own business in the long run. In FacilityLive's view, the SBM is equally scalable as is the market strategy. They tend to adopt a similar approach in every ecosystem they get involved in, from Pavia to Brussels, to Liverpool and more.

According to Lotito, "our SBM encompasses the development of European digital platforms and ecosystems, a network of Small Valleys, the nurturing of talents, but also our approach to finance is to some extent beyond-market".

The funding strategy of FacilityLive

In 2010, at the beginning of FacilityLive, a market strategy of funding for a high-tech venture with global ambitions and with huge potential would have implied to go to Silicon Valley and to enter "the" new venture techno ecosystem, get finance and focus operations immediately on bringing the product to the market (Luca Sangalli, CFO FacilityLive). Lotito and Teroni also here swim against the tide. The rationale of financing the venture is – in line with the DNA of FacilityLive – based on innovative and "beyond market" elements. They stay in Europe and they avoid being backed by large venture capital firms and institutional investors, for two main reasons: first, they want to protect their governance and vision and second, they want to protect the early phases of their venture and grow a sustainable global enterprise starting from Europe. Lotito and Teroni are perfectly conscious that growing a global software company in a European country requires more time than doing this in an established ecosystem, such as the Silicon Valley where a more mature ecosystem boosts any kind of start-ups. Importantly, they started their adventure in a moment of economic turmoil, with a prototype of search to be financed in 2008, and need of capital in the years thereafter – when investors have become very prudent with their targets.

As shown in Table 4.2, the funding to develop the FacilityLive platform has been raised

CASE STUDY *(continued)*

Table 4.2 Visual, auditory and kinesthetics

Year	Shareholders	Company	Equity (cumulated) (Mln EUR)	EV (Mln EUR)
<2010– prototype seed	3	oldco	2.80	..

Year	Shareholders	Company	Equity (cumulated) (Mln EUR)	EV (Mln EUR)
2010	12	holding	0.80	4.00
2012	14	opco	2.20	18.00
2014 (before Elite)	30	opco	6.50	35.00
2016	77	opco	20.00	225.00
2017 (Sept)	90	opco	29.20	225.00
TOTAL	**90**	**facility**	**32.00**	

Note: To further protect the governance the seed funding of the second phase (from 2010 onwards) has been raised in a holding: as of Sept 2017, considering the amount raised and the corresponding company valuation the founders own the majority of the holding which in turn owns 70% of the operative (opco) company. The capital has been raised from individuals and family offices, a private foundation and the University of Pavia.

Source: FacilityLive.

in two different phases from two separate ventures. In the first phase, the "pre-foundation" phase, the prototype was developed. Software development, validation and go to market started with FacilityLive foundation and the FacilityLive holding incorporation in September 2010. At the end of phase one the prototype has been granted to the new venture.

The facts speak for themselves: FacilityLive is still controlled by Lotito and Teroni, the company valuation is €225 million and the company has raised €32 million over seven years. The mechanism of funding, developed at the very beginning of the venture's life, had to guarantee control of governance for the founders and growth for the venture. In FacilityLive they call their approach "perpetual" funding (versus the usual rounds), which was and still is directed towards "physical", private people/families (versus VC or institutional investors who, in the founders' vision, are not adapted to support the FacilityLive's venture in the first stages).

It is a dual mechanism, which associates reputation and legitimation building globally (based on the validation of the company and its trajectory) and the ensuing increase in company valuation. Luca Sangalli, CFO of FacilityLive with a long-standing experience in

CASE STUDY *(continued)*

private equity, explains that funding is a long-term path and that the strategy of FacilityLive funding was and is dictated by the European context, the protection of governance but also by the long-term roadmap and the investments needed to develop a platform. The long-term path of funding implies also to have the proper investor in every phase, private people/ families in the initial one and institutional investors when funds are needed to scale up the market:

> In a period around 2008, the initial fundraising was truly difficult. After the burst of the real estate bubble investors had changed. They were reluctant to invest, not because of a lack of capital but because of a psychological barrier. They were sick and tired to invest in the usual way, they wanted to see, understand, touch (Sangalli).

It was the great intuition by the founders to identify physical persons and wealthy families as a potential target for raising capital in the initial stages. This type of investor was not focused on examining business plans, due diligence or patents, they needed to establish a fit with the founders' vision and style, in order to understand the potential of the venture. More than numbers though, communication and storytelling stands at the basis of such investor relationships, again, a philosophy very different from the market-based one (Figure 4.1). The founders organize several shareholders' meetings throughout the year in order to update and align them, sharing all latest news related to strategy, the technology roadmap, business and communication. Another major advantage that comes with this type of investors is the network and knowledge they bring in, says Sangalli, also because they are carefully chosen. "More than once", says Teroni, "FacilityLive has rejected people willing to invest because we felt they were not aligned with the venture's mission". Sangalli adds that "the high number (89) of investors seems to be unmanageable but we prefer to have many and committed investors than to have one that is unmanageable".

BOX 4.1

FACILITYLIVE AT THE ELITE PROGRAMME

In November 2014 FacilityLive entered the ELITE Programme of the London Stock Exchange. It was the first non-UK company to be admitted to this special programme which aims at supporting ambitious private companies through their next stages of growth. Participation in the ELITE Programme usually leads to a listing at the Alternative Investment Market (AIM), the London Stock Exchange international market for smaller, growing ventures but the anti-conformist approach of FacilityLive to financial disclosure (no business plan, no conventional KPIs) was not well received by LSE investors and analysts. Although we had initially the idea to follow the trajectory of listing "we reject the idea to communicate to markets through a business plan. We instead pioneered a progressively validated storytelling" as Lotito says.

CASE STUDY *(continued)*

The ELITE experience at the London Stock Exchange in 2014, although concluded without listing, was an important milestone for FacilityLive: As is illustrated in Table 4.2, at the entry in ELITE, the firm had a valuation of €35 million and 30 shareholders. In the two following years the shareholders passed from 30 to 77, with a corresponding increase of €14 million in equity and the valuation jumped from €35 million to €225 million. ELITE had provided a benchmark of a recently listed technology venture which helped create the basis of the "new story" to be told – based on validated facts, that is, the benchmark company and its potential. Another important fact that had boosted the company valuation is the presence of patents in 44 countries of the world including the most important industrial and technological countries (e.g. USA, Europe, Canada, Japan, Korea, Russia, Israel, South Africa, Australia).

"Perpetual" funding enables and accompanies company valuation and growth over time with an underlying mechanism that avoids dilution. The philosophy is long-term, based on raising as much as is needed to ensure the next phase of growth in platform development and company valuation:

> Just imagine we would have raised €20 million at the beginning without corresponding company assets – governance would have been quickly lost with the quota requested in such a situation. In the longer term, with raising capital need to develop the platform, the mechanism must take into account the continuity of capital increase at an increasing company valuation to protect governance (CFO Sangalli).

The technicality developed by FacilityLive allows to manage long-term capital increase open at a fixed Company Valuation (i.e. €225 million), bringing a low dilution to all the shareholders, combined with the possibility for the new investor to buy a small part of existing shares at a lower value placed by the historic shareholder in order to leverage the entry value. This mechanism gives flexibility in managing the capital increase without impacting on the expected dilution of the shareholder with a strong protection on governance. Even the "selling investors" see such a reduction of their investment as a small

BOX 4.2

THE MECHANISM

A new investor agrees to invest €1.5 million for 1 per cent of the company (€150 million of Company Evaluation). The investor subscribes 0.625 per cent of new quota at €225 million of evaluation. He invests €1.4 million in the company and at the same time buys from an existing shareholder 0.375 per cent of quotas at €225 million of value paying €0.1 million. At the end the new investor invests €1.5 million for 1 per cent of the company (€150 million of evaluation) subscribing quotas at €225 million (i.e. low dilution).

CASE STUDY *(continued)*

sacrifice by virtue of which overall development and protection of governance is guaranteed. They are compensated by "small positive exits" and more importantly, by an impressive growth of company valuation and the corresponding value increase of their shares.

Beyond this truly innovative technical mechanism, integral parts of the funding strategy are the non-market elements. In FacilityLive SBM is more than swimming against the tide and acting in an anti-conformist manner: the combination of funding with achievements and company validations built the basis of continual (good) storytelling which brought global reputation and legitimacy. The strategy enabled sustainable company growth and development in a European context which is, a priori, not conducive to high-tech venture finance and growth. At the same time, it allowed climbing up the ladder in terms of privileged contacts. FacilityLive has a full-time lobbyist in Brussels helping the company establishing important relationships with European institutions that can help fostering the company growth. In fact, in Silicon Valley, government support has always been a booster for the local businesses.

As we write (2017), Lotito is in Silicon Valley to take part in the Startup Europe Comes to Silicon Valley initiative – organized with the support of the European Commission and European Parliament – which brings together EU policy makers, the best of the new European scaleups and corporation to meet Silicon Valley stakeholders. Lotito has been invited to speak at the European Innovation Day, the central event of this initiative, and to be jury member at the event's Policy Hackathon.

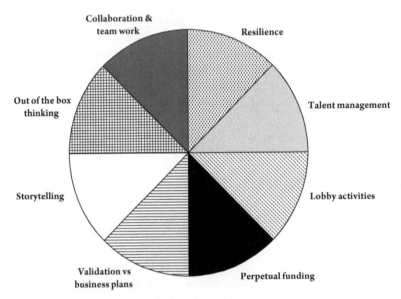

Source: FacilityLive.

Figure 4.1 FacilityLive's SBM distinctive components

CASE STUDY *(continued)*

So far, the story told by FacilityLive and its founders has convinced institutions, investors, and other partners in their ecosystem. Will it become one of the big success stories in the digital economy and will their SBM be confirmed?

What's next in FacilityLive funding when the investment required for making FacilityLive a unicorn will rise exponentially? How can funding then reconcile this need and the objective to maintain governance of the founders and roots in Europe? When the company actually gets to the market, will a non-market strategy still be possible and of advantage?

Case references

BBC World News TV (2016). https://vimeo.com/192623455, accessed 14 October 2017.
CNBC (2016). https://www.cnbc.com/world/?region=world, accessed 14 March 2018.
de Figueiredo, A., Johnston, I.G., Smith, D.M., Agarwal, S., Larson, H.J. and Jones, N.S. (2016). Forecasted trends in vaccination coverage and correlations with socioeconomic factors: a global time-series analysis over 30 years. *Lancet Global Health, 4* (10), e663–e760.
European Parliament (2017). EU TECH STUDY TOUR First Report 2017, Directorate-General for Innovation and Technological Support Directorate for Innovation and Resources Innovation department, available at https://joinup.ec.europa.eu/news/eu-tech-study-tour; accessed 10 November 2017.
FacilityLive: www.facilityLive.com/media, accessed 15 October 2017.
London Stock Exchange's ELITE Programme page about FacilityLive, https://uk.elite-growth.com/en/companies/facilitylive, accessed 15 October 2017.
Personal interviews with Gianpiero Lotito and Mariuccia Teroni on 6 and 28 September 2017.
Personal interview with Luca Sangalli on 11 September 2017.
Rociola A. (2017, October). La startup italiana con la valutazione più alta in effetti è una sorpresa. https://www.agi.it/blog-italia/startup/facilitylive_venturebeat_startup-2309932/post/2017-10-31/ accessed 6 November 2017.

NOTES

1. Resources encompass physical artifacts, skills, knowledge and ideas. Using the lexicon of the resource-based view (Barney, 1991), a firm's resources include tangible assets such as financial, physical, human capital and intangible resources such as reputation, knowledge, culture, and social networks.

2. "Vertical" platforms are two-sided market platforms, while "horizontal" platforms are multi-sided market platforms.

3. FacilityLive registered a trademark for their "Small Valley" (singular) concept with the aim of claiming their paternity and avoiding its improper use by other subjects.

CHAPTER REFERENCES

Alvarez, S. and Barney, J. (2007). Discovery and creation: alternative theories of entrepreneurial action. *Strategic Entrepreneurship Journal, 1* (1–2), 11–26.

Aspelund, A. and Moen, C.F. (2012). International new ventures and governance structures: are international entrepreneurs strategic or entrepreneurial? *Journal of Management and Governance, 16,* 125–146.

Barney, J. (1991). Firm resources and sustained competitive advantage. *Journal of Management, 17*(1), 99–120.

Bellavitis, C., Filatotchev, I. and Kamuriwo, D.S. (2017). Entrepreneurial finance: new frontiers of research. *Venture Capital,* 16 January, *19* (1–2), 1–16.

Bettignies, J. and Brander, J. (2007). Financing entrepreneurship: bank finance versus venture capital. *Journal of Business Venturing, 22,* 808–832.

Bird, B. (1989). *Entrepreneurial Behavior.* Glenview, IL and London: Scott, Foresman and Company.

Blomqvist, K., Hurmelinna-Laukkanen, P., Nummela, N. and Saarenketo, S. (2008). The role of trust and contracts in the internationalization of technology-intensive born globals. *Journal of Engineering and Technology Management, 25* (1–2), 123–135.

Bloodgood, J.M., Sapienza, H.J. and Almeida, J.G. (1996). The internationalization of new high-potential US ventures: antecedents and outcomes. *Entrepreneurship: Theory and Practice, 20,* 61–76.

Cooper, A.C. and Bruno, A.V. (1977). Success among high-technology firms. *Business Horizons, 20* (2), 16–22.

Cooper, A.C. and Daily, C.M. (1997). Entrepreneurial teams. In D.L. Sexton and R.W. Smilor (eds) *Entrepreneurship 2000* (pp. 127–150). Chicago, IL: Upstart Publishing Company.

Cosh, A., Cumming, D. and Hughes, A. (2009). Outside entrepreneurial capital. *Economic Journal, 119* (540), 1494–1533.

Cotta Ramusino E. (2018). Start up innovative e sistema finanziario. In O. Cagnasso and A. Mambriani (eds) *Start up e PMI Innovative.* Bologna: Zanichelli, 94–109.

Coviello, N. and Munro, H. (1995). Growing the entrepreneurial firms: networking for international market development. *European Journal of Marketing, 29* (7), 49–61.

Covin, J.G. and Slevin, D.P. (1991). A conceptual model of entrepreneurship as firm behaviour. *Entrepreneurship Theory and Practice, Fall,* 7–25.

Crowdsourcing week (2015). Top 10 Equity Crowdfunding Platforms in Europe at http://crowdsourcingweek.com/blog/top-10-equity-crowdfunding-platforms-in-europe/.

Cumming, D. and Zhang, Y. (2016). Alternative investments in emerging markets: a review and new trends. *Emerging Markets Review, 29,* 1–23.

Denicolai, S., Hagen, B. and Pisoni, A. (2015). Be international or be innovative? Be both? The role of the entrepreneurial profile. *Journal of International Entrepreneurship, 13,* 390–417.

Eisenhardt, K.M. and Schoonhoven, C.B. (1990). Organizational growth: linking founding team, strategy, environment, and growth among US semiconductor ventures, 1978–1988. *Administrative Science Quarterly, 35* (3), 504–529.

Ensley, M.D. and Hmieleski, K.M. (2005). A comparative study of new venture top management team composition, dynamics and performance between university-based and independent start-ups. *Research Policy, 34*(7), 1091–1105.

Ensley, M.D., Pearson, A.W. and Amason, A.C. (2002). Understanding the dynamics of new venture top management teams: cohesion, conflict, and new venture performance. *Journal of Business Venturing, 17* (4), 365–386.

Ferrua Villanueva, L. (2016). International Entrepreneurial Finance (Class Presentation), University of Colorado Denver: Business School, Jake Jabs Center for Entrepreneurship and Institute for International Business, 3 December.

Forbes (2015), Trends show crowdfunding to surpass VC In 2016, at https://www.forbes.com/sites/chancebarnett/2015/06/09/trends-show-crowdfunding-to-surpass-vc-in-2016/4/#5a06f451772b, accessed 27 October 2017.

Ganotakis, P. and Love, J.H. (2012). Export propensity, export intensity and firm performance: the role of the entrepreneurial founding team. *Journal of International Business Studies*, 43 (8), 693–718.

Greene, P.G., Brush, C.G., Hart, M.M. and Saparito, P. (2010). Patterns of venture capital funding: Is gender a factor? *Venture Capital*, 3 (1), 63–83.

Gulati, R., Nohria, N. and Zaheer, A. (2000). Strategic networks. *Strategic Management Journal*, 21 (3), 203–215.

Gust.com. (2015). *Global Accelerator Report*. (website).

Hagen, B. and Zucchella, A. (2014). Born global or born to run? The long-term growth of born global firms. *Management International Review*, 54 (4), 497–525.

Hambrick, D.C. and Mason, P.A. (1984). Upper echelons: the organization as a reflection of its top managers. *Academy of Management Review*, 9, 193–206.

Harper, D.A. (2008). Towards a theory of entrepreneurial teams. *Journal of Business Venturing*, 23, 613–626.

InvestEurope (2016). https://www.investeurope.eu/.

Jackson, S.E. and Joshi, A. (2011). Work team diversity. In S. Zedeck (ed.) *APA Handbook of Industrial and Organizational Psychology* (vol. 1, pp. 651–686). New York: APA.

Jin, L., Madison, K., Kraiczy, N.D., Kellermanns, F.W., Crook, T.R. and Xi, J. (2016). Entrepreneurial team, composition, characteristics and new venture performance: a meta-analysis. *Entrepreneurship Theory and Practice*, April, 743–771.

Johanson, J. and Vahlne, J. (1977). The internationalization process of the firm: a model of knowledge development and increasing foreign market commitments. *Journal of International Business Studies*, 8 (1), 23–32.

Johanson, J. and Vahlne, J.E. (2009). The Uppsala internationalization process model revisited: from liability of foreignness to liability of outsidership. *Journal of International Business Studies*, 40 (9), 1411–1431.

Kellogg School of Management at Northwestern University, Kellogg Insight (2009). Better Decisions through diversity, heterogeneity can boost group performance, based on the research of Phillips K., Liljenquist K., and Neale M. https://insight.kellogg.northwestern.edu/article/better_decisions_through_diversity accessed on 5 March 2017.

Kerr, W., Jones, B. and Brownell, A. (2016). Supercell. *Harvard Business School Case*, 9-817-052, 17 October.

Klotz, A.C., Hmieleski, K.M., Bradley, B.H. and Busenitz, L.W. (2014). New venture teams: a review of the literature and roadmap for future research. *Journal of Management*, 40 (1), 226–255.

Kozlowski, S.W.J. and Bell, B.S. (2003). Work groups and teams in organizations. In W.C. Borman, D.R. Ilgen and R.J. Klimoski (eds) *Handbook of Psychology: Industrial and Organizational Psychology*, 12 (pp. 333–375). London: Wiley.

Kuemmerle, W. (2004). International entrepreneurship: managing and financing ventures in the global economy-overview, *Harvard Business School*, 9-899-148, 14 September.

Lamb, P.W. and Liesch, P.W. (2002). The internationalization process of the smaller firm: re-framing the relationships between market commitment, knowledge and involvement. *Management International Review*, 42, 7–26.

Lending Club, https://www.lendingclub.com/.

Lin, P.T. (2016). International Entrepreneurial Finance (Class Presentation), University of Colorado Denver: Business School, Jake Jabs Center for Entrepreneurship and Institute for International Business, 3 December.

Loane, S., Bell, J. and Cunningham, I. (2014). Entrepreneurial founding team exits in rapidly internationalising SMEs: a double edged sword. *International Business Review*, 23 (2), 468–477.

Loane, S., Bell, J.D. and McNaughton, R. (2007). A cross-national study on the impact of management teams on the rapid internationalization of small firms. *Journal of World Business*, 42 (4), 489–504.

Lumpkin, G. and Dess, G. (1996). Clarifying the entrepreneurial orientation construct and linking it to performance. *Academy of Management Review*, 21 (1), 135–172.

Ma, W., Osawa, J. and Chu, K. (2016). China's Tencent seeks to buy majority stake in clash of clans maker Supercell, *Wall Street Journal*, 23 May.

McDougall, P.P., Shane, S. and Oviatt, B.M. (1994). Explaining the formation of international new ventures: the limits of theories from international business research. *Journal of Business Venturing*, 9, 469–487.

Mort, G.S. and Weerawardena, J. (2006). Networking capability and international entrepreneurship: how networks function in Australian born global firms. *International Marketing Review*, 23 (5), 549–572.

National Venture Capital Association (2016). https://nvca.org/.

Osawa, J. and Needleman, S. (2016). Tencent seals deal to buy clash of clans developer for $8.6 billion. *Wall Street Journal*, 2 June.

Oviatt, B.M. and McDougall, P.P. (1994). Toward a theory of international new ventures. *Journal of International Business Studies*, 25, 45–64.

Reuber, A.R. and Fischer, E. (1997). The influence of the management team's international experience on the internationalization behaviors of SMEs. *Journal of International Business Studies*, 28, 807–825.

Reuber, A.R. and Fischer, E. (2002). Foreign sales and small firm growth: the moderating role of the management team. *Entrepreneurship Theory and Practice*, 27, 29–45.

Roberts, E.B. (1991). *An Environment for Entrepreneurs. Entrepreneurs in High Technology: Lessons from MIT and Beyond.* New York: Oxford University Press.

Stevenson, H. and Roberts, M. (2002). New venture financing. *Harvard Business School*, 9-802-131 January 2002 (revised August 2006).

Tam, P.W. (2012). Pebble Technology becomes Kickstarter test case. *Wall Street Journal*, 2 July.

van Knippenberg, D. and Schippers, M.C. (2007). Work group diversity. *Annual Review of Psychology*, 58, 515–541.

Weerawardena, J., Mort, G.S., Liersch, P.W. and Knight, G.A. (2007). Conceptualizing accelerated internationalization in the born global firm: a dynamic capabilities perspective. *Journal of World Business*, 42, 294–306.

Wiens, J. and Bell-Masterson, J. (2015). How entrepreneurs access capital and get funded. *Kauffman.org*, 2 June.

Zahra, S.A., Ireland, R.D. and Hitt, M.A. (2000). International expansion by new ventures firms: international diversity, mode of market entry, technological learning, and performance. *Academy of Management Journal*, 43, 925–950.

5

International entrepreneurial entry: implementation processes

5.1 A word on business models and the lean start up perspective

Although we divide here strategic design (Chapter 4) from implementation decisions and present these in a sequential way, we would like to stress the fact that all these elements – from staffing and governance to the development of the value proposition, and market/segment selection, entry mode and marketing programmes are interdependent and are occurring frequently in parallel, especially so in the international start-up. International entrepreneurs ask the questions "Who are my customers? Where are they? How can I attract, reach them and keep them better than competition?" simultaneously and they need to find an answer which resounds well with the resources and capabilities they possess or can mobilize.

Unlike their domestic counterparts, INVs are at the lookout for an internationally viable strategy and so must deal with an additional challenge by bringing the international dimension into these already challenging processes and decisions. For example, the value proposition must be attractive to customers in many markets, governance aspects extend from national to international team composition, from domestic to international networks and partners, and overall marketing programmes must be replicable or easily adaptable abroad.

The business modelling approach and the lean start up methodology – both concerned with simultaneous design and implementation decisions and prominent in entrepreneurship and management literatures and practice – are emerging also in the international arena as a means to cope with the complexities of the early internationalizing firm.

Business models reflect "management's hypothesis about what customers want, how they want it and what they will pay, and how an enterprise can organize to best meet customer needs, and get paid well for doing so" (Teece, 2010, p. 191).

A business model encourages the entrepreneurs to conceptualize the venture as an interrelated set of strategic choices regarding value propositions, choice of customer segments, partners, revenue models and more (see Table 5.1); seeks complementary relationships among these pillars through unique combinations; develops activities around a logical framework; and ensures consistency between elements of strategy, architecture, economics, growth, and exit intentions (Onetti et al., 2012). Business models make the strategic choices that characterize a venture explicit and therefore are a relatively simple way to delimit and organize the key decisions that are made (intentionally or by default) at the outset of any venture. The business model therefore is a "conceptual model", a way to deal with simultaneous design and implementation decisions under conditions of resource scarcity and uncertainty – exactly the business situation in which start-ups must decide and get organized. An illustration of such iteration around selected design elements of the business model and parallel international implementation decisions is well described with the ING Direct example in Box 5.1.

BOX 5.1

ING DIRECT – MILESTONES IN THE EVOLUTION OF A BUSINESS MODEL (IN ITALIC THE CHOSEN OPTIONS)

Strategic intent: be a *low cost, high value provider of financial services* by offering customers an attractive value proposition and high levels of customer service.

Set of various realization options: branch banking, selling retail banking products through the ING insurance network; *model without branches*.

Set of various entry products: brokerage, managed funds, credit cards, consumer loans, *saving account*.

Which market to enter (for a test): Anglo Saxon countries (because of more established direct distribution) and smaller countries – **Australia** and *Canada:* closer to Europe and dominated by five major retail banks which offer consumers little variety or real choice.

Through successful testing clarification of the core business model elements: branch-less banking, simplicity, low cost, value for money/fairness, local teams preferably without banking experience; "fleet of local companies (i.e. subsidiaries)" with high degrees of freedom.

Country selection: two key criteria – local telecommunication/Internet infrastructure needs to be sufficiently developed to support direct banking; country must have market minimum size of > €100 billion held in savings accounts to attain a cost-effective operational scale.

Responding to contextual differences in various countries: individual marketing and promotional campaigns differed significantly. For example positioned as "your other bank" in Australia, "new style of money management – fresh, modern, innovative. . ." in France; some adaptation of product range: balance account in France is higher because savings in France face strong competition with Livret A (a tax free, fee-free saving account) sponsored by the French government; different performance and customer service monitoring systems and levels had to be established because of local regulations of account openings: great differences in "time to open" accounts; call centres in Italy could not record calls due to labour legislation etc.

Source: Dunford, Palmer and Benveniste (2010).

Also in lean start-up terms (Blank, 2013; Ries, 2011), the search for a business model constitutes one of the foundational elements to help find a viable route to customers and to identify more or less (internationally) scalable or repeatable businesses. According to the lean start-up principles, entrepreneurs put their various hypotheses in the business model in order to understand how the business creates value for the customer and the firm. Experimentation with different value creating combinations and early testing with customers and partners here are key: it leads to the formation of the business model or, if necessary, its quick adaptation and change. Quick iteration only demands little resources and allows for "cheap failure" while overall the co-testing with customers brings a priori successful, scalable products and solutions to the market.

Different business models, with their idiosyncratic combination of the various elements shown in Table 5.1, will bring different market offerings and different avenues for international expansion (Hennart, 2014; Autio and Zander, 2016; Tanev et al., 2015; Rask, 2014). For example, Hennart (2014) provocatively posits that it is the business model which brings new ventures "accidentally" to the global stage. He argues that INVs/BGs sell to spatially dispersed customers distinctive niche products that incur low communication, transportation, and adaptation costs so that selling to foreign customers does not require additional time or effort as compared to customers residing at home. Essentially, in Hennart's (2014) terms, the main reason for early and accelerated internationalization is the particular combination of business model elements – what INVs sell, how they sell it, and to whom. Hennart (2014) takes the example of Atlassian to make the case for his view. Atlassian is an Australian international new venture based on a digital business model and an innovative software for expert customers who customize the product themselves according to their needs and simply download it from a platform, wherever they are located. Such expert customers do not require training or (after sales) service, customization of the product is in their hands (and has not to be done by the venture), and the platform is an international distribution and communication channel at the same time. Under a similar line of thought, Autio and Zander (2016) argue that digitization enables "lean internationalization", that is, a novel pattern of early and proactive internationalization, because ICT reduces location-specificity of business operations while at the same time making assets more accessible. The authors argue that through digitization the firm can access value creating resources everywhere and match them better with target markets. They also emphasize simultaneous experimentation with business models in several markets and the ensuing flexible adjustment of their offerings while selecting the most promising markets for closer focus.

Once the venture has formed an initial, internationally viable business model, it will need to replicate it continually and quickly to achieve international growth. Importantly, international replication does not only come with potentially high growth and exploitation of economies of scale, it also bears the potential of generating additional value and skills through the evolution and adaptation of the business model and related learning. If this potential

Table 5.1   Main pillars and questions that underlie business model design and implementation

Pillar 1 offering (value proposition): how do we create value?	Pillar 2 customer segments & customer relationships: for whom do we create value?	Pillar 3 Key activities & key resources?
collection of products and service	customer archetypes/type of organizations	production/operating systems
product itself/ product bundled with other firm's product and services	regional/national/ international customers?	selling/marketing
various elements, e.g. newness, performance, customization, convenience to understand the levers of customer wants	where is the customer in the value chain?	information management/ mining/packaging
image of operational excellence/consistency/ dependability/speed	one/ or multiple segments	technology/R&D/creative or innovative capability/ intellectual
product or service innovation/ quality/features/availability	how do we get/keep/grow customers	financial transactions/arbitrage
intimate customer relationship/ experience	which relationships do we have established? How costly are they?	supply chain management
low cost/efficiency		networking/resource leveraging
Pillar 4: Key partners	**Pillar 5 Cost structure & revenue streams**: How do we **make money**? What are our cost structures?	**Pillar 6** (personal/investor factors): What are our **time, scope, and size ambitions**?
Who are our key partners? Who are our key suppliers?	pricing and revenue sources	subsistence model
Which key resources are we acquiring from our partners?	operating leverage: high/ medium/low	income model
Which key activities do they perform?	volumes: high/medium/low	growth model
	margins: high/medium/low most important costs – most expensive key resources and key activities	speculative model

Source: Adapted from Morris, Schindehutte and Allen (2005); and Osterwalder and Pigneur (2010).

is realized, cross-fertilization across markets and company functions can be leveraged for even faster diffusion and internationalization. Dunford, Palmer and Benveniste (2010) describe the ING Direct experience where the network of subsidiaries through a "steal with pride" principle and sharing of well-working approaches in other countries – co-option across international teams and markets – benefitted from experience and so realized fast internationalization and impressive performance.

Growth, learning from international markets and the innovation potential that may be realized through the "locus" of activities is of particular importance in our context (and underresearched so far in business model literature). "Locus" decisions encompass the capacity to make fast and appropriate selection of the most suitable locations for the different activities of the new venture (e.g. selling; sourcing) jointly with the related decisions of who should or with whom the activity should be carried out (e.g. make or buy, partner). Location selection in international entrepreneurship goes beyond the "home market" and so includes the identification of foreign customers and partners, includes the decision whether to outsource or whether to offshore, or whether to locate the company "at home" or also abroad. Such location choices can make the difference in terms of access to resources, development of knowledge and competence, creation of a network and the various advantages ensuing from internationalization that we have discussed earlier.

The overall set of decisions that must be taken by an international new venture therefore is more complex and must be organized in an effective and fast manner.

Both, the business model and the lean start-up perspectives are based on experimentation and with a view to alignment of design and implementation decisions from the outset. They help cope with uncertainty, business-, product-, customer and/or market-wise, and enable nimble and fast adaptation which is especially in the international arena one of the key factors of success. Therefore, we believe that business modelling and/or the principles of the lean start-up approach will greatly benefit the international start up.

5.2   Selecting markets, customers and partners

One of the key characteristics of international entrepreneurs is their global mindset or international entrepreneurial orientation. Entrepreneurs and entrepreneurial teams of international new ventures do not see foreign markets as a mere addition to their domestic markets, they may be described instead as "citizens of the world". From the outset, they proactively and strategically design and implement offers and business models that are viable and scalable internationally.

Therefore, already in the process of designing the business model and offering, the young small firm is called to evaluate whether, how and in which markets it can grow and which barriers have to be overcome to achieve performance internationally. Market and customer selection, therefore, must strike a balance between attractiveness of markets and customer segments (the opportunity) and the resources and the capabilities the INV has at its disposal. In this section we will discuss the location (locus) decision mentioned above with regard to a market-seeking, selling objective of the international new venture.

5.2.1 "Born global" – multiple and distinct markets from the beginning

Until the emergence of BG firms, international expansion had been predominantly depicted as a stepwise and slow process (Johanson and Vahlne, 1977; Luostarinen, 1979). An important characteristic of this internationalization pattern is that market selection is based on similarity to the home market (i.e. low psychic distance) and experiential learning on foreign markets (Johanson and Vahlne, 1977) before the next, more distant market is envisaged. The market selection and expansion process of SMEs has thus been expected to be risk-averse and to proceed slowly and incrementally. Beyond this dominant stepwise process present in all stage models, other views on market selection modes of SMEs depict them as being reactive or opportunistic at best (e.g. Westhead, Wright and Ucbasaran, 2001).

The international expansion patterns of INVs have challenged these traditional views of market selection. INV actually may ignore their home market altogether and target lead markets or they enter domestic and international markets concurrently (e.g. Bell, 1995; Boter and Holmquist, 1996; Coviello and Munro, 1995, 1997; Madsen and Servais, 1997). In fact, one of the characterizing features of these firms' market expansion, and thus, underlying market selection, is their broad scope and the high number of target countries. They enter multiple, potentially very different international markets at the same time and very early in their life. Thus, they do not seem to follow a psychic distance and experiential learning pattern which determines the subsequent market choice, nor do they react to unsolicited orders or behave opportunistically only – born globals seem to choose their international expansion path strategically (Mudambi and Zahra, 2007). Being young and small and operating under resource constraints of any kind makes the early internationalizer vulnerable. A misstep in the international arena therefore for them may not only threaten growth but may also threaten survival which makes the selection of the "right" target markets and the timing of entry imperative for them.

5.2.2 Approaches to market and/or customer and partner selection

Market selection implies an assessment of where the firm can grow, how fast and what may stand in the way to exploit the firm's offering internationally. In other words, the venture is called to decide upon the most attractive product/service – market combination, be the market defined geography-wise, customer-wise or both.

The context or the environment we have discussed in Chapter 1 re-enters in these considerations. The "big picture", determined by the regulatory environment, by sociocultural trends, and by economic and competitive conditions will determine the opportunity for the firm and, at the same time, describe how the offering should be presented to the market. The external environment therefore will determine whether and how the firm enters a particular market, which entry mode and entry timing it chooses, what shape its marketing programme takes – in short the strategy and the means with which the offering is brought to that market. The interdependencies between the firm's design and its implementation decisions here become very visible and underline the need of an approach to internationalization which matches the firm internal resources (and those it can mobilize and leverage) with the external conditions of the market/customer segments. In the case of the born global firm, the evaluation of the attractiveness of the opportunity and growth prospects inherently includes the evaluation and selection of international markets/customer segments.

While much normative work has been done on how firms should select foreign country markets (for a taxonomy see Papadopoulos and Denis, 1988), much less is available on how young and small firms actually proceed with their international market selection.

In normative models of market selection, the overall attractiveness of a market, which is a function of its sales potential (size and growth) and risk, plays a central role. Normative work emphasizes the systematic and data-based evaluation of market/segment attractiveness and its positive influence on international performance (e.g. Cooper and Kleinschmidt, 1985).

Brouthers and Nakos (2005) for example show that systematic assessment is related to better performance even when controlled for other drivers, namely international experience of the decision makers, firm size (as a proxy for resources) and product adaptation to foreign markets.

Along normative models, the firm identifies the most attractive markets and/ or customer segments and then chooses the strategy and tools to reach the objective. Normative models thus build on causal-deliberate decision making (Sarasvathy, 2001; see Chapter 3 this volume) and the idea that market data and information is available and meaningful. Gabrielsson, Gabrielsson and Seppälä (2012) for example confirm that the definition of foreign market patterns comes first and that marketing decisions are taken in a subsequent step. Further analyses of BG behaviour evidence selection of lead markets and of growth markets (e.g. Bell, 1995; Hagen and Zucchella, 2014) or "watching the post" –markets (Brewer, 2001) which also point to an assessment of business factors and market attractiveness, likely "size", access to advanced and sophisticated customers, and other strategic (long-term) considerations with regard to the choice of foreign markets. For example, USP, an Austrian venture with skin test strips on offer opened a sales office in Singapore because it was considered to become one of the major hubs in global cosmetics and the founder considered "being there" key to future business. YOOX, the Italian company which started an end-of-collection design e-commerce shipped everywhere but concentrated marketing effort in lead markets, for example, Germany, the Netherlands and the UK in order to avoid "overstretching" of scarce resources and to test the market. MolMed, an Italian biotechnology venture, opened clinical centres not only in markets with huge future potential, such as the US but also in those considered strategic for getting centralized approval or reputation in a region, for example, Japan.

Other accounts of BG selection modes report imitation postures, namely a follow the domestic client abroad; follow the competition or the industry trend (e.g. Bell, 1995; Martin, Swaminathan and Mitchell, 1998). Such approaches are determined by "chance" or serendipity (e.g. Brewer, 2001; Crick and Spence, 2005) – the firm is led by others into new country markets and sales are generated by reactive rather than proactive factors and assessment. Chance or serendipitous market selection could also include encouragement to "test" a market, or referral to a particular market by business partners or acquaintances.

Referrals or, in more general, the use of partners and networks also seems to have merit in explaining the market selection of new ventures (e.g. Bell, 1995; Coviello and Munro, 1995, 1997). First, multiple and diverse partners in a network convey timely and business-relevant information and so represent a substitute for market data. Second, as reported by Martin, Gabrielsson and Seppälä (1998) and many others, the inter-organizational relationships of suppliers and buyers lead to a client-following strategy and so affect their pattern of international expansion. Third, other network-related work shows that country market considerations may be of lesser importance than international partner characteristics (Moen, 2004) which can be found within a network (and which underlines the strong interdependence of market selection and market entry mode decisions, see section 4.2). Trudgen and Freeman (2014) report examples where firms had made commitments to the Australian market, a market which neither of the firms considered to be particularly interesting. One of the firms had encountered a very competent distributor, whereas the other knew a person with great skills who wanted to start a foreign subsidiary of the company in Australia. Similarly, one firm argued that a lot of highly interesting markets, especially in Europe, had not yet been targeted because they had not found the right partners to collaborate with. Networks therefore appear to be influential in terms of both market selection and the mode of entry for small international firms. Market selection through networks and contacts may be seen through the lens of effectuation where the firm leverages readily available knowledge and resources (e.g. experience; social and business contacts) and uses these for decisions upon international market/segment or partner selection.

Overall, however, in early internationalizers, neither of the approaches seems to prevail and many questions regarding the interdependencies between market selection, entry mode and marketing programmes remain unanswered. For example, how does the young international firm balance potential and risk involved, or attractiveness and ease of entry, and how does it decide upon the timing? Do international entrepreneurs see markets as countries, specific geographies (e.g. cities and urban areas, university clusters), specific partners, specific customer segments or "pockets" of segments? Extant research has emphasized more the outcome – the international expansion patterns in terms of number and types of countries (e.g. Jones and Coviello, 2005) – than the underlying reasoning which may be well different from country-level considerations.

5.2.3 The international expansion patterns – easy markets first?

One of the characterizing features of born globals is their rapid expansion into a large number of foreign markets – apparently without any sign of the sequence conceptualized in the Uppsala model. The sequence of the model, built on the assumption of market selection according to low psychic distance, is that the "easy", the similar countries are targeted first and the more difficult later. Firms tend to internationalize through country markets from which information flows are relatively unimpeded because those countries can more easily be understood by managers. Also, due to their similarity with the home market, just a minimal need of adaptation of the firm's offering is to be expected. Market selection and a sequence according to psychic distance over time has been supported by many researchers (e.g. Crick, 1995; Rao and Naidu, 1992) but has been challenged by the very existence of born global firms and their pattern-breaking behaviour.

However, the role played by psychic distance in the initial market selection of BGs remains unclear: some argue that it is of little concern to opportunity driven entrepreneurs, selecting lead markets and growth markets wherever they are. Others propose that some BGs initially select psychically proximate markets for the purpose of risk reduction, but are then able to utilize expertise, networks and entrepreneurial skills to move very quickly to psychically distant markets with more opportunities. Studies also show that BGs change quickly to distant and more promising markets if the "close" markets do not stand up to expectations (Freeman et al., 2010).

What also follows, implicitly, from an observation of their international expansion pattern is that born globals decide for breadth instead of depth, that is, they prefer large country portfolios and spreading of (little) resources to smaller portfolios and more dedicated resources to achieve market penetration. This may go hand in hand with a "balancing perspective", in terms of risk, in terms of short- and long-term objectives and performance.

We said above that market selection is a strategic decision where errors, in terms of both "wrong entry" or "lost entry", can be costly. Under such a view market selection should be the result of an assessment of the relative promise of country markets and/or customer segments in function of the firm's objectives, characteristics and resources, especially in an early stage. Tables 5.2 and 5.3 present an illustration of elements that impact market selection.

We turn now to a brief discussion of the two main approaches of market selection – top-down and bottom-up, that is, contractible/restrictive and expansive respectively.

Table 5.2 A summary of market/customer selection approaches

Firm-, management-, product-service related elements influence . . .			
Rationale	Systematic–proactive	Non-systematic opportunistic–reactive	
Decision-making	Causal–deliberate	Effectual	Imitative
Strategies	Top-down – contractible, restrictive	Bottom-up – expansive	
	"Outside-in"	"Inside-out"	
	Breadth	Depth	
	Offensive	Defensive	
	Long-term	Short-term	
Information search	Extensive	Limited	
Type of information	Secondary	Primary (experiential or from others)	

Source: Adapted from Swoboda, Schwarz and Hälsig (2007).

5.2.4 Steps in the market/customer segment selection process

World markets can be seen either from a country market or a customer segment (or partner) perspective. The two approaches we will briefly present in the following reflect these views and either depart from country markets (top-down) or from customer segment considerations (bottom-up) (see Figure 5.1).

Common to both approaches are the main steps, that is, preliminary screening, estimating market potential and estimating company sales (and profit) potential.

The bottom-up process starts with the identification of homogeneous customer groups with the goal of servicing one (or more) groups across several countries. A preliminary screening takes place on a customer basis, while the in-depth screening takes country aspects into consideration. Such an approach is common for firms with homogeneous and distinct customer groups and/or firms that aim to pursue standardized strategies. For example, a venture may decide to enter a market only if a segment of customers exists that views its offering as new, innovative, distinct from available solutions on the market. However, if import restrictions exist or currency fluctuations put margins at risk this country will not be selected. Expansive selection is widespread as it may account for regional preferences and groups of markets that

Table 5.3 Elements that influence market selection

Firm-specific factors		Firm external – host country factors	
Product-service related	Innovative product with global appeal Technology advantage/quality advantage Narrow product offering	Industry	High-tech industries/ knowledge intensive e.g. have shorter life cycles/ windows of opportunity than more traditional industry; first mover advantages
		Host country	Country – market attractiveness; marketing infrastructure; competition; country risk; Entry barriers – tariff– non-tariff; geographic distance; psychic distance
Firm related – age and size	Resource constraints Specialization; flexibility; no path dependencies; quickly learning		
Management related	Experience and knowledge of founders – impacts international orientation and provides network contacts Strong customer orientation Risk taking – risk averse Psychic distance		
Strategy-related	Offensive – defensive; long-term – short term		

Source: Adapted from Papadopoulos and Denis (1988).

are proximate culturally (that is low psychic distance) and geographically and so similar in terms of business environment or customer buying behaviour. The bottom-up approach usually considers fewer countries because the preliminary screening is based on similarity.

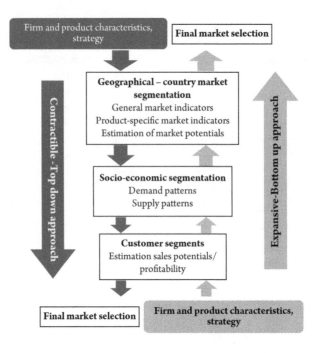

Source: Authors' elaboration.

Figure 5.1 Market selection approaches

The top-down process instead begins with the preliminary screening of markets along macro-economic criteria (e.g. legal and economic conditions), similar to a PEST(LE) analysis[1] for a home market, taking industry- and/or product-specific criteria into consideration. The final selection then takes firm-specific aspects into account. In order to start from a manageable number of countries, pre-decision factors (i.e. knock-out criteria, firm strategic considerations) lead to the exclusion of country markets from further evaluation. For example, YOOX, the e-commerce venture that started out with end-of-season couture at accessible prices, in an initial stage considered only lead countries in terms of "above average" Internet penetration and online purchasing rates. They also chose clusters of markets that were close – not because of their potential similarities but to explore synergies in terms of logistics platforms, and to achieve critical mass. Not only synergies but also trade-offs must be considered, for example, network effects in the case of a competitor's e-commerce business which would make an entry at a later date difficult or no longer possible.

Obviously, data availability, collection and quality is a problem in the process as is the limited information processing time and capacity in new ventures. However, a huge number of free sources are available that can be used for a quick assessment of essential information.

The process of market segment selection has not been described so far in literature but, implicitly, we may conclude that both approaches (in more or

BOX 5.2

RESOURCES FOR MARKET SELECTION

The CIA Factbook, Doing Business in, the World Competitiveness report and various country risk agencies give updated and comparable information for the screening of country markets. Many other sources of assistance are available too. For example, globalEDGE,[2] a knowledge web-portal that connects international business professionals worldwide to a wealth of information, insights, and learning resources on global business issues includes a feature of automatic country comparisons. Partnership opportunities are available for businesses and other organizations as well. StudiaBo, an Italian start up, has put market selection at its core: it provides not only macro-industry data but can provide also information on market share, price level and price ranges on product level using big data from customs documents etc. Their service (www.exportplanning.com) includes not only an assessment of the opportunity, an indication of the risk and accessibility (e.g. logistics, business practices, tariff barriers) of the market involved but also an evaluation of the firm's export readiness, in-depth market research, market entry recommendations and so on. They are now working on a platform which will enable the small firm to use data for market selection autonomously.

Source: http://www.studiabo.it/; https://globaledge.msu.edu/; https://www.cia.gov/library/publications/the-world-factbook/; http://www.doingbusiness.org/; https://www.weforum.org/reports.

less depth) are used. Contractible and causal-deliberate approaches may be expected when the primary motivations are the selection of lead markets or growth markets because they point to assessment of market attractiveness in terms of sales and risk. INVs also seem to start with segment considerations. Very frequently their strategy is the niche (e.g. Aspelund, Madsen and Oystein, 2007; Hennart, 2014; Zucchella et al., 2016), and their competitive advantage is based on specialization and customization – both indicative of the fact that such ventures serve very small "segments" globally. One of their distinguishing characteristics is also intimate customer knowledge which makes identification of segments a priori easier and manageable. Most importantly, customer determination at an early stage is essential for new ventures that look towards global markets. Needs of global customers need to be understood early (already in the design process) and this can be secured through identification and subsequent close cooperation with leading or reference customers.

Market selection has implications for subsequent operational marketing planning, in terms of entry timing but also in terms of adaptation or standardization practice. Similar markets will require just a minimum level of adaptations and thus will save resources and give a time-advantage to the firm. Not necessarily however the similar markets are also the most attractive ones. Firms in which active entry prevails and firms that strategically go to lead markets have been described as being superior performers internationally (McNaughton, 2003; Hagen and Zucchella, 2014). Market selection is also closely intertwined with the entry mode decision. The risks taken with market selection may be traded off with the selection of a risk-sharing or risk-avoiding entry mode or vice versa – a topic which will be discussed in the next section.

5.3   Market entry

Once the company has determined the product (or service) to internationalize and selected the target country, it would have to decide on an entry mode to penetrate the target market. In the international business literature, entry mode discussions have focused on (1) comparing different entry modes, (2) examining the factors influencing the choice of an entry mode, and (3) describing patterns of market entry. More recent studies have enriched the discussion of market entry and have focused on new actors, new modes of entering foreign markets, and different entrepreneurial patterns of entry mode selection.

In this section, we address entry mode selection in entrepreneurial internationalization. Following a brief discussion of market entry from an evolutionary perspective, we highlight new modes of entry that leverage the Internet and digital media. Discussed here collectively as *global e-commerce*, these entry modes have opened new opportunities for entrepreneurs to engage in international business, and have provided new dimensions to the conversation about market entry in international business.

5.3.1   Market entry: evolutionary perspective

Classification of entry modes

In his seminal book on *Entry Strategies for International Markets*, Franklin Root (1987) offered a comprehensive classification of entry modes in international business. He categorized these modes into three principal groups: Export Entry Modes, Contractual Entry Modes, and Investment Entry Modes. Drawing on Root (1987), the following describes these modes of entry and the factors influencing a company's choice of entry mode.

In export entry modes, a company manufactures the product outside of the target country and transfers it to the latter either through intermediaries in the company's home country who does the actual exporting of the product (indirect exporting) or on its own with or without the assistance of middlemen in the target country (direct exporting). In the latter scenario, the company that transfers the product to the target country may use a third-party distributor or export it to the company's own subsidiary in the target country.

Contractual entry modes are non-equity deals and involve the transfer from an international company (i.e. principal company) of a process, technology, brand, or skill to another company (i.e. recipient company) in the target country. Licensing, franchising, technical agreements, management/service contracts, and contract manufacturing agreements are examples of these contractual modes of entry.

Investment entry modes involve equity participation and ownership by a foreign investor of production facilities or other assets abroad. The assets may be fully, majority, jointly, or minority owned by the investor. A company engages in foreign direct investment either through cross-border merger/ acquisition or greenfield ventures.

Factors influencing the choice of entry mode

According to Root (1987), both external and internal factors influence a company's foreign market entry mode decision. External factors include the target market's environmental factors (e.g. political, economic, social, and technological environment); the target market's industry and competitive factors (e.g. size and growth of the market, competitive positions), the target market's production factors (e.g. production costs and infrastructure); and home country factors (e.g. size of the domestic market, incentives offered by home governments).

Internal factors include a company's product factors, as well as its resource/ commitment factors. A company's product profile, such as its product's level of differentiation and service intensity requirements could influence the company's choice of international entry mode. For example, a product that requires high levels of pre- and post-sales services will necessitate the company's presence in the target country, thereby compelling the company to choose an investment mode of entry. Likewise, profitable margins earned from highly differentiated products enable companies to engage in direct investment in the target country.

Internal factors related to company resources and commitment could influence a company's ability to choose a mode of entry over another. Of particular importance in this regard is human resource availability, particularly the availability of an executive or general manager from the home market to oversee a company's involvement in a foreign market. For example, a company that does not have sufficient leadership or management bandwidth to oversee a foreign market may choose contractual or partnership modes over investment modes of entry.

Evolutionary perspectives in entry mode selection

The Process Theory of Internationalization views internationalization as a gradual and incremental process. Companies initially focus on the local market and expand their foreign sales only after a period of domestic market maturation. By focusing on the local (i.e. home) market, the company is assumed to gain scale and experience which are essential elements for the company to offset liabilities of size and foreignness when venturing internationally (Johanson and Vahlne, 1977; Hennart, 2014; Serapio, 2018).

As mentioned earlier, internationalization under this view tends to be slow and gradual because firms have inadequate information on the opportunities, challenges and risks of serving foreign markets and the only way to assess these is to enter these markets. As the company gains experience in these markets, it builds confidence to do business internationally leading to a cycle of upward commitment and greater engagement internationally. This also explains how companies neutralize the liability of foreignness and newness by choosing to initially enter familiar and less distant markets, from a geographic and/or cultural perspective (Hennart, 2014).

Likewise, from the viewpoint of the process theory of internationalization, the choice of entry modes is considered to be evolutionary. Companies will weigh risk versus reward in selecting entry modes and generally favour less risky modes of entry, such as indirect or direct exporting, licensing, and contract manufacturing during early stages of their internationalization. Only after a company has achieved success and gained experience from its initial mode of entry will it consider and select investment modes (e.g. joint ventures, fully-owned subsidiaries) that entail greater financial exposure and risk.

5.3.2 Market entry: entrepreneurial perspective

Emerging entry modes

Advances in digital globalization have opened new options for companies to reach international customers through cross-border transactions. McKinsey's 2016 Report on Digital Globalization captures the significance of this development (Manyika et al., 2016):

- While flows of goods and finance have lost momentum, used cross-border bandwidth has grown 45 times larger since 2005. It is projected to grow by another nine times in the next five years as digital flows of commerce, information, searches, video, communication, and intracompany traffic continues to surge.
- Digital platforms change the economics of doing business across borders, bringing down the cost of international interactions and transactions. They create markets and user communities with global scale, providing businesses with a huge basis of potential customers and effective ways to reach them.
- Small businesses worldwide are becoming "micro-multinationals" by using digital platforms such as eBay, Amazon, Facebook, and Alibaba to connect with customers and suppliers in other countries. Even the smallest enterprises can be born global: 86 per cent of tech-based start-ups (surveyed by Manyika et al., 2016) report some type of cross-border activity.
- Individuals are participating in globalization directly, using platforms to learn, find work, showcase their talent, and build personal networks. Some 900 million people have international connections on social media and 360 million people take part in cross-border e-commerce (Manyika et al., 2016).

Cross-border sales that leverage the internet or digital media (i.e. global e-commerce) have grown significantly during the past decade and are projected to increase exponentially in the coming years. For example, worldwide retail e-commerce sales reached $1.86 trillion in 2016 and are projected to grow to $4.48 trillion by 2021 (Virgillito, 2017). Although retail e-commerce sales started predominantly as domestic sales, cross-border e-commerce or global e-commerce have increased considerably in recent years. A 2017 Forbes survey across 24 countries and six continents showed 57 per cent of online shoppers bought from an overseas retailer, including 63.4 per cent from Europe, 57.9 per cent from Asia Pacific, 55.5 per cent from Africa, 54.6 per cent from Latin America, and 45.5 per cent from North America (Orendorff, 2017).

Cross-border e-commerce can be found in different spaces, such as B2B, B2C, and C2C; in various sectors in both goods (e.g. apparel, books, household goods, industrial and commercial goods, etc.) and services (e.g. education, music, gaming, etc.); and accessible through multiple devices (e.g. mobile phones, tables, desktops). Today, a growing number of entrepreneurial ventures are leveraging e-commerce to engage in international business, using one or a combination of the following modes of entry: (1) online shopping sites for retail sales directly to customers (e.g. Wonderbly, YOOX; blacksocks); (2) online marketplaces which process third-party business to consumer sales (e.g. Lazada.com) or consumer to consumer sales (e.g. eBay); (3) B2B marketplaces (e.g. Alibaba); (4) B2C online service sites (e.g. Tutor Vista for online education); (5) social media and video platforms (e.g. YouTube for Musicians); (6) social gaming (e.g. Supercell), and others.

5.3.3 Entry modes and international entrepreneurship

In contrast to the Process Theory of Internationalization, the Theory of International New Ventures posits that for entrepreneurial companies, international expansion does not follow a staged process. Domestic maturation is not a necessary condition for internationalization and entrepreneurial firms do not necessarily choose to expand first to proximate markets (see section 5.2).

In regards to selecting entry modes, international entrepreneurial ventures do not always follow a pattern of moving from export entry modes to contractual entry modes, and then on to investment modes of entry. In fact, international entrepreneurial ventures may exhibit a preference for entry modes that leverage partnerships and networks early in its internationalization. Further, risk and reward may not be the only factors that influence the choice of market entry; speed may be a primary consideration driving the selection of an entry mode, particularly for born global companies.

An interesting special case supporting early and fast international growth is represented by franchising. Through this arrangement some firms, especially in some industries, have been able to grow quickly in diverse foreign markets, without huge investments in money and human resources (Doherty, 2007; Alon, 2010). With franchising, a firm internationalizes its brand and distribution format. Franchising supported for example the global expansion of McDonalds, and a number of well-known multinationals in the fast food, cafeterias and catering businesses. The same happened in a number of retail stores in the apparel industry and an increasing number of sectors and activities have increasingly relied on this solution to boost international growth.

In 2015, 32 per cent of the units of the Franchise Times top 200 franchises in the United States were located outside of US borders. The number of international locations franchised by companies grew by 10.3 per cent in 2015, while domestic US growth was just 1.3 per cent (Kaiser, n.d.). As mentioned, also industries involved tend to diversify and there is an exponential growth of franchising in the fast casual restaurants and in fitness (especially small box gyms), beauty and personal care and senior people home care. In these businesses not only large firms but mostly smaller and younger ventures find a space to explore and exploit international entrepreneurial opportunities (Kaiser, n.d.).

Calzedonia Group, founded in Italy in 1986, is an early and fast international-izing firm, which relied extensively on franchising to achieve its ambitious growth targets. Thirty years of business have seen constant, solid growth in terms of turnover and expansion, the creation of successful products and brands, the establishment of an international fashion retail presence, with 4200 shops in the world mostly under franchising agreements. The company claims "We are in a period of rapid expansion and consolidation in the heart of Europe, with the goal of commercial growth in the Far East and the United States and an always attentive eye towards new challenges in markets with interesting potential" (https://it.calzedonia.com/home.jsp).

At the same time the franchisee can be seen as a case of international en-trepreneurship: firms abroad access to foreign resources, in terms of brand and commercial format, thus realizing a sort of inward entrepreneurial internationalization. Some authors have called this latter case frantrepreneur (Sundbo et al., 2001), discussing the role of franchisees in introducing inno-vations to better respond to local market needs, thus contributing to refining and adapting the original format.

Partially similar consideration can be applied to the case of international licensing: this is another entry mode which relies on partnerships and con-tractual arrangements and permits to internationalize quickly an innovation, a brand, a process, without committing vast resources to the foreign market entry (Clegg, 1990).

The emergence of new modes, mentioned above, has added new dimensions to the discussion of entry modes in internationalization. Not only have entre-preneurial companies established global e-commerce to enter foreign mar-kets on their own, entrepreneurial companies can now leverage other online sites (i.e. online marketplaces) to reach customers in foreign countries. For example, Lazada.com, an online marketplace specializing in Southeast Asian markets, has provided an effective channel for entrepreneurial companies in the US, Canada, Hong Kong, and other countries to reach customers in the region (https://www.lazada.com/).

The growth of e-commerce has enabled companies to develop and imple-ment business models that lead to early and rapid internationalization, such as the case with born global companies. For example, Hennart has observed that born global companies "sell niche products and services to internationally dispersed customers using low cost information and delivery methods . . . and which does not require additional time or effort on the part of the company" (Hennart, 2014, pp. 117, 129). As previously noted in this chapter, Hennart has referred to these companies as "Accidental Internationalists" (Hennart, 2014).

In contrast to Hennart's argument, however, we contend that the effort required selling through online marketplaces and engaging in global e-commerce is not minimal or zero. On the contrary, in today's world where e-commerce has emerged as an important mode of entry for international markets, there is nothing "accidental" about companies that use e-commerce in becoming international. Most of these companies craft their business models deliberately to reach foreign customers. In addition, route to international market considerations (i.e. choice of delivery and communication channels) require considerable time and effort.

In fact, the growth of e-commerce, including advances in mobile commerce, e-payments, electronic data interchange, online transaction processing, and other facets of e-commerce, has led to the development of created entrepreneurial opportunities (see Chapter 3 this volume), new business models, and novel approaches to international market entry. For example, AirBnB pioneered a novel business model in the lodging industry that leveraged the growth of e-commerce and the global sharing economy.

Finally, exit considerations have received minimal coverage in the literature when discussing international entry modes. In practice, companies in today's fast-moving marketplace concurrently think of issues related to exit (as well as pivoting options) as they contemplate their entry strategy for international markets.

5.4 Entrepreneurial marketing as a key driver of entrepreneurial internationalization[3]

Reaching customers globally and building a global brand and market presence is a demanding task for any firm. For early and rapidly internationalizing small firms this is exceptionally challenging due to the restraints that ensue from the liabilities of smallness, newness and foreignness and the speed of their internationalization.

For example, the small and young firm lacks structures and it has no established brand to build upon; at the same time it must identify and approach customers worldwide which requires the development and implementation of an internationally viable value proposition and strategy – challenging endeavours given their potentially very diverse and dynamic international markets and given the scarcity of financial and human resources they have at their disposal.

In this section we argue that entrepreneurial marketing is a driver of entrepreneurial internationalization and one of the – neglected – explanations for their superior international performance. Extant work that deals with the topic of international marketing strategy in the early and rapidly internationalizing firm has mainly been confined to the discussion of the niche strategy and differentiation advantages based on innovation, product quality and intimate customer knowledge (e.g. Aspelund, Madsen and Oystein, 2007; Hagen et al., 2012; Knight and Cavusgil, 2004). Market selection, one of the key strategic decisions in the international marketing context, has been related to the concepts of the founders' international entrepreneurial orientation, psychic distance (i.e. in general the absence of psychic distance patterns) and network relationships or has been explained with dynamics of global industries and related pull effects into lead markets and global niches (e.g. Coviello and Munro, 1995; Johanson and Vahlne, 2009). Similarly, market entry mode research has been mainly discussed against the background of networks and partnerships or in terms of the "virtual" entry via the Internet (e.g. Gabrielsson and Gabrielsson, 2011). Little work has gone further in order to understand how one of the firm's key functions, that is, marketing, can contribute to confront the many simultaneous firm foundation and internationalization challenges of such firms.

Here we discuss the role of marketing in entrepreneurial internationalization by approaching it under the lens of entrepreneurial marketing. Entrepreneurial marketing is an emerging topic in (international) entrepreneurship and marketing literatures (Hallbäck and Gabrielsson, 2013; Mort, Weerawardena and Liesch, 2012). It has been conceptualized in terms of marketing activities in small and new (resource-constrained) firms (e.g. Gruber, 2004), marketing in turbulent environments (e.g. Morris, Schindehutte and LaForge, 2002; Becherer, Haynes and Fletcher, 2006), non-traditional and/ or digital marketing, a stage in the evolution of marketing's sophistication within an organization (Kotler, 2003) or a combination of entrepreneurial- and market-oriented postures (e.g. Morris, Schindehutte and LaForge, 2002; Hills, Hultman and Miles, 2008).

We follow the idea of the intersection of entrepreneurship and marketing and view and describe entrepreneurial marketing as a distinct set of marketing

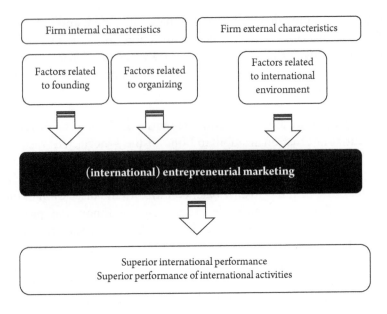

Source: Adapted from Aspelund, Madsen and Oystein (2007).

Figure 5.2 Marketing under "special conditions": the young, small, international organization

abilities and processes.[4] This set fits with the idea of parallel design and implementation decisions and processes and helps the firm to deal with the challenges related to venturing abroad with or close after foundation.

The founding and organization factors in Figure 5.2 relate to the liabilities of newness and smallness. New firms have to define new roles and tasks, which, with a general lack of human resources (quantity- but also quality-wise), may lead to temporary inefficiencies and mistakes. They are not only challenged to establish internal structure and relationships, they are also challenged to create relationships with external stakeholders – be they customers, suppliers or intermediaries, just to mention a few. The absence of a brand, reputation or a track record makes such relationship-building time consuming and costly and potentially a barrier to entry (Gruber, 2004).[5] Further, the newness and small size come with resource constraints which relate to financial capital but also to gaps in required skills. Such constraints make the small firm vulnerable because they limit the room to move and the scope of marketing strategies that the new venture can imagine and/or pursue. On top, the young and new firm has no history, no experience on which to base its decisions and also market data may be contradictory, unreliable or not be available at all. Turbulent environments, characterized for example with convergence of industries, rapidly changing customer expectations, decreasing customer loyalty, high transparency and so on, increase uncertainty. Such internal and external conditions require different, entrepreneurial and agile marketing approaches – one of the reasons why it has been proposed in such contexts (e.g. Morris, Schindehutte and LaForge, 2002; Becherer, Haynes and Fletcher, 2006).

The newly established firm and its entrepreneurial project is comparable to a real-life experiment in which hypotheses on the utility of an innovative solution are tested vis-à-vis existing solutions and other innovative approaches (Gruber, 2004). This comes very close to the idea put forward in the business model and lean start-up movement (Blank, 2003; Ries, 2011) and the *ability to innovate through experimentation*,[6] the first ability and set of activities where entrepreneurial marketing plays a major role. Experimentation copes with the problem of predictability of the nature and the level of demand for an innovation because it co-creates and tests the new offering jointly with the potential customers. This is well expressed by Drucker (1973) who said that firms need to realize that the purpose of a business is not to create a product but to create a customer. The intimate understanding of customers and their wants and the ensuing development of value propositions and roads to reach the customer are core areas of marketing. Marketing influences here not only the design of the firm's offering (through the development of hypotheses for experimentation) but impacts also implementation and exploitation: it leads the customers to choices and thus determines the market success of the innovative solution.

Experimentation with series of alternative hypotheses opens the range of options although the venture may not have the possibility to pursue them at once (and immediately). At the same time, experimentation *leverages and extends (scarce) resources*, the second ability identified for entrepreneurial marketing (e.g. Morris, Schindehutte and LaForge, 2002; Mort, Weerawardena and Liesch, 2012). Taking the example of experimentation, entrepreneurial marketing leverages one core resource of the small firm that is its intimate customer knowledge (e.g. Hagen et al., 2012). Customer knowledge however does not automatically imply that the venture is able to *read and act on signals* – the third ability of entrepreneurial firms that we identify. The identification and translation of signals or, in other words, of (latent) needs into hypotheses for marketable offerings is the contribution of entrepreneurial marketing.

At the same time, entrepreneurial marketing builds on and leverages *relationship management* (with various partners and potential customers included), the third ability in the set of entrepreneurial marketing. Relationship

BOX 5.3

FROM BURBN TO INSTAGRAM – AN ILLUSTRATION OF "READING AND ACTING ON SIGNALS" AND "INNOVATION THROUGH EXPERIMENTATION"

Instagram was still in its infancy when it was purchased by Facebook. An app that had existed for just 551 days, and had made absolutely no revenue, sold for $1 billion. How exactly did the 28-year-old company founder, Kevin Systrom, manage to pull off this feat?

In the beginning of January 2009, Systrom, who had no formal computer science education, started to put time and energy into teaching himself to code. It was around this time that Foursquare was beginning to become popular, which resulted in the increased interest of location check-in apps. Although Systrom had a few concepts developed for these type of apps, in late 2009 he started to pour all of his attention into an app that combined many elements that were popular at the time, including Foursquare.

"I figured I could build a prototype of the idea in HTML5 and get it to some friends", Systrom said, in an interview. "Those friends ended up using the prototype without any branding elements or design at all."

This initial app was called Burbn, and its primary function was to allow users to check in to locations and earn points by meeting with friends and posting pictures. However, although he let his close friends trial the app, he needed a large investment of money to be able to release it as a full product. In March 2010 he decided to leave his full-time job behind, to pursue making Burbn a fully-fledged company. Within two weeks he managed to raise $500,000 and was able to start putting a team together. Mike Krieger, who was an engineer for Meebo, was Systrom's first hire and eventually became the co-founder of Instagram.

"Once he joined, we took a step back and looked at the product as it stood", Systrom reminisced. "We decided that we wanted to focus on being really good at one thing." The pair felt that Burbn had too many features and was cluttered with the photo feature being definitely the most popular. So they decided to strip Burbn of everything except for its basic features like photo upload, commenting, and like capabilities.

They both came up with the name Instagram from the words instant and telegram. For the next eight weeks, Systrom and Krieger worked night and day to perfect and refine their new project. Their friends and families were used to test the app in its beta stages and to help them fix bugs. They also helped with the decision to only have 11 filters on launch, rather than the 30+ that were originally proposed.

On 6 October 2010, at 12:15 in the morning, Instagram went live: 10,000 users downloaded the app within a couple of hours, from all across the world. After the first week, 100,000 users had downloaded the app, and by December the Instagram community had grown to an astonishing million.

Here is the simplified version of the creation of Instagram:

- Kevin Systrom started to learn to code
- Built his prototype in HTML5, and called it Burbn

➡

←

- Gave out the unbranded version to friends and family for feedback
- Met investors and showed them Burbn
- Quit his job to pursue making his own company
- Managed to get $500,000 in funding
- Started to collaborate with Mike Krieger
- Decided to focus on the photo niche
- Created a new photo app from scratch, but scratched it
- Went back and started to look at Burbn again
- Turned Burbn into an iPhone app
- Felt that the app was too cluttered, so discarding everything except for the photo sharing features
- Renamed it Instagram
- Launched, and within a few hours became the number one photo app on the iOS store.

Source: https://instamacro.com/blog/the-exciting-story-of-instagram, accessed 3 May 2017.

building and managing is discussed as networking ability in the context of entrepreneurial internationalization where it is, in line with our perspective, described as a core competence of early internationalizers and a source of timely and business-relevant information and a substitute for owned resources and capabilities. When mobilized and leveraged for marketing purposes, relationships with customers and business partners may not only help to establish hypotheses and validate them through testing, they may also be used to reach marketing objectives such as constant sourcing of new product ideas, that is, co-creation with customers, parallel innovation with suppliers; co-promotion with partners and cheap access to distribution, free promotion and publicity, or positive word-of-mouth of enthusiastic customers.

The fifth, and last ability of entrepreneurial marketing, is the *coordination of multiple functions and partners*, a boundary-spanning role within the firm and across value-chain partners. This coordination ability is probably the most focused on implementation or value delivery of the firm. The resource scarcity demands a high degree of effectiveness and efficiency which demands imaginative forms of marketing that are low-cost but, at the same time, have a strong impact on the market. Morris, Schindehutte and LaForge (2002) call this "doing more with less", others have elaborated on it in terms of resource enrichment (Mort, Weerewardena and Liesch, 2012) internally and externally. Enrichment, or creative and innovative combination of resources for value delivery can be well illustrated with the case of blacksocks.com, one of the e-commerce pioneers (founded in 1999 in Switzerland) with black

---

BOX 5.4

BAD BREWERS

In 2013, Andrea Ciliberti, a young Italian with a lot of entrepreneurial initiative and experience in fashion, noticed a lack of dedicated craft beer for the emerging street food gourmet scene. Convinced about the business idea, Andrea and some friends soon started visiting the shops they had identified: in around one month they sought to better understand the emerging street food scene, the wants and ideas of their potential customers, and the value and potential of their idea of new and dedicated beers. Feedback confirmed the lack of adequate beers, especially in terms of quality, and it validated the value proposition – the dedicated high-level street beer. The team also visited national and international food fairs to discuss the idea with the B2B segment. Many of the people consulted were so enthusiastic to provide contacts and ask for updates. Andrea thus moved and started thinking of new and different types of beer recipes, supported by a quick market analysis regarding the most appreciated beer characteristics, taste, gradation, "recipes", size and style of bottles and so on. Together with an internationally experienced expert brewer who was passionate about the idea to develop street beer recipes, they finally developed three beers to be tested. They also got endorsement and support from one of the most famous and important Italian brewers who decided to cooperate with experience, competence and reputation. A small stock of around 100 bottles for each recipe was produced and tested, improved upon feedback and re-tested "on street" and "in shops" with old and new customers. Two beer recipes fully met customer expectations after two rounds of testing and went into fully fledged production and online distribution.

Source: Giambarresi (2017).

---

socks on offer (for a detailed case description please see Hagen and Zucchella, 2014).

As is evident from the example above, blacksocks launched and sustained their venture internationally through "doing more with less", through mobilizing, leveraging and enriching owned resources and those from value chain partners. Back in 1999 they were pioneers in e-commerce with an innovative way of coordination both upstream and downstream. Value delivery was made easy through an e-commerce model and a subscription formula that enabled close customer contact and perfect service, repeat shipments enriched with little and funny surprises to get customers emotionally involved. The "simple" product of premium quality, although positioned in a niche, enabled realization of economies of scale and it was possible to upscale and grow rapidly.

In international marketing, the question of adaptation versus standardization is subject of lively and continued discussion. Blacksocks, through its offering

BOX 5.5

TELLING A GOOD STORY – BLACKSOCKS STORY OF RESOURCE EXTENSION AND ENRICHMENT

The founder and managing director of blacksocks.com, Samy Liechti started off with a marketing budget of only 500 Swiss Francs to launch and drive traffic to a website which offered black socks (essentially a commodity easy to find everywhere) in times when Internet and broadband penetration were low. Liechti built on his extensive marketing experience from working as a key account for advertising agencies at home and abroad – and a good story. He claimed that the business idea – black socks on subscription – was born during a Japanese tea ceremony with clients where he had to put off his shoes and felt terribly embarrassed. His black socks were not of the same colour, and even worse, his big toe was poking out. Liechti said that destiny had picked him to free the world – more precisely, business men in medium to higher positions – from socks sorrows. This story was judged funny and convincing enough to get featured in talk shows and business press across the globe, from *The Zuercher Zeitung* to *The Handelsblatt* to the *Financial Times*, from Bloomberg to CNN to Swiss broadcasting, yielding huge impact through free publicity. Liechti managed, according to the headline of the *Financial Times*, to make a product as boring as black socks a topic for lunch conversations. Blacksocks also participated in competitions and was constantly awarded – with "the best product" in Germany's popular consumer tests, the American Copernican award for outstanding customer relationship, the Best of Web design award in Switzerland, just to mention a few – yielding again much buzz, traffic to the site and, importantly, reputation. Blacksocks entered in "countertrade" agreements with business press publishers and major airlines where loyalty points or miles could be used for blacksocks subscriptions, an efficient and efficacious way to get co-promoted towards the target group, profit from high-level reputation partners, and, importantly, getting early and constant sales. Liechti and his friend participated in marathons, wearing their black socks and showing that they did not slip, launched limited editions such as perfumed Valentine's socks – activities intended to keep the level of attention in the press and free publicity constantly high.

They created a virtuous cycle in driving traffic to their site, created positive word-of-mouth, reputation and a brand, for free. Blacksocks reached its first year target after four months and they had shipped in 30 countries in the same period. Importantly, their outstanding customer relationship is proven by a retention rate as high as 80 per cent, reinforced by a winning subscription idea, and a percentage of around 30 per cent of new customers that are brought in through existing clients.

Source: Hagen and Zucchella (2012, 2014).

and its positioning in a niche, approaches a global segment and thus avoids the necessity of adaptation to specific country needs (e.g. Zucchella et al., 2016). It also deliberately standardizes as their web-based international approach does not only bring the promise of multiplying effects and spill-overs but also brings international transparency, for example, in terms of prices.

Now, along the example of blacksocks we also argue that entrepreneurial marketing is able to alter the risk profile of the venture. Blacksocks' subscription formula, for example, as well as the countertrade agreements brings early and continued sales, which is an overly important aspect in small and resource constrained firms. Additionally, subscribers as well as loyal customers can be served with lower cost; through positive word-of-mouth they bring new customers in at no cost, thus enabling the venture to save and/or allocate the resources to other activities, for example continued innovation. Customer relationship management enables better customer understanding, co-creation of new products and experimenting and testing with a friendly audience in an economic and in a timely manner. These aspects unite entrepreneurial marketing and lean start-up elements. Through its focus on experimentation and on value generating activities, lean start-ups eliminate waste and inefficient activities and thus speed up development cycles. At the same time this will considerably reduce market risk or false starts, which may be extremely costly. Together with the fact that loyal customers are less sensible to competition and more inclined to buy products from the same company outstanding customer relations also allow protection and growth in times of economic downturns. Blacksocks for example "leveraged" its existing customer base in difficult times to propose new products like T-shirts or underwear to achieve growth.

Reducing risk on one side will permit the venture to take more risk on the other, for example through internationalizing earlier and faster.

The final argument we make here is that the new venture should be uniquely equipped to develop these abilities *because of* being new and small. The organization is more flexible, communication is more direct, decision-making is faster (e.g. Chen and Hambrick, 1995) and the firm can act speedier when opportunities are recognized. The absence of a path dependency or organizational inertia of more established firms makes them (re)act to change in a more nimble fashion. Similarly, Autio, Sapienza and Almeida (2000) introduced the learning advantage of newness as a distinct characteristic of early internationalizers. In summary, international new ventures leverage their smallness and newness – they do more with less.

5.5 From childhood to maturity – managing long-term growth

While the last decades have provided us with a multitude of studies examining the initial stages of entrepreneurial internationalization, we lack knowledge about how early internationalizers evolve over time, what happens to them once they become more established mid-size firms, nor do we know how successful they remain over time. Little systematic research has been carried out examining such ventures once they mature (Cavusgil and Knight, 2015; Coviello, 2015).

We have a first understanding of the effects of early entry on the performance and survival of the firms (e.g. Efrat and Shoham, 2012; Fernhaber, 2013; Sui and Baum, 2014), an idea how internationalization patterns continue and develop over time and a first glance on drivers along time to understand the evolution and growth of these firms better (e.g. Hagen and Zucchella, 2014; Morgan-Thomas and Jones, 2009; Prashantham and Young, 2011).

Still, we need much more insight on what ultimately happens to early internationalizers regarding their (international) growth trajectories. Do they struggle to determine when, where and how to move the venture beyond its initial growth spurt? Is rapid growth maintained, and if so, what are the drivers of continued growth and performance?

5.5.1 What are the longer-term implications of early entry?

It seems to be the case that the degree to which organizations are able to change and alter themselves is dependent on their size and age. As firms grow and age they become more complex and they develop an interdependence between the various organizational functions and domains.

It is this interdependence which reduces the firms' ability to change organizational strategies and structures (e.g. Hannan and Freeman, 1984) – the firm becomes path-dependent. From this reasoning follows the suggestion that the actions and environments at creation have long-term impacts on the firm's strategy and structure and on the development and growth of the venture (e.g. Eisenhardt and Schoonhoven, 1990). For example, a new firm which expands early and in an accelerated manner into many different foreign markets chooses a strategy and (risk) position that is very different from its domestic or traditional counterparts which enter markets slowly and incrementally. Such a choice will determine subsequent resource choices and decision sets of the firm and its development in general. In the context of early internationalizers Knight, Madsen and Servais (2004) remark that the pattern remains with the firm for decades. Beyond the confirmation that strategy at foundation is an important determinant for a new venture, these views also suggest that growth drivers have a temporal locus and thus may be more or less influential in the various stages of the venture's life cycle, in line with the models of growth we present in the next section.

5.5.2 Conceptualizations and empirical analyses of growth models

The conceptualizations of venture long-term development usually assume growth and imply that growth occurs in stages along the life cycle of the firm or the product.[7] Transition from one stage to the other hinges on the successful management of dominant problems that arise in these stages and which influence the venture's internal organization (Kazanjian, 1988). The number of the stages varies across the different conceptualizations but all share the underlying assumption that growth is linear and that ventures proceed through a predictable pattern that can be related to the problems and challenges a firm finds pressing along time (Kazanjian, 1988).

The role of dominant problems is important, not only in defining the stages, but also in understanding the transition from stage to stage. The conflicts and tensions created by these problems trigger learning and so stimulate the search for knowledge and competence to resolve those problems. Only if the venture deals successfully with the dominant problem, it proceeds further and the problem–search–resolution process then will recur in subsequent growth cycles. Importantly, survival is at stake in all phases and companies can fail at any point during their growth if they do not manage crises (Churchill and Lewis, 1983). The increase or decrease of the influence of problems and the relations among them are important for our understanding of the challenges that the ventures confront. Strategic positioning for example is one of the drivers whose importance cuts across all stages while others are of importance only in specific growth phases (Kazanjian, 1988).

In Table 5.4 an example of a general model of venture growth (Kazanjian, 1988) and an IE conceptualization are illustrated (Gabrielsson et al., 2008). The comparison helps to better understand both the underlying thought of life cycle models and the challenges and drivers that early internationalizers face long-term. They do however not account for the fact that organizations also may die or need retrenchment (Gabrielsson and Gabrielsson, 2013) and of the many different growth strategies and combinations thereof that the ventures may choose.

We turn now to research findings that have looked into long- and short-term performance drivers of venture development and their outcome in early internationalizers in more detail.

Table 5.4 Examples of growth models and dominant problems

Kazanjian, 1988	Gabrielsson et al., 2008
1st stage: conception and development	**1st stage: the introductory phase**
Structure and formality are nonexistent;	Underdeveloped structure; limited resources
Creation of idea – Construction of prototype	Select channels/networks
Find financial backers	(Inter)national funding
Strategic positioning	Strategic positioning
	Integrated operation – market strategy
	Deliberate system for organizational learning
2nd stage: commercialization	**2nd stage: growth and resource accumulation**
Org task system becomes a consideration; functions are created	Resource accumulation through organizational learning
Single owner, few people dominate	Self-finance though growth
Strategic positioning	Planning – strategy
3rd stage: growth	**3rd stage: break out and required strategies**
To produce, sell and distribute products in volume and to avoid being shaken out of the market as ineffective or inefficient	Ties with global player/network
Pressure to attain profitability	Effective implementation of strategies
Balance profits against future growth	Global vision and commitment to rapid entry and market penetration
Growth of hierarchy; advent of functional specialization; move toward professionally trained, experienced people	
Strategic positioning	
4th stage: stability	
Maintain growth momentum and market position	
Second generation product;	
Professional/experienced team support original owner	

Source: Kazanjian (1988); Gabrielsson et al. (2008).

5.5.3 Drivers of continued venture growth

The analysis of the drivers along time follows the idea that ventures face different challenges along their (international) life and that the key factors which lead to early entry in the international arena are not necessarily the same as those needed for further expansion. Similar to the identification of recurrent problems in growth stages, such an analysis helps entrepreneurs and venture teams to understand how to prepare and manage continued growth in changing internal and external contexts. They are better-informed on key issues that need attention, need to be developed or need to be preserved (e.g. entrepreneurial behaviour with growing hierarchy; quick decision making).

A multitude of drivers (see examples in Table 5.5) has been analysed in the search for understanding the initial superior performance, that is, the speed, scope and intensity of early internationalizers, while the influencers of continued internationalization, post-entry dynamics and long-term (international) performance remain to be uncovered. Two questions are of particular interest: first, we are interested in determining the importance and the temporal locus of the various drivers; second, we need an answer to the question whether the accelerated and broad pattern of international

Table 5.5 Drivers of (continued) entrepreneurial internationalization (illustrative)

Internal drivers	External drivers
Founder and team-related: international, industry entrepreneurial experience, management experience, commitment to growth, education; decision making logics; team openness and team composition (diversity, completeness)	Profile of target markets (e.g. institutional environment; growth potential, customer sophistication)
Entrepreneurial orientation at individual and firm level	Affiliation to industrial districts
Niche strategy; marketing differentiation; innovative high-quality products; different types and combinations of growth strategies	Networks
Various resources and capabilities: finance, R&D, techno, marketing, networking; resource acquisition	Industry (dynamics)
	Macro conditions (technology, ICT, globalization etc.)

Source: Authors' elaboration.

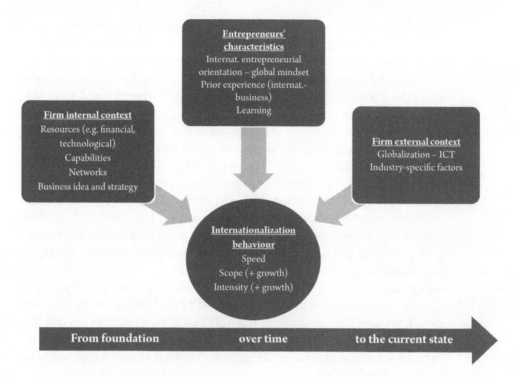

Source: Adapted from Hagen and Zucchella (2014).

Figure 5.3 Drivers of continued entrepreneurial internationalization

expansion seen in the initial phase does continue and whether it translates into survival and growth on the longer run.

Hagen and Zucchella (2014) for example propose to study the drivers along a set of variables regarding: (1) the entrepreneur's capabilities; (2) the firm's internal environment; and (3) the firm's external environment. These variables and their interactions impact the process of internationalization over time and permit to understand which factors mostly affect the persistence along the years of an international entrepreneurial organization (Figure 5.3).

The authors – based on their empirical evidence – conclude that "many companies can be born global but only some are born to run. . ." (i.e. ventures that show continued and even accelerating international growth over time). The second conclusion is that a born to run company experiences growth cycles, which involve waves of innovation (across governance, strategy, organization, product/services) and associated reconfiguration of capabilities and/or enlargement of actual capabilities. Each innovation wave is triggered by a combination of factors, the first of which is the "openness" of the entrepreneurial and managerial team, also through outside advice. Openness has to be interpreted both as initial diversity in competencies and their variation over time, which simultaneously shape and accompany the firm's evolution and its growth needs. This process requires that the organization learns from team members, from new market opportunities and from key partnerships. Thus, long-term growth depends on a delicate balance between openness and stability of key entrepreneurial and managerial resources, and on the integration of different sources of learning at the organizational level and around innovative projects (Hagen and Zucchella, 2014). Another gatekeeper to long-term growth is the entry in strategic and complex (in terms of accessibility, structure, institutions and cultures) markets in combination with strategic partners and committed entry modes. The features of complex markets are triggering mechanisms not only for selling but also for high-quality learning and capability building and continued innovation (Hagen and Zucchella, 2014; Efrat and Shoham, 2012). For example, YOOX, an Italian fashion luxury e-retailer entered the Chinese market through partnering with Armani, one of the most renowned fashion brands in the Chinese market, set up a logistic platform and only in a subsequent step opened the virtual YOOX stores in the market. Also, blacksocks, a Swiss venture with socks on subscription on offer, entered the US market successfully with, in this case, a local partner.

Regarding uncontrollable external factors, Efrat and Shoham (2012) suggest that market growth, technological turbulence, and target-country risk influence strongly the initial phases but then lose their impact on the long run. Market growth and turbulence, for example, positively influenced short-term performance showing that high market potential drives entrepreneurial internationalization while target-country risk level had a negative impact on BGs' early strategic performance, underlining the vulnerability of the new and young firm. Similarly, the confluence of multiple weak and inefficient institutions has a direct and negative effect on new venture growth as shown by Batjargal et al. (2013). While these results emphasize the importance of identifying the "right" arena prior to entering multiple markets concurrently (please see section 5.2 for details), the impact was lost later when the internal factors – managerial, technological and marketing capabilities – were of utmost importance. Once the early internationalizers begin to diversify and penetrate markets or new market segments, their focus changes. In the firm's ongoing efforts to better-address their market wants, innovation, marketing and management capabilities become important. In later stages, once the ventures' operations become more diversified and their products more established, marketing capabilities and maintaining a mindset for growth and innovation is key.

Complementing and constantly renewing knowledge and capabilities (through openness, hiring professionals along the way, networks, internal learning) the high-growth firms constantly innovate and find successful growth formulae to realize the next steps to growth.

Internationalization, in a first step, is a strategy of fast growth but the venture must determine its future path and with it the growth strategies for their "second act". Here Hagen and Zucchella (2014) underline the role of extension of the initial niche strategy and the ability of the "born to run" firms to successfully conceive and implement complementary growth strategies, avoid niche lock-in and cover multiple segments of the market. Maintaining growth momentum over time requires the evaluation of alternatives to build and exploit growth opportunities. On the growth agenda may be complementary strategies to internationalization: the venture may simply extend its core into additional contexts, leverage assets from existing markets to innovate in old and new markets and segments, sell more to existing customers, or diversify through acquisition and integration of companies to enter adjacent markets (Ansoff, 1957).

In line with the assumption that initial strategy sets the venture on its future development path, born global companies do not behave like typical niche companies that remain small. Instead, after having established in their initial global niches they examine different options for continued growth along product and market/segment scope. Internationalization in Hagen and Zucchella's (2014) study is an important but not the only source of company growth. Blacksocks continuously adds new products to its portfolio, YOOX extends its business in different segments to cover all segments of the fashion industry, becomes a reference point in building e-commerce platforms for the industry, and another venture, Valvitalia, grows through successful acquisitions (see also Almor, Tarba and Margalit, 2014). This bears similarities to Kazanjian's (1988) strategic positioning if understood as a continual development of the firm's position in its various segments and markets which must be decided and developed in parallel with the firm's resource and capability base.

Hagen and Zucchella (2014) also note that high-growth firms plan and prepare for growth well ahead of taking the next "big step" and that long-term growth, overall, depends on a delicate balance between innovation and growth (in terms of new people, new markets, new products) and stability across multiple time horizons. Growth hinges not only on the "right" decision (or a response to the dominant problem), it requires also the right timing. In summary, as a firm evolves, the importance and the impact of different drivers shifts with the stages in the firm's life cycle.

5.5.4 International growth patterns, post-entry dynamics and their performance implications

We have mentioned above that the initial strategy and with it the firm's internationalization decisions are of the most critical factors for the survival, performance and future growth potential of new ventures. However, what needs to be clarified in our context of entrepreneurial internationalization is whether the early, accelerated and geographically broad internationalization pattern is superior to incremental and slower internationalization behaviour beyond the initial stage and how early and intense internationalization affects the ventures' long-term survival, growth and performance.

Sui and Baum (2014) provide a comparison of three alternative paths to international expansion namely: (1) the entrepreneurial internationalization pattern (early, accelerated, geographically broad and intense); (2) the incremental and slow pattern which represents the dominant process model (based on similarity of markets, experiential learning and increasing commitment over time; Johanson and Vahlne, 1977); and (3) the born regional path[8] proposed by Rugman and Verbeke (2004) standing for an intermediate position along the dimensions of time and geographic scope. Sui and Baum (2014) in line with earlier studies (Mudambi and Zahra, 2007) find no significant differences between these three internationalization strategies with respect to their effect on survival, suggesting that small ventures, similar to larger firms, are rational and efficient in choosing the internationalization strategies that best fit their resource base. They also underline the importance of resources and innovation to adapt efficiently to changes in demand and the cultural and institutional multiplicity of their many international markets. Innovation therefore is not only a driver of early internationalization but also an important factor for staying alive in the international environment.

We turn now to post-entry growth or the question of speed in the continued international endeavours of early internationalizers. Do born globals maintain their quasi explosive development and initial speed in market expansion, do they slow down, change to more gradual patterns or even de-internationalize? Similar to an initial decision on the path to take, also the subsequent decisions will hinge on the firm's internal and the external conditions to confront. Clearly, we may assume that the pursuit of early and accelerated internationalization aims at achievement of greater international growth also at later stages, an assumption which has been confirmed in empirical studies (Carr et al. 2010; Efrat and Shoham, 2012; Fernhaber, 2013). Hagen and Zucchella (2014) illustrate the evolution of internationalization paths of born global cases. They find non-linear growth with some recurring patterns that distinguish low-growth from high-growth born globals. The high-growth firms do not only maintain rapid growth, they seem to accelerate in scope, intensity and in commitment – in line with Garnsey, Stam and Hefferman's (2006) proposition that growth drives growth. Other paths, those of the lower-growth firms, continue with periods of stasis, consolidation or also de-internationalization, followed by incremental or rapid growth periods. The fact that patterns are prone to interruptions and setbacks too is important to further understanding of drivers, critical events and ways to deal with upcoming challenges.

In summary, the IEO can maintain over time its distinctive characteristics, but this requires the capacity to face and confront successfully a number of challenges. The process is far from being predictable and linear; it is instead partially conditioned by non-controllable factors and partially shaped by entrepreneurial volition and organizational dynamic capabilities.

CASE STUDY

Blueseed: if you build it, will they come?

Manuel G. Serapio

In 2011, Max Marty and Dario Mutubdzija set out to launch Blueseed. Right out of the starting gate, Blueseed's business model was met with both excitement and scepticism. Marty and Mutubdzija's idea was to locate a ship twelve nautical miles off the coast of Northern California to serve as a home for international entrepreneurs to live and work in proximity to one of the world's most dynamic innovation hubs – Silicon Valley. The excitement around Blueseed was that foreign entrepreneurs will not need a visa to work in the United States because they will be living and working on a ship located in international waters. Blueseed will provide ferry boats and a helicopter to transfer these entrepreneurs back and forth to the US mainland. All that these international entrepreneurs will need for entry into the United States was a business (B-1) visa which was easier to obtain (Marty, 2013).

For sceptics, Blueseed's business model seems unworkable because of the many legal, regulatory, and operational hurdles that the company had to overcome. For example, how will the US government view Blueseed's attempt to circumvent immigration laws with its clever business model? Likewise, will anchoring a boat twelve nautical miles off the coast and ferrying its tenants back and forth onshore be perceived as a security risk? Even if Blueseed was able to overcome the regulatory hurdles, would operating a large ship be too cost-prohibitive?

Indeed, despite Blueseed's initial success in signing up prospective customers and the promise of funding from an influential investor, Peter Thiel, the company has not been able to launch (Platt, 2012). Was the idea too ambitious in the first place? Were the sceptics right in that the business model was unworkable? Did the founders underestimate the risk versus

CASE STUDY *(continued)*

reward profile of the business, thereby leading to their inability to attract enough investors to fund Blueseed's first venture in Silicon Valley? Or, was it just an issue of poor launch planning and execution? Was it reasonable to expect that investors, partners, and customers would come after the founders have built Blueseed?

The US visa landscape: no visas for international entrepreneurs

The process of applying for and obtaining work and immigrant visas to the United States was problematic for entrepreneurs as there were no entrepreneur visas to the United States and the existing alternatives were inadequate. For example, the E-2 visa allowed treaty investors and their employees to work in or be self-employed in the United States. Investors were required to make investments of $100,000 or more and must own at least 50 per cent of the business. However, this visa was renewable only in two-year increments and was not convertible to a green card. Restrictions also applied to certain countries such as China, India, Brazil and Russia (https://blueseed.com/).

The EB-5 investor visa allowed the investor to work and be self-employed in the United States. The visa had no expiration and may provide a pathway to permanent residence. The required investment amount varied by location (i.e. high versus low unemployment areas) and ranged from $500,000 to over $1 million. The programme also required the investor to create at least 10 jobs. While popular, the EB-5 programme has been dominated by Chinese investors, thereby crowding out applicants from other countries (https://blueseed.com/).

Two other programmes are the H1-B and L-1 visas. H1-B provides a work visa for skilled workers but does not allow for self-employment. The visa is good for three years and is renewable for another three years. H1-B recipients can apply for a green card after meeting labour certification and other requirements. The programme requires a company sponsor for the applicant which often was a large company with an established track record. Additionally, the number of visas issued per year was capped at 65,000 in 2012 and had a rejection rate of 50 per cent. The L-1 visa was a specialized intra-company transfer visa and applies to applicants who have worked for foreign branches abroad. As with the H1-B visa, more than 50 per cent of applicants for the L-1 visa are rejected (https://blueseed.com/).

Political efforts to establish a visa for entrepreneurs have not been successful. By May 2012, four legislative attempts have all failed, namely the Startup Visa Act (March 2011), the Startup Act (June 2011), the IDEA Act (December 2011), and the Startup Act (May 2012). Additionally, there was no indication that the US Congress would pass a comprehensive immigration reform that would increase visas for entrepreneurs (https://blueseed.com/).

It was in this context that Marty and Mutubdzija conceived the Blueseed idea. The challenging and lengthy process of applying for a visa and the low chances of getting one was not lost on Marty and Mutubdzija as both men were first generation immigrants, from Cuba and Yugoslavia, respectively. Both men also shared a similar background having worked for the Sea Steading Institute. They were passionate about the Institute's mission

CASE STUDY *(continued)*

to further the establishment and growth of permanent, autonomous ocean communities, enabling innovation with new political and social systems. Marty and Mutubdzija wanted a solution to the work visa problems of international entrepreneurs. They wanted to give them a platform where entrepreneurs can work in close proximity to their US partners, customers, and investors and not be constrained by US immigration laws and regulations. This novel solution and platform was Blueseed.

Creating the solution: Blueseed's business and financial model

Anchored twelve nautical miles off the coast of Silicon Valley, Blueseed will be registered and carry the flag of the Bahamas. The ship will accommodate 1,000 entrepreneurs living in a high-tech "googleplex of the seas" atmosphere. It will have different living configuration spaces for different budgets, customizable office space, and various amenities and recreational spaces, including gyms, game rooms, movie theatre, concierge, medical services, and 24-hour security. Internet access will incorporate wireless 1Gbps+ link to shore, liquid robotics ocean drone relays mesh network, and O3b satellite back-up. Fibre optic cable connection was planned for the future (https://blueseed.com/).

Blueseed has looked into retrofitting a 6-plus-year-old former cruise ship as its inaugural ship. There was a good inventory of these ships in the market because cruise lines have moved away from mid-size ships to mega-size ships. In preparation for its launch, Blueseed had commissioned various vessel concept designs (Garling, 2012). Estimates put the cost of chartering and adapting a cruise ship at $15 to $50 million, depending on the size of the ship (Marty, 2013).

Blueseed planned to offer two to three trips per day to the mainland, making it possible for their tenants to meet with potential investors, customers, and partners. The primary mode of transfer will be via large capacity round-trip ferry boats; the trip will take 30 minutes each way. For more urgent transfers, Blueseed will provide helicopter services that will take about 20 minutes to Palo Alto. Blueseed's tenants will use their business (B-1 visas) to travel to the mainland which allows them to stay for up to 180 days. The company will work with border authorities for a streamlined customs checkpoint similar to Global Entry (https://blueseed.com/).

The company's founders envisioned building an awesome start-up community and technology-oriented space that had the feel of a high-tech university dorm and 24/7 hackathon and co-working space. The company's website touted the benefits of being aboard Blueseed, including: (1) No visas or immigration restrictions; (2) Much lower regulatory costs and the flexibility to choose where to incorporate; (3) Simplified business and regulatory environment; (4) An international location where companies can bring in talent from anywhere in the world; (5) No stressful commuting; no traffic; and (6) "Perpetual hackathon" atmosphere (https://blueseed.com/).

Blueseed's initial choice of location, Silicon Valley, was also its biggest selling point to international entrepreneurs. Silicon Valley is the top hub for innovation in the United States

CASE STUDY *(continued)*

accounting for the lion's share of US patents and trademarks and 40 per cent of all venture capital in the United States in 2011. Most importantly, Silicon Valley is a coveted location for many current and aspiring international entrepreneurs. Many of the entrepreneurial ventures that have grown into household names are Silicon Valley located or affiliated firms. These firms, such as Google, Uber, Tesla, App Dynamics, and Cloudera, were established by at least one immigrant or international entrepreneur founder (Manjoo, 2017).

Under its financial model, Blueseed will generate revenues from a combination of rent and a start-up equity in the tenant company. Cash rent was estimated from $1,200 per person per month for a shared room for four and up to $3,000 per person per month for a private room with ocean view. This cost includes an office space, a savings for tenants of about $2,200 per month for the equivalent office space rental in San Francisco (or $500 for desk space). Blueseed will claim up to 6.5 per cent equity in their tenant's company in exchange for them being aboard Blueseed. Tenant clients will have a choice to either pay more cash upfront for less equity that Blueseed will take in their company, or less cash for more equity (https://blueseed.com/).

Investors concerns and Blueseed's future

Blueseed had initial success in attracting companies who have expressed interest in the company's idea of an international community for international entrepreneurs. These included 496 start-ups and 1516 entrepreneurs from 72 countries. Interestingly 23 per cent or more than 80 companies were start-ups from the United States. This was followed by India (10 per cent), United Kingdom (6 per cent), Canada (4 per cent), Australia (4 per cent), France (3 per cent), Brazil (3 per cent), Spain (3 per cent), China (2 per cent), Germany (2 per cent), Italy (2 per cent), Russia (2 per cent) and Singapore (2 per cent) (https://blueseed.com/).

Of the motivations given by these companies and entrepreneurs for wanting to move to Blueseed, 55 per cent cited "living and working in an awesome start-up and technology oriented environment" as critical. Thirty six per cent rated "proximity to Silicon Valley" as being critical. "Having an alternative to securing US work visas" was rated as important by the majority of respondents but came in only as the fifth most critical factor behind the two above-mentioned factors, as well as the "ease of finding talent" and "streamlined legal and regulatory environment and low overheads" (https://blueseed.com/).

Blueseed has not had the same level of success in attracting investors as it has with potential customers. Floodgate, Correlation Ventures, and Zhenfund Beijing were reported to have invested in the company's seed round (Marty, 2013). Peter Thiel initially supported the Blueseed idea but did not participate in the seed round (Banister, 2013). In June 2014, the San Jose *Mercury News* reported Blueseed as having hit a wall, unable to raise $30 million to support its launch (Quinn, 2014). Mutubdzija was reported to have approached Chinese investors to fund the venture while other sources have indicated that the most

CASE STUDY *(continued)*

funding commitments Blueseed has been able to obtain was $9 million, way short of its targeted launch funding of $30 million (Quinn, 2014).

Among others, investors were concerned about the Blueseed's risk–reward profile. Given that it takes an estimated 5–7 years on average for a start-up company to make an exit, investors were concerned about the length of time before Blueseed would be able to book gains from its 6.5 per cent ownership of a tenant client (Babonas et al., 2012). Furthermore, the financial model did not seem realistic in that rental earnings will not be sufficient to cover Blueseed's high start-up costs and operating expenses. Investors were also not convinced about the US government's willingness to allow Blueseed to exist outside of US laws. Finally, should the US government relax visa regulations for international entrepreneurs, it will strike a blow to Blueseed's unique value proposition.

The company had targeted to launch its first Blueseed ship in 2015 but this has yet to materialize. In 2013, Max Marty, Blueseed's co-founder and CEO, left the company. Dario Mutabdzija, formerly Blueseed's President, has taken over as the company's CEO. According to Blueseed's website, the venture is on hold while the company seeks additional funding. It remains to been seen whether Blueseed will finally be able to raise the funds to launch its first ship or if the venture will become one of Silicon Valley's failed big ideas in recent years.

Note: Dr Manuel G Serapio wrote this case using secondary information from Blueseed and other resources. The author gratefully acknowledges previous case research conducted on Blueseed by Richard Babonas, David Bohman, Alec Brewster, Christie Hickman, Carly Matteson, and Ben Remer. This case is intended for teaching purposes only.

Acknowledgement: CU Denver's Institute for International Business and Center for International Business Education and Research provided support for the preparation of this case.

Case references

Babonas, R., Bohnam, D., Brewster, A., Hickman, C., Matteson, C. and Remer, B. (2012, 11 December). *Blueseed.* Unpublished case study.

Banister, C. (2013, 12 December). Mike Maples gets on board Blueseed's sea platform. *TechCrunch.* Retrieved on 14 March 2018 from https://techcrunch.com/2012/12/13/mike-maples-gets-on-board-blueseeds-sea-platform/.

Blueseed, https://blueseed.com/. International entrepreneurs in international waters. Accessed August 2017; https://blueseed.com/come-aboard/results/; https://blueseed.com/faq/.

Bruder, J. (2011, 14 December). A start-up incubator that floats. *The New York Times.* Retrieved on 14 March 2018 from https://boss.blogs.nytimes.com/2011/12/14/the-start-up-boat/.

Chatterjee, R. (2011, 16 December). How Blueseed plans to host "visa-free" entrepreneurs off US coast. *The Economic Times.* Retrieved on 14 March 2018 from https://

CASE STUDY *(continued)*

economictimes.indiatimes.com/slideshows/corporate-industry/how-blueseed-plans-to-host-visa-free-entrepreneurs-off-us-coast/slideshow/11133923.cms.

Cities on the Ocean. (2011, 3 December). *The Economist*. Retrieved on 14 March 2018 from http://www.economist.com/node/21540395.

Garling, C. (2012, December). Startup ducks immigration law with Googleplex of the Seas. *Wired.com*. Retrieved on 14 March 2018 from https://www.wired.com/2011/12/blueseed/.

Guynn, J. (2013, 13 March). Tech's new wave: Limits on visas for skilled foreigners. *Los Angeles Times*. Retrieved on 14 March 2018 from http://articles.latimes.com/2013/mar/13/business/la-fi-high-seas-immigration-20130313.

Hathiramani, J. (2012, 12 September). Indian startups flock to Silicon Valley's "seastead" Blueseed. *The Sunday Times*. Retrieved on 14 March 2018 from http://www.sundaytimes.lk/120902/business-times/indian-it-startups-flock-to-silicon-valley-seastead-blueseed-10204.html.

Knowles, D. (2013, 13 March). Silicon Valley investors seek to raise $27 million to fund Blueseed, a floating tech-world community off the California coast, to bypass US visa restrictions. *New York Daily News*. Retrieved on 14 March 2018 from http://www.nydailynews.com/life-style/real-estate/int-waters-eyed-tech-workers-avoid-visa-laws-article-1.1287863.

Lee, T. (2011, 28 November). Startup hopes to hack the immigration system with a floating incubator. *Ars Technica*. Retrieved on 14 March 2018 from https://arstechnica.com/tech-policy/2011/11/startup-hopes-to-hack-the-immigration-system-with-a-floating-incubator/.

Manjoo, F. (2017, 8 February). Why Silicon Valley wouldn't work without immigrants. *NY Times.com*. Retrieved on 14 March 2018 from https://www.nytimes.com/2017/02/08/technology/personaltech/why-silicon-valley-wouldnt-work-without-immigrants.html.

Marty, M. (2013, 31 July). Two years of Blueseed/Blueseed-the startup community on a ship [Web blog post]. Retrieved on 3 September 2017 from https://blueseed.com/blog/two-years-of-blueseed/.

Newton, C. (2012, 20 May). Blueseed to entrepreneurs: your ship may come in. *SF Gate*. Retrieved on 14 March 2018 from http://www.sfgate.com/business/article/Blueseed-to-entrepreneurs-Your-ship-may-come-in-3570961.php.

Partnership for a New American Economy. (2011, June). *The New American Fortune 500*. Report by Partnership for a new American Economy. Retrieved on 14 March 2018 from http://www.newamericaneconomy.org/sites/all/themes/pnae/img/new-american-fortune-500-june-2011.pdf.

Platt, J. (2012, 16 May). PayPal co-founder funds floating city for entrepreneurs. *Mother Nature Network*. Retrieved on 14 March 2018 from https://www.mnn.com/green-tech/research-innovations/stories/paypal-co-founder-funds-floating-city-for-entrepreneurs.

Quinn, M. (2014, 6 June). Blueseed is a big idea that isn't this tech boom's kind of startup. *The Mercury News*. Retrieved on 14 March 2018 from http://www.mercurynews.com/2014/06/06/quinn-blueseed-is-a-big-idea-that-isnt-this-tech-booms-kind-of-startup/.

NOTES

1 Political, economic, social, technological, legal and environmental analysis.
2 Created by the International Business Center at Michigan State University.
3 Part of this section builds on Hagen and Zucchella (2018).
4 A propensity to act entrepreneurially or marketing oriented does not necessarily include the matching ability to do so.
5 Note that in the early stage of the firm elements and impact of the liability of newness equate to the liability of foreignness – the firm, at foundation, is a stranger at home and abroad.
6 Usually, in an entrepreneurial context, causation and effectuation logics are discussed (see Chapter 3, this volume). Experiments, based on hypotheses, are different from both approaches. They follow the idea that what is difficult to predict can be discovered and validated through experimentation with and through customers (Blank, 2003; Ries, 2011).
7 The product life cycle view is relevant here because typically new ventures experience their initial growth around a single new product.
8 Ventures here internationalize quickly into a larger number of similar (regionally close) markets.

CHAPTER REFERENCES

Almor, T., Tarba, S.I. and Margalit, A. (2014). Maturing, technology-based born-global companies: Surviving through merge and acquisition. *Management International Review, 54* (4), 421–444.

Alon, I. (2010). *Franchising Globally: Innovation, Learning And Imitation.* New York: Palgrave.

Ansoff, I. (1957). Strategies for diversification. *Harvard Business Review, 35* (5), 113–124.

Aspelund, A., Madsen, T. and Oystein, M. (2007). A review of the foundation, international marketing strategies, and performance of international new ventures. *European Journal of Marketing, 41* (11/12), 1423–1448.

Autio, E., Sapienza, H.J. and Almeida, J.G. (2000). Effects of age at entry, knowledge intensity, and imitability on international growth. *Academy of Management Journal, 43* (5), 909–924.

Autio, E. and Zander, I. (2016). Lean internationalization, paper presented at the 2016 AIB Conference, New Orleans, 1–33.

Batjargal, B., Hitt, M.A., Tsui, A.S., Arregle, J.L., Webb, J.W. and Miller, T. (2013). Institutional polycentrism, entrepreneurs' social network and new venture growth. *Academy of Management Journal, 56* (4), 1024–1049.

Becherer, R.C., Haynes, P.J. and Fletcher, L.P. (2006). Paths to profitability in owner-operated firms: the role of entrepreneurial marketing. *Journal of Business and Entrepreneurship, 18* (1), 17–31.

Bell, J. (1995). The internationalization of small computer software firms: a further challenge to "stage" theories. *European Journal of Marketing, 29* (8), 60–75.

Blank, S. (2003). *The Four Steps to the Epiphany: Successful Strategies For Products That Win.* Stanford, CA: Stanford University Press.

Blank, S. (2013). Why the lean start-up changes everything? *Harvard Business Review, May,* 1–9.

Boter, H. and Holmquist, C. (1996). Industry characteristics and internationalization processes in small firms. *Journal of Business Venturing, 11* (6), 471–487.

Brewer, P. (2001). International market selection: developing a model from Australian case studies. *International Business Review, 10* (2), 155–174.

Brouthers, L.E. and Nakos, G. (2005). The role of systematic international market selection on small firms' export performance. *Journal of Small Business Management, 43,* 363–381.

Calzedonia Group, https://it.calzedonia.com/home.jsp; https://it.calzedonia.com/custserv/cust serv.jsp?pageName=Corporate; https://it.calzedonia.com/custserv/custserv.jsp?pageName=Fr anchising.

Carr, J.C., Haggard, K.S., Hmieleski, K.M. and Zahra, S.A. (2010). A study of the moderating effects of firm age at internationalization on firm survival and short-term growth. *Strategic Entrepreneurship Journal, 4* (2), 183–192.

Cavusgil, S.T. and Knight, G.A. (2015). The born-global firm: an entrepreneurial and capabilities perspective on early and rapid internationalization. *Journal of International Business Studies, 46* (1), 3–16.

Central Intelligence Agency. *The World Factbook.* Retrieved on 14 March 2018 from https://www.cia.gov/library/publications/the-world-factbook/.

Chen, M.J. and Hambrick, D.C. (1995). Speed, stealth, and selective attack – how small firms differ from large firms in competitive behavior. *Academy of Management Journal, 38* (2), 453–482.

Churchill, N.C. and Lewis, V.L. (1983). The five stages of small business growth. *Harvard Business Review.* Retrieved on 14 March 2018 from https://hbr.org/1983/05/the-five-stages-of-small-business-growth.

Clegg, J. (1990). The determinants of aggregate international licensing behaviour: evidence from five countries. *Management International Review, 30* (3), 231–251.

Cooper, R.G. and Kleinschmidt, E.J. (1985). The impact of export strategy on export sales performance. *Thunderbird International Business Review, 27* (3), 12.

Coviello, N. (2015). Re-thinking research on born globals. *Journal of International Business Studies, 46* (1), 17–26.

Coviello, N.E. and Munro, H.J. (1995). Growing the entrepreneurial firm: networking for international market development. *European Journal of Marketing, 29* (7), 49–61.

Coviello, N.E. and Munro, H.J. (1997). Network relationships and the internationalisation process of small software firms. *International Business Review, 6* (4), 361–386.

Crick, D. (1995). An investigation into the targeting of UK export assistance. *European Journal of Marketing, 29* (8), 76–94.

Crick, D. and Spence, M. (2005). The internationalisation of "high performing" UK high-tech SMEs: a study of planned and unplanned strategies. *International Business Review, 14* (2), 167–185.

Doherty, A.M. (2007). The internationalization of retailing: factors influencing the choice of franchising as a market entry strategy. *International Journal of Service Industry Management, 18* (2), 184–205.

Drucker, P.F. (1973). *Management: Tasks, Responsibilities, Practices.* New York, NY: Harper & Row.

Dunford, R., Palmer, I. and Benveniste, J. (2010). Business model replication for early and rapid internationalisation: the ING Direct experience. *Long Range Planning, 43* (5/6), 655–674.

Efrat, K. and Shoham, A. (2012). Born global firms: the differences between their short- and long-term performance drivers. *Journal of World Business, 47* (4), 675–685.

Eisenhardt, K.M. and Schoonhoven, C.B. (1990). Organizational growth: linking founding team, strategy, environment, and growth among US semiconductor ventures, 1978–1988. *Administrative Science Quarterly, 35* (3), 504–529.

Fernhaber, S. (2013). Untangling the relationship between new venture internationalization and performance. *Journal of International Entrepreneurship, 11* (3), 220–242.

Freeman, S., Hutchings, K., Lazaris, M. and Zyngier, S. (2010). A model of rapid knowledge development: the smaller born-global firm. *International Business Review, 19* (1), 70–84.

Gabrielsson, M. and Gabrielsson, P. (2011). Internet-based sales channel strategies of born global firms. *International Business Review, 20* (1), 88–99.

Gabrielsson, P. and Gabrielsson, M. (2013). A dynamic model of growth phases and survival in international business-to-business new ventures: the moderating effect of decision-making logic. *Industrial Marketing Management, 42,* 1357–1373.

Gabrielsson, P., Gabrielsson, M. and Seppälä, T.T. (2012). Marketing strategies for foreign expansion of companies originating in small and open economies: the consequences of strategic fit and performance. *Journal of International Marketing, 20* (2), 25–48.

Gabrielsson, M., Kirpalani, V.H.M., Dimitratos, P., Solberg, C.A. and Zucchella, A. (2008). Born globals: propositions to help advance the theory. *International Business Review, 17* (4), 385–401.

Garnsey, E., Stam, E. and Hefferman, P. (2006). New firm growth: exploring processes and paths. *Industry and Innovation, 13* (1), 1–24.

Giambarresi, M. (2017, April). *Lean startup methodology: Comparing the outcomes of two different project implementations.* Unpublished Master Thesis: University of Pavia.

GlobalEDGE, https://globaledge.msu.edu/.

Gruber, M. (2004). Marketing in new ventures:theory and empirical evidence. *Schmalenbach Business Review, 56* (2), 164–199.

Hagen, B. and Zucchella, A. (2014). Born global or born to run? The long-term growth of born global firms. *Management International Review, 54* (4), 497–525.

Hagen, B. and Zucchella, A. (2018). Entrepreneurial marketing as a key driver of early and sustained internationalization. In N. Dominguez and U. Mayrhofer (eds) *Key Success Factors Of SME Internationalisation: A Cross-Country Perspective* Bingley, UK: Emerald Publishing.

Hagen, B., Zucchella, A., Cerchiello, P. and De Giovanni, N.(2012). International strategy and performance: clustering strategic types of SMEs. *International Business Review, 21* (3), 369–382.

Hallbäck, J. and Gabrielsson, P. (2013). Entrepreneurial marketing strategies during the growth of international new ventures originating in small and open economies. *International Business Review, 22* (6), 1008–1020.

Hannan, M.T. and Freeman, J. (1984). Structural inertia and organizational change. *American Sociological Review, 49* (2), 149–164.

Hennart, J.-F. (2014). The accidental internationalists: a theory of born globals. *Entrepreneurship Theory and Practice, 38* (1), 117–135.

Hills, G.E., Hultman, C.M. and Miles, M.P. (2008). The evolution and development of entrepreneurial marketing. *Journal of Small Business Management, 46* (1), 99–112.

Instamacro, https://instamacro.com/blog/the-exciting-story-of-instagram.

Johanson, J. and Vahlne, J.E. (1977). The internationalization of the firm: a model of knowledge management and increasing foreign commitment. *Journal of International Business Studies, 8* (1), 23–32.

Johanson, J. and Vahlne, E. (2009). The Uppsala internationalization process model revisited: from liability of foreignness to liability of outsidership. *Journal of International Business Studies, 40* (9), 1411–1431.

Jones, M.V. and Coviello, N.E. (2005). Internationalisation: conceptualising an entrepreneurial process of behaviour in time. *Journal of International Business Studies, 36* (3), 284–303.

Kaiser, T. (n.d.). Franchise Times Top 200+. Retrieved on 14 March 2018 from http://www.franchisetimes.com/Resources/Top-200/.

Kazanjian, R.J. (1988). Relation of dominant problems to stages of growth in technology-based new ventures. *Academy of Management, 31* (2), 257–279.

Knight, G.A. and Cavusgil, T. (2004). Innovation, organizational capabilities, and the born-global firm. *Journal of International Business Studies, 35* (2), 124–141.

Knight, G.A., Madsen, T.T. and Servais, P.P. (2004). An inquiry into born-global firms in Europe and the USA. *International Marketing Review, 21* (6), 645–665.

Kotler, P. (2003). *Marketing Management.* New Jersey, US: Prentice Hall.

Lazada, https://www.lazada.com/.

Luostarinen, R. (1979). *Internationalization of the firm.* Helsinki School of Economics. Dissertation. Series A: 30, Helsinki School of Economics, Helsinki.

Madsen, T.K. and Servais, P. (1997). The internationalization of born globals: an evolutionary process? *International Business Review, 6* (6), 561–583.

Manyika, J., Lund, S., Bughin, J., Woetzel, J., Stamenov, K. and Dhingra. D. (2016). *Digital globalization: the era of global flows.* McKinsey Global Institute Report. Retrieved on 19 March 2018 from https://www.mckinsey.com/business-functions/digital-mckinsey/our-insights/digital-globalization-the-new-era-of-global-flows.

March, J.G. (1991). Exploration and exploitation in organizational learning. *Organization Science*, 2 (1), 71–87.

Martin, X., Swaminathan, A. and Mitchell, W. (1998). Organizational evolution in the interorganizational environment: incentives and constraints on international expansion strategy. *Administrative Science Quarterly*, 43 (3), 566–601.

McNaughton, R.M. (2003). The number of export markets that a firm serves: process models versus the born-global phenomenon. *Journal of International Entrepreneurship*, 1 (3), 297–311.

Moen, Ø. (2004). Internationalization of small, computer software firms. *European Journal of Marketing*, 38 (9/10), 1236–1251.

Morgan-Thomas, A. and Jones, M.V. (2009). Post-entry internationalization dynamics. Differences between SMEs in the development speed of their international sale. *International Small Business Journal*, 27 (1), 71–97.

Morris, M., Schindehutte, M. and Allen, J. (2005). The entrepreneur's business model: toward a unified perspective. *Journal of Business Research*, 58 (6), 726–735.

Morris, M.H., Schindehutte, M. and LaForge, W. (2002) Entrepreneurial marketing: a construct for integrating emerging entrepreneurship and marketing perspectives. *Journal of Marketing Theory and Practice*, 10 (4), 1–19.

Mort, G.S., Weerawardena, J. and Liesch, P.(2012). Advancing entrepreneurial marketing: evidence from born global firms. *European Journal of Marketing*, 46 (3/4), 542–561.

Mudambi, R. and Zahra, S.A. (2007). The survival of international new ventures. *Journal of International Business Studies*, 38 (2), 333–352.

Onetti, A., Zucchella, A., Jones, M.V. and McDougall-Covin, P. (2012). Internationalization, innovation and entrepreneurship: business models for new technology-based firms. *Journal of Management & Governance*, 16 (3), 337–368.

Orendorff, A. (2017, 1 September). Global ecommerce: statistics and international growth trends [Infographic] [Blog post]. Retrieved on 19 March 2018 from https://www.shopify.com/enterprise/global-ecommerce-statistics.

Osterwalder, A. and Pigneur, Y. (2010). *Business Model Generation*. Hoboken, NJ: John Wiley & Sons.

Oviatt, B.M. and McDougall, P.P. (2005a). Defining international entrepreneurship and modelling the speed of internationalization. *Entrepreneurship: Theory and Practice*, 29 (5), 537–553.

Oviatt, B.M. and McDougall, P.P. (2005b). The internationalisation of entrepreneurship. *Journal of International Business Studies*, 36 (1), 2–8.

Papadopoulos, N. and Denis, J.-E. (1988). Inventory, taxonomy and assessment of methods for international market selection. *International Marketing Review*, 5 (3), 38–51.

Prashantham, S. and Young, S. (2011). Post-entry speed of international new ventures. *Entrepreneurship Theory and Practice*, 35 (2), 275–292.

Rao, T.R. and Naidu, G.M. (1992). Are the stages of internationalisation empirically supportable? *Journal of Global Marketing*, 6 (1/2), 147–170.

Rask, M. (2014). Internationalization through business model innovation: in search of relevant design dimensions and elements. *Journal of International Entrepreneurship*, 12 (2), 146–161.

Ries, E. (2011). *The Lean Startup: How Today's Entrepreneurs Use Continuous Innovation to Create Radically Successful Businesses*. New York, NY: Crown Business.

Root, F. (1987). *Entry Strategies for International Markets*. Massachusetts/Toronto: Lexington Books.

Rugman, A. and Verbeke, A. (2004). A perspective on regional and global strategies of multinational enterprises. *Journal of International Business Studies*, 35 (1), 3–18.

Sarasvathy, S.D. (2001). Causation and effectuation: toward a theoretical shift from economic inevitability to entrepreneurial contingency. *Academy of Management Review, 26* (2), 243–263.

Serapio, M. (2018). *International Entrepreneurship.* Retrieved from http://www.venturehighway. com.

Sui, S. and Baum, M. (2014). Internationalization strategy, firm resources and the survival of SMEs in the export market. *Journal of International Business Studies, 45* (7), 821–841.

Sundbo, J., Johnston, R., Mattsson, J. and Millett, B. (2001). Innovation in service internationalization: the crucial role of the frantrepreneur. *Entrepreneurship and Regional Development, 13* (3), 247–267.

Swoboda, B., Schwarz, S. and Hälsig, F. (2007). Towards a conceptual model of country market selection: selection processes of retailers and C&C wholesalers. *The International Review of Retail, Distribution and Consumer Research, 17* (3), 253–282.

Tanev, S., Rasmussen, E. S., Zijdemans, E., Lemminger, R. and Svendsen, L.L. (2015). Lean and global technology start-ups: the two research streams. *International Journal of Innovation Management, 19* (3), 1–41.

Teece, D.J. (2010). Business models, business strategy and innovation. *Long Range Planning, 43,* 172–194.

The World Bank. Doing Business. Retrieved on 14 March 2018 from http://www.doingbusiness. org/.

Trudgen, R. and Freeman, S. (2014). Measuring the performance of born-global firms throughout their development process: the roles of initial market selection and internationalisation speed. *Management International Review, 54* (4), 551–579.

Virgillito, D. (2017, 14 August). Global ecommerce: massive opportunity ahead for the borderfree business [Blog post]. Retrieved on 19 March 2018 from https://www.shopify.com/ enterprise/global-ecommerce-opportunities.

Westhead, P., Wright, M. and Ucbasaran, S. (2001). The internationalization of new and small firms: a resource-based view. *Journal of Business Venturing, 16* (4), 333–358.

World Economic Forum. The World Competitiveness report. Retrieved on 14 March 2018 from https://www.weforum.org/reports.

Zucchella, A., Hagen, B., Denicolai, S. and Masucci, M. (2016). Early and accelerated internationalization: the role of the niche strategy in a new generation of exporters. *International Journal of Export Marketing, 1* (1), 27–47.

Index